Narrating the Law

DIVINATIONS:
REREADING LATE ANCIENT RELIGION

Series Editors:

Daniel Boyarin, Virginia Burrus, Derek Krueger

A complete list of books in the series
is available from the publisher.

Narrating the Law

A Poetics of Talmudic Legal Stories

Barry Scott Wimpfheimer

PENN

UNIVERSITY OF PENNSYLVANIA PRESS

PHILADELPHIA

Copyright © 2011 University of Pennsylvania Press

All rights reserved. Except for brief quotations used for purposes of review or scholarly citation, none of this book may be reproduced in any form by any means without written permission from the publisher.

Published by
University of Pennsylvania Press
Philadelphia, Pennsylvania 19104-4112
www.upenn.edu/pennpress

Printed in the United States of America on acid-free paper

10 9 8 7 6 5 4 3 2 1

Library of Congress Cataloging-in-Publication Data
Wimpfheimer, Barry S.
 Narrating the law : a poetics of talmudic legal stories / Barry Scott Wimpfheimer.
   p. cm. — (Divinations : rereading late ancient religion)
 Includes bibliographical references and index.
 ISBN 978-0-8122-4299-7 (hardcover : alk. paper)
 1. Talmud—Criticism, Narrative. 2. Narration in rabbinical literature. 3. Aggada—History and criticism. 4. Jewish law—History. 5. Judaism—History—Talmudic period, 10-425. 6. 6. Talmudic academies—Iraq—Babylonia—History. I. Title.
BM509.N37W56 2011
296.1'2066—dc22

2010027771

For Shana

Contents

Introduction	1
Chapter 1. Privileging Legal Narrative: Resisting Code as the Image of Jewish Law	9
Chapter 2. Deconstructing Halakhah and Aggadah	31
Chapter 3. A Touch of the Rabbinic Real: Rabbis and Outsiders	63
Chapter 4. Social Dynamics of Pedagogy: Rabbis and Students	96
Chapter 5. Torah as Cultural Capital: Rabbis and Rabbis	122
Chapter 6. Lengthy Bavli Narratives: A New Theory of Reading	147
Conclusion	164
Notes	169
Bibliography	214
Index	229
Acknowledgments	237

Introduction

Contemporary books are familiar. A patron selecting a recently published volume in a bookstore instantly knows its kind. Bright cover colors and cheap construction indicate a beach or plane read. Footnotes and endnotes announce scholarly work. My three-year-old son identifies his books by their glossy dust jackets and large illustrations. The familiarity of contemporary books derives from one's experience of similar ones. Today's books classify themselves. Classification is helpful for library cataloging or gift purchasing alike; it is also important in directing readers toward particular ways of reading. One does not expect scholarly conclusions from a children's picture book or entertainment from a dry academic tome. One knows to compare a John Grisham book to its oeuvre and not to a Toni Morrison novel. The familiarity of contemporary books often masks the importance of a reader's assumptions in approaching a work of literature.

The Babylonian Talmud (henceforth Talmud), by contrast, is quite unfamiliar. From its composition in two ancient languages—Hebrew and Aramaic—to the way it floats from topic to topic without much justification to its equal interest in theology, ethics, magic, law, medicine, history, and biblical interpretation, the Talmud is an unusual text. Though it is a religious text, it rarely feels particularly spiritual. Often described as a commentary, the Talmud is unlike other commentaries in its easy distraction from the commentarial task. Were there not two of them—the Palestinian (or Jerusalem [Yerushalmi]) and Babylonian (Bavli)—one could say that the Talmud is *sui generis*. The existence of two Talmuds marks neither as familiar.

One might have expected that the Talmud—as an unusual text—would languish unread on a musty library bookshelf or have a small group of devotees. But the Talmud has been one of the best read works of all world literature. Since coming into being, the Talmud has been the proving ground of the rabbinic elite, who rigorously analyze its every word with monastic devotion. The magnetic pull of this text has remained strong enough that all contemporary denominations of Judaism expend significant resources learning and teaching it.

Even as the Talmud has been well studied for more than a millennium, its readers have generally pursued a cherry-picking approach that allows them to focus on small passages, ignoring those that are irrelevant for the respective reader's concern. In this way, readers do not need a full set of assumptions about the way the Talmud works as a whole. This explains how the Talmud is both the primary source of elaborations on biblical narrative cited in synagogue sermons and the forum for discussing pressing matters of Jewish law. The foremost division of the Talmud into usable smaller parts is the dichotomy of Halakhah (law) and Aggadah (everything nonlegal),[1] a binary that explains how the Talmud is father both to Maimonides' *Mishneh Torah* and to the literature of Sholem Aleichem and H. N. Bialik.

This book teaches how to read the Talmud, not by detailing the mechanics of talmudic logic, but by describing how the Talmud functions as a work of literature. At its most basic structural level, the Talmud is a commentary on the Mishnah, a second-century code of Jewish law. It is misleading to call the Talmud a commentary since talmudic passages are only loosely predicated upon individual Mishnaic statutes. The smallest literary units of the Talmud, known as *sugyot* (plural of *sugya*), present themselves to the reader as literary versions of recorded rabbinic conversation. The sense that the Talmud is a rabbinic conversational archive is furthered by the Talmud's practice of attributing assertions, rationales, stories, and other parts of talmudic discourse to named rabbis in a manner that puts elements of the text in dialogue with one another. The attributions give the Talmud the feel of a screenplay; one could stage a passage of Talmud by distributing different rabbinic parts.

This book attempts to describe the Talmud by targeting a small subset of its writing—talmudic legal stories. Though only a small subset of talmudic text, talmudic legal stories are perfectly situated to represent the entirety of the Talmud for these comprise some of the messiest bits of an already untidy work of literature. The combination of their story form and legal content makes it difficult to catalog talmudic legal narratives within the division of Halakhah (law) and Aggadah (non-legal material). This book argues for a mode of reading that refuses to resolve the Talmud's incongruities by division. Rather, the book suggests that the untidiness of talmudic legal narratives—and the Talmud as a whole—mimics the messiness of life itself. By introducing a way to read the Talmud that embraces such complexity, this book produces rich readings of rabbinic literature and history and invites readers to meaningfully connect rabbinic lives with their own.

In the millennium since its composition, the Talmud has come to occupy a central position as the canonical text of Jewish law. All discussions of Jewish law, whether theoretical or practical, are conducted within a rubric that begins in the Talmud. Even though codes like the twelfth-century *Mishneh Torah* or the sixteenth-century *Shulhan Arukh* are often the public address of Jewish law, their statutes remain in force only inasmuch as these reflect compelling readings of the Talmud; innovations within Jewish law are executed through a process of return to the canonical Talmud and its rabbinic conversation.

The heretofore dominant mode of studying talmudic law privileges the statute as a genre of writing. While this is clearest within the work of those talmudic readers who produce legal codes, it is true of other talmudic commentators who signal their privilege by evaluating all legal texts on the basis of their ability to cohere with one another.[2] This privilege is evident in the attempt, ubiquitous within both the Talmud and its commentarial literature, to challenge all legal texts that appear incoherent because their statutory content is in conflict with other such texts.

As a result of the privileging of code and statute, talmudic legal narratives are regularly misread by traditional and critical readers. In the course of producing statutory coherence, the dominant mode of reading (sometimes already within the Talmud itself) forces legal narratives into statutory form and suppresses that part of the narrative that is inexpressible in statutory form. The transformation of narrative into statute erases some of narrative's distinguishing features—such as temporality, plurality, and affect. In addition to these seemingly ancillary erasures, the dominant mode of talmudic reading must often work to suppress the basic legal message of a talmudic legal narrative because the very dramatic twist that makes a story interesting is often inconsistent with the cultural expectations preserved in normative statutes.

This book both encourages and models a new way of reading talmudic legal narratives. Rather than working within an understanding of law as a statute book to which legal narratives must conform, this book uses the opportunity of legal narrative to reimagine law. Law is a cultural discourse or a language through which a culture makes meaning. The two primary advantages to defining law as discourse are escaping the sense that law is synonymous with prescription and recognizing the ways in which law works alongside other discourses both to control behavior and to constitute cultural meaning. In framing law as discourse, this work resists the tendency (common among practitioners and theorists in Jewish and other legal contexts) to presume the dominance of legal norms. The notion of law as discourse is one that emerges if we use legal narratives to represent law. It makes sense, then, to follow the narrative's own construction of law as discourse in order to create the framework of reading.

The new reading practice described and implemented in this volume enables a novel understanding of talmudic law as a site for cultural investigation. This work is in conversation with a small cadre of legal scholars (working in American and European law) who resist the temptation to work within law as an operative practice and instead explore law as a locus of cultural meaning. Law is thus a field of the humanities rather than the arm of the state. This is not to say that this book shies away from treating law as a mechanism for control and social discipline. On the contrary, this volume targets rabbinic power at the levels of the depicted characters, the depicting authors, and the interpreting readers. The book uses talmudic legal narratives as a location to examine rabbinic power within the multiple discourses of culture, appreciating both the legal and nonlegal discourses through which such power is constituted and negotiated. It is in this vein that, though this volume makes little attempt to intervene in contemporary Jewish law, its argument is relevant for that practice. By focusing on legal narrative to put Jewish law in conversation with other cultural discourses, this book highlights the choices halakhic interpreters have made and continue to make while hinting at ways in which contemporary halakhic thinkers could reimagine the relationship between Halakhah and evolving contemporary mores.

Talmudic legal narratives are themselves part of the talmudic legal discourse that has structured a millennium of Jewish law. In seeking to revisit these texts and resist the dominant hermeneutics of that legal discourse, this volume subverts from within, calling attention to the ways authoritative texts are sometimes marginalized through interpretation. This effort is akin to attempts within American legal scholarship to recover the voices of those (slaves, women) whose words were repressed when first verbalized even within the authoritative discourse.[3] The deconstructive act of refocusing attention on the hitherto marginalized (or interpretively suppressed) evidence is made more powerful through its ability to claim the authority of the tradition. The ubiquity of talmudic legal narrative throughout the Talmud, in its most important legal passages, marks this volume's call for a new hermeneutics to handle such texts as fundamental.

The multidiscursive approach to law advocated through the example of legal narratives need not be limited to narrative. Rather, once one recognizes the way that law functions as one of several cultural discourses and should be read together with, rather than separate from, those discourses, one can apply the same thick reading practice both to nonnarrative legal genres and to the nonlegal materials usually classified as Aggadah. The long-standing distinction between Halakhah and Aggadah is a dichotomy of reading practices that has long masqueraded as a division into two textual corpora; readers have divided unified rabbinic sources in order to determine hermeneutic operating procedures for each corpus. By applying a complex hermeneutics that reads law together with other discourses, this volume opens the door for a reconsideration of the value of the exclusionary gesture that separates Halakhah from Aggadah. This deconstruction of the Halakhah/Aggadah binary is analogous to the similar gesture performed by those within the "law and literature" subfield who refuse to import material from one field into the other and insist on exploring both law and literature through a lens of cultural meaning.

Students of the Talmud in traditional settings generally work under the assumption that the attributed dialogue of a talmudic passage reflects an actual conversation that took place in one of the great Babylonian yeshivas during the amoraic period. Critical scholars recognize several facts that undermine this traditional picture: They note that the scholars named in the Talmud lived and operated in different areas of both Babylonia and Palestine; that these named scholars were often removed from one another by a century or more; that the great Babylonian yeshivas did not yet exist in the amoraic period (ca. 200–500 C.E.);[4] and that the significant portion of unattributed matter in the Talmud that binds the talmudic conversation together stems from the later period of the Talmud's redaction.[5] Critical scholarship recognizes that the Talmud's archival appearance is a posture artfully created by its editors, not a simple transcription of rabbinic conversations.

Few works have directly targeted the Talmud's fashioning from a literary rather than a compositional perspective.[6] One reason for this is that the sedimentation preserved on the surface of the text and the text's free-associative style suggest a randomness that belies the unity often presumed as the basis for strong literary analysis.[7] Another reason is the sheer size of the Talmud and the bias (inherited from traditional Talmud study) within the field toward comprehensive essentialist claims. Few scholars, including myself, have the capacity to speak from a place of comprehensive knowledge of the Talmud in toto.

The choice to limit attention to a specific genre of text within the Talmud helps to both narrow the book's realm of analysis and clarify the dilemma that the Talmud's layering poses for literary analysis. Even with the limitation to genre, this book does not claim to treat all instances of legal narrative in the Talmud. While such work would likely be fruitful, the size of that corpus with all of the attendant passages is overwhelming. In this volume, readings focus on both the legal narratives as hermetic units and on the literary and legal collages surrounding the narratives.

Over the past two hundred years (beginning with the nineteenth-century movement known as Wissenschaft des Judentums), scholars have developed a set of methodological tools essential to establishing a textual laboratory despite the challenge of inconsistent and even contradictory transcription from oral works to medieval manuscripts and print editions. This volume utilizes these lower critical tools in analyzing texts. Critical rabbinics scholarship has also evolved a set of assumptions about the meaning of texts, crafted as a corrective to the unrestrained treatment of such texts within some traditional scholarship. These higher critical assumptions form the starting point for this volume's treatments of the Talmud and other rabbinic sources. But this work is not limited to the assumptions of higher critical reading, which assumes as its task the recovery of a text's original meaning. Rather, this work is also informed by regnant literary theory, which identifies both the difficulty of confidently recovering original intent and the strong role the reader plays in constructing meaning. There is valuable tension here between the intentionalist hermeneutics of Wissenschaft and the reader-centric possibilities of contemporary theory.

Two of my mentors, David Weiss Halivni and Shamma Friedman, have together been responsible for the most important transformation within talmudic hermeneutics—the approach that makes dividing the Talmud into its historical layers a consistent a priori rule rather than an occasional post facto necessity.[8] This volume, which focuses on a specific subgenre of talmudic text, is enabled by their insight and approach. This book also owes a debt to Daniel Boyarin's *Carnal Israel*.[9] When I first encountered *Carnal Israel* as a rabbinical student, it inspired me to imagine rabbinics as part of a broader humanities discourse. Like *Carnal Israel*, this volume hews to the close reading styles of New Criticism and its postmodern heirs. It considers all of its texts within a hermeneutics of suspicion that presumes multiple registers beneath the surface. The goal is to produce a sense of these texts that is persuasive and compelling. Strong literary analysis produces a rich meaning from these texts by enabling their full flourishing as a literature with all of the unknowing knowledge that good criticism is capable of unveiling.[10]

Though the major work of this book is its contribution to talmudic poetics, the book also contributes to a historiographic picture of the Babylonian rabbinate. While the initial chapters engage most explicitly in identifying and responding to the hermeneutic challenge of talmudic legal narrative, the latter chapters implicate the method of reading such narratives and their attending *sugyot* thickly. These applications of the book's method of reading Talmud uncover the ways in which the complex reading practice encouraged by legal narratives yields anthropological insight into Babylonian rabbinic culture. The passages treated provide a glimpse of the instability of rabbinic authority by shining a light on the boundaries within Babylonian rabbinic culture: the boundary between rabbinic insiders and outsiders, between rabbinic teachers and their students, and between one rabbi and another. At each of these liminal points, the analysis demonstrates extreme cultural anxiety where one might have expected confidence; more important than the fact of this cultural anxiety, though, is the genealogy of its manifestation in the Talmud.

Book Program

The opening two chapters of this book identify talmudic legal narrative as a form and transform it into a literary genre. Drawing together legal, literary, and cultural theory, the first chapter imagines law as a space of cultural meaning large enough to embrace even those details of legal stories that deliberately subvert the expectations of normative statutes. Along similar lines, the second chapter continues the expansion of law as a discourse by challenging the traditional dichotomy of Halakhah/Aggadah usually employed to characterize rabbinic texts; by noting the ways in which this dichotomy is most significant for its determination of a reader's assumption, this chapter deconstructs it by asking readers to refrain from classifying legal narratives as one or the other as an initial step.

The hinge connecting the book's genre thesis and its thick description of Babylonian rabbinic culture is located at the beginning of Chapter 3. The prologue to this chapter introduces the treatment of Babylonian rabbinic culture comprised within Chapters 3, 4, and 5. While talmudic legal narratives have played a little acknowledged role as the basis of much Babylonian rabbinic historiography, rabbinic historians have mined this material for their own interests in describing static institutions and relationships. This book's readings are interested in the social dynamics evidenced by literary tensions—within the legal narratives themselves and within the larger talmudic passages in which these are juxtaposed. Chapters 3, 4, and 5 each address a social relationship essential to any understanding of rabbinic culture. Chapter 3 examines the complicated relationship between rabbinic insiders and outsiders, the legal response to that relationship, and the tension between ethics of equality and the compulsion to protect group interests. Chapter 4 targets the pedagogical scenario of rabbis and their students, highlighting the local struggles and means through which individuals established their standing as teachers in the community. Chapter 5 examines the relationships of rabbis and their colleagues through an economic lens that views the rabbinic intellectual community as a marketplace driven by competition for Torah capital. The three chapters together further our understanding of the ways the Babylonian rabbis constituted, negotiated, and authorized their own communal power both collectively and individually.

The final chapter reconnects the historical treatment of Babylonian rabbinic power with the book's earlier focus on talmudic genre. While the book's earlier readings focus on terse single-scene amoraic legal narratives incorporated within legal passages suffused with the active voice of the Talmud's anonymous editors, Chapter 6 considers the genre of the elaborate multi-scene talmudic narrative that scholars have largely attributed to the Talmud's anonymous editors. This examination applies the hermeneutics employed in the reading of concise legal narratives to longer talmudic stories and suggests that scholars look to rabbinic narratives not as vehicles for transmitting discrete morals but as literary attempts to process contemporaneous culture. In this vein, literary analysis highlights the ways in which talmudic storytellers themselves embrace the cultural complexity often resisted by the editors of talmudic conversational passages. This insight partially reconstructs the Halakhah/Aggadah dichotomy along different lines as a distinction between literary genres.

Chapter 1

Privileging Legal Narrative: Resisting Code as the Image of Jewish Law

Jewish history witnesses a long-standing tension over legal codes.[1] Though there have been attempts to reduce Jewish law to a code of mandates and prohibitions, each such attempt has encountered resistance.[2] The earliest codes of Jewish law are embedded within the Torah; Bible critics long ago hypothesized their originally independent documentary origins. Though they are blatantly separable, the fact of their embedding speaks to redactors who resisted the codificatory impulse by contextualizing such codes within the narratives of ancient Israel.[3] Even while canonizing controversy, the second-century Mishnah organizes Judaism through its code; but the later Talmuds that preserve and comment upon the Mishnah undo much of its codificatory work. Maimonides and Rabbi Joseph Karo are the best-known post-talmudic codifiers; each of their codes encountered strident contemporary opposition.

Codifiers of Jewish law have been driven by an assumption, often implicit, that codes are the ideal form for representing law. This assumption is sensible: since law is often equated with its normative function, a code would seem to offer the most efficient way to represent the mandates and prohibitions that determine a legal subject's behavior. But law is not composed entirely of its normative function, and the code—like other metonymies—is blind to nonnormative aspects of the law. Codes present mandates and prohibitions, ignoring questions of genealogy, legal authority, and the relationship between theoretical law and lived life. Even the most well conceived and executed codes (*Mishneh Torah*, for example) can, as a result, still be found lacking.

The strained relationship between Jewish law and code provides a key to precisely situating the difficulty of legal narratives in the Talmud. In his work on court case accounts in the Babylonian Talmud, Eliezer Segal notes the general perception that legal stories featured in talmudic legal discussions are often incoherent with other talmudic legal texts.[4] This incoherence is often challenged by named rabbis or the anonymous voice of the Talmud; when it survives unnoted in the Talmud's text, it is usually the basis for serious post-talmudic commentary. The perceived incoherence of legal narrative within the Talmud can be explained by recognizing the complicated relationship between Talmud and code.

One way to characterize the Talmud is to see it as a reaction to the Mishnah and its code features. The Mishnah's code organizes Judaism, dividing Jewish law into sensible categories and subcategories. The Mishnah's six orders are themselves divided into subject tractates, which are in turn divided into topical chapters. From extant pre-Mishnah texts that survive in other works of rabbinic literature it is clear that the Mishnah's language is edited for brevity and that, despite its fame for canonizing controversy by preserving multiple viewpoints, the Mishnah does not include all extant opinions within its reports of scholarly debate.[5] The Mishnah's fealty to the statute as a genre is evident when we consider its exclusion of the prevalent tannaitic method of biblical interpretation, midrash. The rare midrashic justifications found in some Mishnaic passages serve as reminders of the large extant midrashic corpus excluded from the Mishnah.

The Talmud can be understood as an attempt to reopen the Mishnah to the material excluded during the Mishnah's compilation. The Talmud reverses the Mishnah's code by reintroducing the longer rhetoric and alternative positions of other orally preserved statutes. More significantly, the Talmud regularly challenges the Mishnah to justify its law through citation of a midrashic reading of the Bible.[6] The Talmud regularly asks for the biblical (or logical) basis for a given Mishnaic proposition—challenging the code to justify a law's authority. Within its extensive amoraic and post-amoraic discussions of Mishnaic law, the Talmud regularly foregrounds discussions of both a law's genealogy and its lived application in ways that are anathema to the Mishnah's code. It is in this context that talmudic discussions incorporate tannaitic and amoraic statutes and midrashim, amoraic and unattributed legal reasoning, and stories about contemporary life in the tannaitic and amoraic periods.

It would be easy to characterize the Talmud as an anticode because of its undoing of the Mishnah.[7] But such a characterization is imprecise. Though the Talmud undoes the Mishnah's code, its rhetoric is charged by a dynamism that is itself driving toward a code.[8] When the Talmud reintroduces alternative divergent positions and midrashic texts, it regularly does so within a framework that seeks to make all of these materials cohere. The Talmud will, for example, introduce an alternative tannaitic position by posing it as a contradiction to the Mishnah. Then the Talmud will resolve the contradiction—by aligning the deviant text with a known canonical outlier or by distinguishing the cases. Though the Talmud is famous for refusing to be driven by a desire for final legal rulings, its discussions are animated by a drive toward resolving contradictions.[9] Thus while the Talmud can be considered anticode vis-à-vis the Mishnah, it can be viewed as an attempt (however successful) at code in its own right.[10] Because of the Talmud's split relationship with code, it is possible for both codifiers and their opponents to find a basis for their work within the Talmud.[11] The post-talmudic geonim who composed codes leaned heavily on the Talmud and conceived of their project as completing Talmud's own code; the sixteenth-century central European rabbis who opposed *Shulhan Arukh* pointed to the Talmud as the model of a legal discourse that opposes codification.[12]

Stories appear on nearly every page of the Talmud. Some talmudic discussions consist of nothing but stories; others include lengthy and even fantastic stories; still others combine stories with other text types, incorporating the story's ideational content within a collage constructed from a number of different text types or genres. Many talmudic stories have nothing whatsoever to do with the law. Some borrow bits of Jewish statutes as part of their narrative construction but take significant liberties.[13] A smaller group of talmudic stories seriously engage law. It is this last group that I have in mind when I refer to talmudic legal narratives.

Talmudic legal narratives run counter to the Talmud's coherent energy; as such, these embedded stories are inherently antisystemic. Since the Talmud is sometimes considered antisystemic as well, there would seem to be little import to the claim that legal narratives oppose system. But recognition of the ways in which the Talmud's literary energy inclines toward coherence explains how and why legal narratives are perceived as deviant both within the Talmud and in its commentary. Because the Talmud regularly juxtaposes sources in a manner (natural for statutes and legal reasoning) that forces direct normative contradictions and resolutions, legal narratives are often perceived as problematic.

Among those scholars of Jewish law who critiqued codification in the wake of the proliferation of various codes in the sixteenth century, Rabbi Ḥayyîm ben Bĕṣalēl articulated the most radical antisystem understanding of Jewish law. In his critique of Rabbi Moshe Isserles's *Tōrat Ha-Ḥaṭa't*

Rabbi Ḥayyîm objects to the attempt at codification because Jewish law is supposed to be radically open-ended.[14] As Rabbi Ḥayyîm explains it, Jewish law must permit the possibility that a single rabbinic decisor could encounter the identical legal scenario on consecutive dates and rule differently in each.[15] Within his critique, Rabbi Ḥayyîm both names the impulse to codification and critiques it. The assumption, Rabbi Ḥayyîm avers, is that noncode legal writing is a failed attempt at the more perfect mode of representation in a code.[16] The failure of Ashkenaz to produce a code, the assumption goes, is a function of the scholarly failing of this Jewish subculture. Rabbi Ḥayyîm objects by declaring the failure to codify a function of the Ashkenazic aversion to system. Only a completely flexible mode of writing permits the kind of open-endedness that allows a rabbi to decide the law one way today and the opposite way tomorrow.

This book follows Rabbi Ḥayyîm in identifying and upending an implicit assumption that law is best articulated as a codified system. Where Rabbi Ḥayyîm advocates open-endedness in the *practice* of law, this study posits open-endedness as the foundation of meaning *within* law—a foundation, that is, that precedes its practice.

Jewish law is actively embraced by contemporary Conservative and Orthodox Judaism. Each of these movements has been pulled in the last decades toward a description of Jewish law as a "system."[17] Within academic scholarship, Jewish law is studied by Talmudists, comparative legal scholars, religionists, and ethicists. Each of these fields has similarly seen Jewish law described increasingly as a system. The advantages of this pull toward system are manifold. The system allows for ease of comparison, internal integrity, and weaker critiques of individual actors within the political world of Jewish law. The turn toward system in Jewish law dovetails with parallel developments within the study of the law in statist contexts worldwide.[18]

This book follows the efforts of feminist scholars in challenging the notion of Jewish law as "system."[19] By focusing on talmudic legal narratives, a set of canonical texts that inherently resist the systematizing force of the Talmud, this work provides a new set of texts through which to describe law as a cultural discourse or language rather than a systemic code. My approach emphasizes the subjectivity of individual actors and the politics that enter into moments of legal decision making. Opening talmudic narratives to this more subjective interpretation also permits an embrace of the particulars of lived life that defy comfortable categorization. Ultimately, what we gain in reading Talmud along these lines—in insisting on a less systematic and more subjective reading practice—amounts to a richer, more complex description of life within Jewish legal culture. What is excavated, then, is Jewish law as it might be *lived*, rather than codified.

Bakhtin and Cover in Dialogue

This chapter, which maps the theoretical space in which the book's methodology operates, draws on the work of an unlikely pair of scholarly fathers—Robert Cover and Mikhail Bakhtin—to posit law in nonsystemic terms. The image of law as a set of rules is neither the literary desideratum nor the working assumption of this chapter. Rather, I look to the union of Cover and Bakhtin so as to fashion an image of law that is both attentive to the particular and open to the complexities of cultural life.

Mikhail M. Bakhtin was a Russian literary scholar active in the first half of the twentieth century whose prescient brilliance was only awarded its due following his death in 1975. As both a dissenter to the orthodoxies of Russian formalism and a victim of Soviet state persecution, Bakhtin is ideal for thinking through the project of resisting the image of law as a code.

Russian formalism engaged in poetics—the analysis of how literary works produce meaning. The formalists' primary focus was great literature, and the highest position in the canon of great literature was reserved for poetry. The Russian formalist project focused heavily on poetry at the expense of prose, striving to articulate a clear set of rules to capture the many ways in which a poem produces meaning.[20] Russian formalist poetics was not limited to poetry; but formalists treated prose using rules established within the study of poetry. In this sense, prose writing was considered a lesser form of literature that worked—when it did—by imperfectly employing the techniques of poets. Novels, as a genre, were thought inferior forms of literature because of their failure to adhere to the rules of poetics. Poems were linguistic productions elevated to high art by their manifold poetic techniques; novels were low art because their language had more in common with ordinary speech than with the creative brilliance of poetry.

In contrast to his peers, Bakhtin would come to celebrate prose and particularly the novel; he did so by embracing the very feature of ordinariness that was so despised by contemporary theorists.[21] In order to establish a poetics that privileges the novel in its ordinariness, Bakhtin challenged assumptions about poetics. Instead of judging prose on the basis of poetry, Bakhtin reversed the relationship to privilege prose as the literary ideal.[22] Unlike poetry, he claimed, prose refuses to force the ordinary everyday into the artificial imposed frame of poetry.[23] The very untidiness of prose—the fact that it cannot be reduced to a simple set of rules—becomes for Bakhtin that which makes it valuable. Prose, and particularly novelistic prose, is a better mirror to the complexity of life, language, and the world than the rigid genre of poetry.[24]

Mapping Bakhtin onto the Talmud, one can see a parallel phenomenon in the relationship between talmudic legal narrative and legal statutes. It has been said that talmudic legal narratives are, as a whole, incoherent with legal statutes.[25] The reason for this is that the default mode of analyzing law has been one that compares all legal texts as if they are statutes; within such a mode legal narratives cannot but be incoherent because, as prose narratives, they are messier than statutes. In order to properly read such narratives, one needs to demote the position of statute in legal culture and, instead, situate law around the messy legal narrative.

Bakhtin's resistance to formalism has been understood as a critique of "semiotic totalitarianism."[26] Bakhtin is suspicious of rigid systems of thought that claim to assert total mastery or control. Within the context of ethics, Bakhtin expressly critiques ethicists who reduce the ethical imperative to a set of rules.[27] This reduction, Bakhtin argues, dissolves the urgent sense of responsibility that a specific event demands. Rules-based ethics become mechanical and sometimes, in that mechanical process, miss the individual subjective demands of the specific scenario.[28] Bakhtin, it turns out, shares striking similarities with the rabbinic resistance to code within Jewish legal history. In fact, he seems to advocate the same open-endedness as Rabbi Ḥayyîm ben Bĕṣalēl but with a heavier focus on the fact that what is good for the individual ethical event is necessary for the overall integrity of ethics in general. In their resistance to the reductionism of codes, legal narratives represent what Bakhtin calls the "eventness" of a particular crisis. That legal narratives messily add elements deemed nonessential for those interested in law as code is precisely why legal narratives should be preferred for Jewish law: because those individual details reflect the individual and unique moment. It should be stressed that Bakhtin's preference for messy prose has nothing to do with historical context; the prose works he celebrates are fiction. The advantage Bakhtin gives to prose over poetry is rooted in the former's refusal to edit out "irrelevant" details or squeeze them into the mold of a rigid genre. The same can be said for legal narratives that, in their details, refuse to submit to the rudiments of statute or code.

In his work on U.S. constitutional law Robert Cover shares Bakhtin's suspicion of systems. In fact, it is because Cover is theoretically open to the advantages of anarchy that his work surpasses his legal liberal colleagues.[29] Cover is deeply suspicious of the institutions that legal liberals are interested in transforming for the public good.[30] To begin with, Cover recognized that the field of American law was (and continues to be) dominated by the actual practice of that law. Even within legal academe, practical considerations win the day.[31] The job of describing law's self-authorizing maneuvers or the assumptions of legal actors gets relatively short shrift.[32] The "law and literature" subfield of legal academia is one place in which descriptive work takes place.[33] But even here much of the scholarship is prescriptive—asking lawyers to read literature in search of legal remedies or submitting literary cases to the processes of contemporary U.S. courts. Only those scholars who use the opportunity of the multidiscursive nature of law and literature to break down disciplinary conventions are able to richly situate law within a descriptive mode that allows law to be analyzed as a field in the humanities.[34] Arguably the first and best to do this was Cover in his landmark essay "*Nomos* and Narrative."[35]

In "*Nomos* and Narrative" Cover illustrates his theory of the relationships between legal precepts and narrative through the example of a biblical contradiction regarding primogeniture. The statute of primogeniture in Deuteronomy is contradicted by narratives of primogeniture in Genesis. Deuteronomy 21:15–17 writes the law of primogeniture as a statute:

> If a man has two wives, one loved and the other unloved, and both the loved and the unloved have borne him sons, but the first-born is the son of the unloved one—when he wills his property to his sons, he may not treat as first-born the son of the loved one in disregard of the son of the unloved one who is older. Instead, he must accept the first-born, the son of the unloved one, and allot to him a double portion of all he possesses; since he is the first fruit of his vigor, the birthright is his due.[36]

The statute is cognizant of the love that might mitigate a legal precept requiring a double portion to go to the eldest son; despite that love, it is the eldest son who must receive the double portion.[37] The statute is clear and unequivocal. And yet, as any Torah reader who begins with Genesis knows, the inheritance of the younger child at the expense of the eldest is the most prevalent trope of that first book of the Hebrew Bible.[38] Time and again, the heroes of Genesis are younger siblings who attain the rightful legacies of their elder brethren.[39] As Cover notes, the Genesis narratives do not indicate that the rule articulated in Deuteronomy was not the norm.

This does not mean that the formal precept was not obeyed. Indeed, the narratives in question would lose most if not all of their force were it not for the fact that the rule *was* followed routinely in ordinary life. What is distinctive about the biblical narratives is that they can never be wholly squared either with the formal rule—though some later rabbis tried to do so—or with the normal practice.[40]

The quandary of Genesis and Deuteronomy—of biblical legal narratives that do not cohere with the precedent of biblical statute—provides Cover with a canvas on which to elaborate his alternative description of law. Before looking at Cover's resolution to the seeming contradiction of Genesis and Deuteronomy, it is helpful to further contextualize some of what is only implicit in "*Nomos* and Narrative."

The section of "*Nomos* and Narrative" that employs the biblical primogeniture example is entitled "The Thickness of Legal Meaning."[41] The term "thickness" is taken from Clifford Geertz's famous essay "Thick Description: Toward an Interpretive Theory of Culture,"[42] referenced explicitly by Cover in an early footnote of the essay.[43] In "Thick Description," Geertz calls for anthropologists to adopt a semiotic approach that defines culture as "the webs of significance man himself has spun."[44] This definition of culture encourages anthropologists to abandon "thin" descriptions that focus on the observable physical world for "thick" descriptions that aim to capture all of the nuances of the various systems of meaning that operate within that physical world. Cultural analysis, Geertz asserts, is "not an experimental science in search of *law* but an interpretive one in search of meaning."[45] The term "law" in the quotation is synonymous with a predictive rule; Geertz's point is that the anthropologist needs to abandon the tendency for single-cause descriptive rules in favor of a sense of overdetermined cultural realities.

Cover is attracted to Geertz's language because Cover is similarly interested in moving from simplicity to complexity, from a legal discourse that privileges legal rules and institutions to one that is capable of thinking through the myriad ways in which law produces meaning within a culture. One of the central dichotomies of "*Nomos* and Narrative" is a distinction between law as practice and law as meaning. The field of law in the United States is an academic one tied closely to a professional practice. For this reason, even at its most theoretical, the field of law structures itself in prescriptive rather than descriptive ways. Articles in theoretical journals, for example, are almost always designed with explicit prescriptive consequences.[46] "*Nomos and Narrative*" uses several dichotomies (jurispathic/jurisgenerative; imperial/paideic) to signal its preference for an understanding of "law as meaning." One of the reasons for the essay's foray into Jewish law is Cover's feeling that the Jewish legal context has a stronger tradition of "law as meaning" than does American law.[47]

In order to think about "law as meaning," Cover attempts to move the theoretical space of law away from the rules and institutions that tend to embody law within theoretical "law as practice" conversations. This focus on rules and institutions privileges those who make and adjudicate such rules and those who operate the machinery of such institutions as the sole agents for legal meaning. A true "law as meaning" perspective, Cover argues, includes an audience broader than these generally privileged adjudicators and legislators, extending to all legal subjects and their relationship to law; all members of society are agents of legal meaning. Narratives play a significant role in the ways that legal subjects meaningfully interact with law. These narratives situate the law as a locus of semiotic meaning within a cultural world that includes several such sites. Cover uses the term *nomos* to describe the legal space in which "law as meaning" can be evaluated; the *nomos* is the "normative world," or the cultural world seen from the perspective of normativity or law.[48] The *nomos* is a thickly described legal space—a space in which rules and institutions must interact in a balanced fashion with the narratives that frame such rules and institutions for minority and disempowered legal subjects.[49] This space is one in which the incoherence of narrative with statute does not compute as an exegetical difficulty for narratives, but as an opportunity for a thicker description of "law as meaning."

Cover introduces the contradiction of Deuteronomy and Genesis in the context of the thickly described *nomos*. Previous biblical commentaries had identified this contradiction and presumed that the Genesis narratives had to be explained or justified on the basis of the legal statutes of Deuteronomy.[50] By contrast, Cover resolves the contradiction of Genesis and Deuteronomy by using Genesis as an opportunity to think about law as meaning and to recognize that in the cultural legal space of the *nomos*, the expectation of the legal mandate creates the energy that drives narratives to buck its demands: "To be an inhabitant of the biblical normative world is to understand, first, that the rule of succession can be overturned; second, that it takes a conviction of divine destiny to overturn it; and third, that divine destiny is likely to manifest itself precisely in overturning this specific rule."[51]

The native inhabitant of biblical culture lives with the expectation reflected in the legal statute, but also with the cultural awareness of the larger narratives in which such expectations are contextualized. By contextualizing the legal precept within the larger theological narrative of ancient Israel, Cover preserves the truth value of both statute and narrative. To extrapolate from Cover's example, a cultural native is one who knows the explicit rules of law, but also the implicit narratives that contextualize those explicit rules, even holding out the possibility of overruling them. This does not mean that statutes are not law or that they are not taken seriously; the narratives in question would often lose their energy, drama, or humor if they did not have the expectation of the legal statute in their background.[52] Characters in narrative are aware of the cultural expectations encoded in the legal statute; they have a deep sense, in other words, of the rules that they follow or defy—and they intuitively grasp when it is acceptable, socially if not legally, to defy them. Such expectations so penetrate the subconscious that it is impossible for cultural natives not to conceptualize their behavior with respect to such expectations; for this reason, we sometimes have characters in such narratives (think Jacob blessing his grandsons) who stage both their awareness of the expectation and their resistance to it.[53]

The upshot of the biblical example is a dichotomy not between legal theory and legal practice, but between the explicit theoretical mandate of a rule book and the implicit theoretical knowledge of a native living within a culture.[54] The narrative is employed within the example as a text that encourages thick description by discussing law within a complex cultural *nomos*. The narrative is antinomian only in the sense that it resists the statutory presentation of law.

Cover's strategy of preserving the truth value of both precept and narrative offers an important model for analyzing talmudic legal narrative. There is a perception, referenced earlier, that talmudic legal narrative is often at odds with juxtaposed legal precepts in the Talmud.[55] The biblical example and Cover's approach creates a model for reading talmudic legal narrative that does not privilege the precept by considering the legal narratives deviant or antinomian. Rather, the legal narrative provides a new opportunity for thickly describing the Babylonian rabbinic *nomos*, a complex cultural world in which cultural natives internalize their legal rules as one of several semiotic frameworks through which they structure their lives. Cover interprets the biblical contradiction in light of the grand theological narrative of ancient

Israel, but one could explain the perceived contradiction of talmudic legal narrative with other talmudic legal texts through other narratives that connect normative behavior with nonlegal cultural semiotic systems.

Among the shortcomings of "*Nomos* and Narrative" is its often unspecific utilization of "narrative" and its failure to explore or articulate a theory of narrative. For this reason, the essay elides over the possibility that the dynamic of Genesis-Deuteronomy is in no small measure determined by the respective genres in which these texts are written. Part of what creates the contradiction between Deuteronomy and Genesis is that the former is a statute and the latter a set of nested narratives. Recent work in narrative theory has suggested that the resistance to legal precepts inherent in the Genesis stories and often observed in talmudic legal narratives is no accident, but is part and parcel of what narrative requires.

In his work on psychological narratives, Jerome Bruner coins the terms "canonicity" and "breach" to unify the works of various narrative theorists who argue that only the unusual or abnormal rises to the level of narrative.[56] Narrative theorists since Aristotle have recognized the importance of event sequence for the definition of narrative, but contemporary theorists generally consider such sequence a necessary but insufficient criterion for constituting narrative.[57] As proof of insufficiency, theorists often point to scripts, like the detailed sequence of a recipe's instructions, as texts that describe a sequence but would not generally be considered narrative.[58] A narrative can be differentiated from a script by the way in which it describes events that are inherently "tellable."[59] Narratives are tellable because of the interplay between canonicity and breach: "For to be worth telling, a tale must be about how an implicit canonical script has been breached, violated, or deviated."[60] A narrative becomes a narrative, in other words, because it describes events and actions that violate expectations, especially legal ones. A legal narrative often rises to the level of narrative because the expectation it violates is the one clearly articulated in legal statutes. The clash between statute and narrative creates a contradiction in content preceded by a contradiction in form—a collision course set in motion by the different generic aims of each form. On the basis of this theory of narrative, one could talk about Cover's movement from "law as practice" to "law as meaning" as a move from law as defined by its rules to law as defined by narratives—a move, that is, from statute to story.

Within American legal scholarship, there has been a recent turn toward storytelling as a mode of resistance to the dominant modes of thinking or structuring the field.[61] One deficiency in this turn has been the fact that, like most theoretical legal work in the United States, legal storytellers still generally operate within the "law as practice" mode critiqued by Cover. Despite this deficiency, there is some measure of overlap between the legal storytelling movement and the theoretical frame I am developing for reading talmudic legal narratives.[62] The perceived advantage of stories within American legal storytelling is their subjectivity—the way they narrate unique events in individual lives rather than generalizing to describe the world at large.[63] In Bakhtin's terms, storytelling preserves the "eventness" of the particular event. Martha Minow draws upon Cover's language of "imperial" forces in law to talk about this aspect of legal stories:

> Stories disrupt these rationalizing, generalizing modes of analysis with a reminder of human beings and their feelings, quirky developments, and textured vitality. Stories are weak against the imperializing modes of analysis that seek general and universal application. But their very weakness is a virtue to be emulated. A story also invites more stories, stories that challenge the first one, or embellish it, or recast it. This, too, is a virtue to be copied. And stories at the moment seem better able to evoke realms of meaning, remembrance, commitment, and human agency than some other methods of human explanation. All this might change if theorizing picks up some of the themes of stories, but, then again, it might not.[64]

Like contemporary U.S. legal stories, talmudic legal stories are generally considered disruptions within an established legal system. Minow suggests that such disruption can be inherently advantageous since it invites additional stories with other perspectives. I would recharacterize Minow's preference in Geertzian terms as one component of thick description; part of thickness is recognition of the variety of different subjective experiences. Minow's claim that stories are currently better ways of evoking "realms of meaning, remembrance, commitment, and human agency" speaks to both the affective quality of legal narratives that is absent from other modes of legal writing as well as to a certain multidiscursiveness inherent in narrative. Minow claims that explicit legal theorizing currently misses the themes captured by legal narratives, but that such a condition might change. I consider such a change impossible because the difference between legal stories and other legal texts amounts to a difference between a multidiscursive genre especially suited for thick description and a single discourse that generalizes in broad strokes.[65]

This cynicism vis-à-vis the potential for systems to absorb the lessons of narrative returns us to Bakhtin and his objection to semiotic totalitarianism. Bakhtin is best known for his preference for dialogical writing. This is often misunderstood to refer to the dialogue of characters, like those in a play. In this sense the Talmud has, in the past, been inaccurately (for Bakhtin, at least) described as dialogical.[66] Bakhtin's preference is for a dialogue of independent entities in which neither entity is contingent upon the other and both are capable of being affected by the other.[67] Bakhtin sees such dialogue as an essential feature of all language and critiques the semiotic totalitarianism of Saussurean linguistics in favor of an understanding of linguistic fluidity that recognizes the ways in which words are forever in dialogical relationships with one another.[68] Such dialogue also describes human ontology with individual consciousnesses always socially interacting with one another in a state of perpetual dialogue. Bakhtin prefers the novel over poetry because the former is a dialogical and the latter a monological genre, and this in both linguistic and social senses.[69] While the poet imposes rigid linguistic considerations on its content, the novelist embraces the ordinary dialogical features of a living language, incorporating multiple registers within its "heteroglossia."[70] At the same time, the poem exclusively reflects the consciousness of the poet, while the well-conceived novel pits the novelist against the novelist's own characters, permitting a genuine dialogical relationship that affects both the characters and the author.

The comparison between the novel and the poem for purposes of evaluating their relative dialogical position provides a model for the comparison of talmudic legal narrative and legal statute. Like the poem, the genre of statute or code rigidly imposes heavy restrictions on its use of language; the legal narrative, by contrast, has the dialogical potential of prose. This is not to say that all legal narrative reaches the dialogical level of a Dostoevsky novel, but that it is relatively more dialogical as a genre by virtue of its flexibility. Likewise, the statute is similar to the poem in that it reflects the single consciousness of the lawgiver, tolerating no dissent.[71] The legal narrative, in contrast, can depict multiple perspectives and permit a dialogical divide between writer and character along novelistic lines.[72]

In some of his writings, Bakhtin transfers the notion of "dialogical" from the context of individuals in dialogue to the context of a dialogue between linguistic or semiotic discourses.[73] Put differently, Bakhtin does not confine his notion of "dialogical" to an actual human encounter, but suggests that an idea is inherently dialogical, both linguistically and socially, because it presents an opportunity for different systems of meaning to encounter one another. The contemporary ideational world, for example, is often subdivided into different academic fields—psychology, sociology, religion, literature, law, and others—that each provides a means of constructing and evaluating one's culture. All entities that operate within culture—like all words in language—are always already sites of dialogical meaning making. In this sense, Bakhtin's dialogical entity overlaps with Geertz's description of culture as a semiotic web. It is often the case that individual cultural languages—the fields mentioned above—presume their own authority and resist their situatedness among parallel cultural languages.

Jewish legal discourse is not unlike other legal discourses or other cultural languages in presuming its own authority monologically.[74] This is one of the reasons why that discourse—sometimes in the Talmud itself and sometimes in post-talmudic literature—struggles with talmudic legal narrative. The more dialogical such a narrative is—framing the normative in the context of conflicting semiotic characterizations—the more palpable the sense that the narrative resists the authoritarian single consciousness of a uniform legal discourse.

In an essay on storytelling in contemporary American jurisprudence, Martha Minow justifies the preference for this legal praxis in the following way: "Modes of analysis and argument that maintain their exclusive hold on the truth are suspect. By casting doubt on alternative modes, they shield themselves from challenge and suppress alternative ways of understanding. They also render ordinary and explicable all they encounter: 'To a hammer, everything looks like a nail.' . . . Storytelling offers a worthy challenge to these modes."[75]

Bakhtin would term "modes of analysis and argument that maintain their exclusive hold on the truth" monological modes of reasoning. The challenge inherent to both contemporary legal storytelling and talmudic legal narratives lies in the fact that such texts narrate dialogically. The contemporary American legal narrative and the talmudic legal narrative share a connection to the dialogical realities of lived life; unlike poetry or statutory law, the legal narrative does not impose a maximal all-encompassing framework for processing a given fact pattern or sequence of events. The inherent "tellability" of narratives creates the "extraordinary" nature of such stories. Their refusal to impose strong structural rigidity on their own narrations allows such stories to be dialogical in the manifold sense of Bakhtin's use of the term.

The inherently dialogical quality of legal narrative makes it less than surprising that Cover was drawn to the narratives of Genesis as a means of articulating a thickly described or dialogical *nomos*. Even as Cover gravitates toward Jewish law to find support for his notion of "law as meaning" in a narrative iteration of the law, his own example demonstrates the extent to which the dominant hermeneutic of Jewish exegesis suppresses the tellable qualities of legal narrative. Cover was himself aware of this rabbinic hermeneutic: "What is distinctive about the biblical narratives is that they can never be wholly squared either with the formal rule—*though some later rabbis tried to do so*—or with the normal practice" (emphasis mine).[76]

That some rabbis would attempt to make the precept of Deuteronomy cohere with the narratives of Genesis by privileging the formal rule and distinguishing the narratives is not surprising. This type of dialectical work is at the heart of talmudic—ergo all of Jewish—legal discourse.

The Talmud is often described as a dialectical text.[77] More precisely, many of the Talmud's legal pericopes are structured around questions of canonical contradiction. The rules for such contradiction are somewhat idiosyncratic since the Talmud is comfortable with flat-footed disagreements among hierarchical equals, but uncomfortable with the possibility that a later authority can disagree with an earlier one or that an attributed position will be contested by an unattributed one, even of the same weight. Frequently such contradictions are distinguished dialectically. Many talmudic legal pericopes contain such dialectic resolutions; so ubiquitous is this phenomenon in the Talmuds, in fact, that the title of the works in toto—*Talmud* or *Gemara*—derives from a term sometimes employed within these works for the dialectical resolution of contradiction.[78]

Bible scholars have increasingly resisted the very contradiction that forms the basis for Cover's example.[79] After all, Deuteronomy and Genesis, taken together, do not compose a unified work, and it is more than possible that the Deuteronomy precept is itself anomalous within an ancient Near Eastern cultural world that generally permitted a man to alter his estate in light of love.[80] But this critique is somewhat beside the point. That the Genesis narratives are still tellable in the sense of defying cultural expectations can be evidenced from the ways in which the stories themselves perform the normative expectation of primogeniture before subverting it. Even so, a similar critique—separating sources from each other—is impossible to register on talmudic legal narratives since such texts inhabit the same textual atmosphere as their statutory and midrashic counterparts. These narratives sit cheek by jowl with legal statutes or midrashim that directly contradict some of their legal content, and this contradiction is frequently the basis for explicit dialectical conversation within the Talmud.

To explore the dialogical nature of talmudic legal narrative is, to some extent, an exercise in reading against the grain. The dominant hermeneutic of dialectical interpreters both within the Bavli itself and in the post-Bavli commentarial literature generally challenges the legal narrative to "square with the formal rule." The exercise of reading talmudic legal narratives involves, therefore, the utilization of source criticism to separate the legal narrative unit from its intra-talmudic interpretation. Such reading practice also involves reckoning with the disparity between the inherently dialogical legal narrative and the generally monological frame of interpretation that seeks to limit the juridical content of legal narratives to that which can be firmly established by formal statute, midrash, or reasoned argument.

Měgîllâ 7b: Imperative Drunkenness

An example of the perceived incoherence of talmudic legal narrative instantiates the above theoretical framework. In its discussion of the laws of drinking on the Purim festival, Měgîllâ 7b has the following juxtaposition of explicit legal precept and legal narrative:

> Rabbâ [ca. 260–320 c.e.] said, "one is obligated to become intoxicated[81] on Purim until one does not know [the difference] between 'cursed is Haman' and 'blessed is Mordecai.'"

> Rabbâ[82] and Rab Zêrā [ca. 260–320 c.e.] made the Purim feast with one another.
> [After Rabbâ had gotten drunk][83] Rabbâ went and slaughtered Rab Zêrā .
> Rabbâ[84] asked forgiveness on Rab Zêrā and brought [Rab Zêrā] back to life.
> A year later, [Rabbâ] said to [Rab Zêrā], "let the master come and let us do Purim [together[85]]."
> [Rab Zêrā] said to [Rabbâ], "miracles do not happen every[86] time."

Rab Zêrā's refusal sets the stage for a protracted discussion among later interpreters of whether drunkenness is required or forbidden on Purim. The Talmud does not pose story and dictum as contradictory nor does it resolve any tension between the two. Some participants in the post-talmudic Jewish legal discourse, though, saw these two adjacent texts as incoherent. The first extant text to note the story's contribution to law cites Rabbênû 'Eprayim of Qalʿat Ḥamad, a student of Rab Yiṣḥaq Alfasi [1013–1103 C.E.], the author of *Hilkōt Rabātî*. *Hilkōt Rabātî* attempts to make the Talmud more usable as a decision-making text by digesting the Talmud, leaving out competing legal rulings in favor of a single position and eliminating nonnormative materials. In its treatment of this passage, *Hilkōt* cites only the dictum requiring inebriation and makes no mention of the story that follows it. Rabbênû 'Eprayim, however, finds normative content in the story that contradicts the dictum. The message of the story, Rabbênû 'Eprayim avers, runs counter to the mandate for inebriation: the moral of Rabbâ's murderous act is that inebriation is a bad idea. The language of Rabbênû 'Eprayim, cited by Rab Zĕraḥyâ Halēwî [1125–1186 C.E.] in *Hamā'ôr Haqāṭān* is noteworthy for the intensity of its rhetoric: "From that incident [in which] Rabbâ went [and] slaughtered Rab Zêrā, [and the] next year he said to him let the master come and let us do etc. the dictum of Rabbâ was edged out, and the law does not follow [his dictum] and *it is inappropriate to act accordingly*."[87]

Rabbênû 'Eprayim is not content to understand this as a debate between two equally weighty texts. Rather, the later narrative text with its dire consequences overwhelms the legal dictum and eliminates its mandated behavior even as optional behavior; *the legal narrative has changed the law from mandate to prohibition*! The subsequent commentarial literature and legal codes debate the law's requirements, splitting into two camps: those who require inebriation according to Rabbâ's dictum, and those who follow Rabbênû 'Eprayim in reading the story as a cautionary tale that contradicts and overrules Rabbâ's dictum.[88]

Even as the commentaries and codes take this legal narrative seriously as law, their reading of the narrative places the story within a narrow legal frame, transforming its content so that it becomes the mirror image of the dictum that precedes it. The story is made to look like a formal rule that states that one may not get inebriated on Purim. The discourse of reading that is interested in a prescriptive understanding of the law is *only* interested in the prescriptive content of the story and mines the story for that alone.

Though the medieval commentarial literature effectively rewrites the story as a contradictory dictum, there remains in postmedieval exegesis an awareness of the violence of this rewrite and its insufficiency to fully appreciate the story of Rabbâ and Rab Zêrā. In his commentary to *Shulhan Arukh*,

Rab 'Eprayim Zalmān Margōlîyōt of Brody (1760–1828 C.E.) revisits the question and claims a prophetic basis for a new compromise:

> One is obligated to become inebriated . . . many wish to explain what is meant by this and to me the youngster this was explained in a night-time vision . . . the great obligation of drinking is *up until the point where one cannot differentiate* between hero and villain, for beyond this point [inebriation] nullifies the intent of the obligation . . . and it is thus explained why the Talmud juxtaposed the story of Rābā and Rab Zêrā which *at first glance seems like it contradicts*. . . . On the contrary, I cite a proof from this that that which one is obligated to celebrate has a limit.[89]

Rab 'Eprayim finds the basis for compromise in the ambiguous word "until" within the dictum. While the simple explanation of "until" is a minimal standard of inebriation that one must reach to satisfy the precept, Rab 'Eprayim suggests that "until" means a maximal line beyond which one cannot tread; the narrative interprets the precept by demonstrating the inherent danger of going over the line. Rabbâ's narrative behavior, read by many medieval authorities as a contradictory dictum, now confirms the legal precept that precedes it.

Even though Rab 'Eprayim Margōlîyōt's reading makes the hermeneutic choice of preferring the story to the dictum, reading the dictum on the basis of the story, it still conceives of the story as if it were a dictum saying that one may not get too drunk on Purim. In confining the story's poetic register to the realm of normative legal rules, such a reading misses out on much of the story's thickness. That thickness is important not only for the insights it provides into rabbinic culture, but also for its contribution to the understanding of the rabbinic *nomos*.

Reading Mĕgîllâ 7b Thickly

The passage in Mĕgîllâ provides a vivid instantiation of the clash between the breach of canonicity that inheres in tellable narrative and the confining expectation of legal precedent. Scholars of rabbinic narrative have debated whether such narratives were produced as popular folk literature or as part of the rhetorical training of an intellectual elite.[90] Narrative theory suggests that irrespective of its compositional context a narrative rises to the level of narrative if it depicts something extraordinary. The drunken beheading and reheading in this legal narrative are what make the story fascinating. Only an extremely formalist legal reading of this passage would focus on the story's didactic moral, obliterating the rest of the tale.

We find just such a formalist reading within talmudic commentary because this formalist hermeneutic is part and parcel of the Talmud itself.[91] On page after page, the Talmud juxtaposes contradictory passages in order to generate distinctions that conceptually enrich rabbinic law. This process inherently flattens all of the sources it treats, since it looks to them only for their contradictory relationships. In the case of Bavli legal narrative, the flattening is of a different level altogether. The very juxtaposition of narrative with statute within a framework of comparative contradiction creates the impression of a flat narrative that could easily be replaced with a statutory analogue—a headline summarizing the law at the expense of the tale.

But there are greater differences between legal narratives and nonnarrative legal texts. While legal statutes are generally articulated in present time in order to evoke a universality of temporal application, the legal narratives out of which they are drawn construct their tales using a diachronic sequencing that allows for character and plot development over time. Legal narratives often utilize surface and latent emotions to generate tone and nuance; they sometimes employ multiple characters and voices, enabling predictable and unpredictable shifts in register and perspective. If rabbinic legal codes mark issues of law through binary decisions tantamount to black and white, the legal narrative represents a far richer palette, allowing not only for legal shades of gray, but for a wide range of possibilities. These differences between legal narratives and other legal texts call for different modes of reading, indeed for a broader legal discourse, as I will illustrate by returning to the example of Rabbâ and Rab Zêrā.

Purim is Judaism's day of carnival. Bakhtin famously theorized that there is, within all society, a carnivalesque energy constituted by various centrifugal forces that each resists the centripetal pull of political or religious authority.[92] For Bakhtin, carnivalesque energy becomes viewable in two ways—through the prose novel that embraces the dialogue of centripetal and centrifugal energies and through the carnival holidays on which the carnivalesque energy surfaces and coexists in tension with political or religious authority. Bakhtin's work on carnival days draws heavily on medieval Christian festivals suffused with drunken feasting, ritualized parodies of authority, and antinomian tendencies. We know of such festivals, many of them local, from the writings of church authorities struggling to suppress them.

Scholars often note that biblical holidays have pre-Israelite antecedents, and the Bible reads religious significance into these days. Along these lines, scholars have suggested that the biblical story of Purim, an event difficult to contextualize as historical, was created to offer religious meaning to a carnival holiday.[93] In Bakhtinian terms, this suggestion imagines the authors of Esther as spokespersons of authority attempting to rein in the carnivalesque energy of the day by authorizing and sacralizing it. We can understand the rabbis of rabbinic literature as performing similar work. Though the rabbinic Purim is a topsy-turvy inversion day with an antinomian bent, the rabbis gave painstaking attention to the few commandments that apply on Purim. Rabbinic literature mines Esther for its laws, turning the niceties of biblical comedy into specific mandates whose every nuance is legislated.[94] This punctilious legislation is an attempt to assert control over folk cultural practices. There is significant irony in contemporary traditional communities on Purim; rabbinic overexertion of the laws of Purim has led legal-minded individuals to compel themselves and others to attend punctiliously and with all seriousness to the reading of the Mĕgîllâ—a work of bawdy comedy.[95] The image of a costumed clown ritually reading the Mĕgîllâ with more precision than the weekly Torah reading is more than a bit farcical.

The story of Rabbâ and Rab Zêrā is itself reminiscent of some of the upheaval of Purim. Two distinguished rabbis with no hint of violent tendencies dine together and get inebriated, following not only the mandate of law, but also the precedent of King 'Aḥašwêrōš and the Jews of Persia. As a result of their excess drinking, one rabbi kills the other, slaughtering him in cold blood. There is humor in the way in which this killing is narrated without affect, as if the slaughtering of a rabbi were as mundane as the initial invitation to dinner. Like King 'Aḥašwêrōš, Rabbâ remembers his actions in the morning and undoes them (overturns them) by bringing Rab Zêrā back to life.[96] The next year Rabbâ invites Rab Zêrā again, an invitation that presumably includes feast, drinking, and the possibility of decapitation. Rab Zêrā's comic refusal ends the story in blatant comedy.

Inasmuch as the story comments on the practice of becoming inebriated, it does not appear, upon fuller reading, to undermine or contradict the practice. After all, if the violence of year one were to impact the behavior of year two, Rab Zêrā would not have to rely on a miracle. It is precisely the expectation that the two rabbis will perform their Purim feasts in exactly the same manner as previously that yields the reader's laughter following Rab Zêrā's retort. The story's comedy, in other words, draws energy from its play with the expectations of mandate.[97]

Having expanded the discourse of reading to appreciate the story's comic qualities, I would like to suggest a broader reading of the dictum as well. The dictum, it should be noted, does not say *simply* that one must get inebriated on Purim. Rather, the dictum includes a reference to the two male protagonists of the book of Esther, Haman and Mordecai. Inebriation is supposed to create a confusion of characters such that one does not know whether to bless the hero or curse him, to curse the villain or bless him. This confusion perfectly captures the quality of Purim as carnivalesque masquerade. On this day on which people dress up to assume a different identity, inebriation allows for the breaking of personal boundaries. Rabbâ's dictum is both an attempt to assert control over the practice of inebriation by legislating it and an attempt to make the ultimate hedonistic activity—getting drunk—a purposive religious event. A law demanding inebriation is bizarre, and the dictum returns to its biblical source to connect the practice with the day's character. The dictum's rhetoric marks Rabbâ's own ambivalence about legislating to control a day characterized by antinomian, base tendencies. While the dominant monological hermeneutic of Jewish law has looked to this dictum as analogous to other dicta that embody normative requirements (and asked whether inebriation is, in fact, a legal requirement), contemporary yeshiva students have (without any sense of irony) turned this statutory attempt to authorize (and thus control) drinking into a popular Purim drinking song; both are reasonable interpretations of a highly ambivalent text.

From this thick perspective, the story and the dictum work well together. The story describes the very rabbi who struggles to control the uncontrollable as being himself out of control. And yet, the next year Rabbâ is willing to do the whole thing all over again. Rab Zêrâ's comic relief stands as a comic critique of the interaction of rabbinic legislative control and the carnivalesque character of the holiday of Purim. Any attempt to read story and dictum entirely within a framework of rules underreads this material by preventing the story from critiquing the normative strategies themselves and the ambivalent impulses that stand behind them.

The Měgîllâ 7b example illustrates the disjunction between the content of talmudic legal narrative and the typical frame for reading such narratives. The monological frame is motivated by its own interests—the creation of a single precedent through a process of dialectical resolution—to read legal narratives as if they were legal statutes. Such a reading practice seeks and consistently finds the rule of law in a story that may or may not contain it. Invariably, there is content in the complex narrative that resists the simplification inherent in flattening the story into a statute. In order to account for such residue, the reader must work within a *nomos* that recognizes the extent to which the cultural world consists of semiotic systems beyond legal rules and that these systems, in crucial and nondoctrinal ways, also determine behavior, even to the point of making competing normative claims on legal subjects. The carnivalesque energy is also a normative impulse, even if this impulse is often deliberately antinomian in the sense that it typically resists extracarnival authority.

There is often an assumption that legal texts constitute the legal realities that they demand. But often, the law develops as a response to extant cultural forces. The example of Rabbâ's dictum nicely illustrates the ways in which assertions of law can themselves represent attempts to claim authority and control in the face of fluid and dialogical cultural battles. We will see a more profound instance of this below in Chapter 2, with the example of doctors and rabbis explicitly vying for control over a dying man's physical body.

Chapter 2

Deconstructing Halakhah and Aggadah

> We have indeed paved other ways
> to the writing of laws and legal traditions;
> These are the finest sifted white flour,
> But aggadot are the leavings.
> —Samuel ben Ḥofnî Gaon[1]

The dichotomy that divides rabbinic literature into "Halakhah" and "Aggadah" (meanings elaborated below) is extremely well entrenched both because it is seemingly self-evident and because it can be exceedingly helpful. When it comes to assigning talmudic legal narratives to one of these classifications, the categorization is not self-evident and, as this chapter will demonstrate, the limitations on interpretation that derive from the dichotomy cease to be helpful. Talmudic legal narratives constitute a genre that elides the division between Halakhah and Aggadah; this liminal status marks this set of texts as an ideal site to reflect upon the nature of the dichotomy, its genealogy, and the ramifications of using it as a heuristic tool. This chapter argues against the conventional wisdom that Halakhah/Aggadah is a binary classification that inheres within rabbinic text. From its origins to the present this distinction has always been most forceful in determining the ways in which readers approach texts—that is, as a hermeneutic lens. It is not that a given text *is* Halakhah or Aggadah but rather that it is treated in the conventional manner such texts have come to be treated. Moreover, the distinction between Halakhah and Aggadah as reading practices has not divided two discourses of equal weight; rather, the distinction elevates Halakhah over Aggadah. The example of a talmudic legal narrative about lovesickness, discussed in this chapter, helps illustrate the ways in which the legal discourse beginning already within the Talmud seeks to suppress the story as an incoherent legal source; the Talmud's uncanny resolution of this incoherence in a text that has been categorized as Aggadah illustrates the need to deconstruct this dichotomy for the purpose of reading legal narrative and suggests that the division might helpfully be challenged in other contexts as well.

All expositions of rabbinic literature—from broad introductions to specific analyses—operate within the framework of the well-established dichotomy between Halakhah and Aggadah.[2] "Halakhah" refers to Jewish law. "Aggadah" (sometimes *Haggadah*) is harder to define both etymologically and categorically. Because the two categories are presumed to encompass all of rabbinic literature, scholars since Sĕʿadiyâ Gāōn have found it helpful to define "Aggadah" as the complementary opposite of "Halakhah": Aggadah is everything nonlegal. Since Halakhah includes all law and Aggadah everything else, all of rabbinic literature is wholly subsumed.

Rabbinic literature is not divided a priori into halakhic and aggadic corpora. Its books are not internally marked nor are its genres of composition determinative. While one could make the case for the Mishnah as a work whose genre is dedicated to Halakhah, it is not uncommon to find nonlegal materials in the Mishnah. Though some rabbinic works of midrash seem unconcerned with legal issues, one is hard pressed to find any such work that avoids the law entirely. It is thus fair to say that there are no works of rabbinic literature that are written exclusively in a specifically halakhic or aggadic mode.[3] This failure to distinguish at the compositional level leads to the conclusion that the rabbinic process of textual production did not include a self-conscious pigeonholing along these lines.[4]

Though the evidence of composition downplays the self-evidence of a Halakhah/Aggadah dichotomy, scholars generally consider the dichotomy to emerge within the rabbinic period itself because of several rabbinic texts that divide between the two discourses.[5] It is important to note, though, that few of these rabbinic texts juxtapose the terms "Halakhah" and "Aggadah," and fewer still consider these to be a set of categories that together encompass all of rabbinic literature.[6]

If the dichotomy existed in rabbinic times, it did not have much force or consequence.[7] In the post-rabbinic world that would change. The Babylonian geonim who followed on the heels of the rabbis responsible for the Talmud succeeded in institutionalizing rabbinic Judaism by creating large yeshivas to train rabbis, proliferating responsa to advise world Jewry on matters of Jewish law and currying the political favor of the Abbasid rulers who controlled the majority of the known world in their day.⁸ It is no exaggeration to suggest that the period of geonic institutionalization solidified the dissemination and adoption of rabbinic Judaism throughout the Jewish world.⁹

Part of the geonic project involved consolidating global Jewish authority within their own confines, proximate to the Abbasids. It is fair to claim that the geonim sought to use proximity to power as a vehicle for their own coronation. The term "coronation" is appropriate for scholars who wrote succession lists for their institutional directors using the rhetoric of royalty. Claims to royalty were not the only geonic assertions of authority. Babylonian geonim grappled with Palestinian intellectuals for control of the hearts and minds of the Jewish diaspora. The geonim attempted to win this battle by establishing themselves as the contemporary version of the legendary Sanhedrin, the supreme court of Jewish law in pre-rabbinic times.¹⁰ While the yeshivas were headed by geonim described as kings, descriptions of the internal workings of the yeshiva make the deliberate analogy to the Sanhedrin as described in rabbinic literature.

The responsa genre was instituted by the geonim as a way of turning the yeshiva into a functional correspondence court. Though geonic responsa include many types of questions and answers, geonic descriptions of the genre highlight the role of a responsum in resolving difficult matters of law. The connection between yeshiva students and the production of responsa made the yeshivas institutions of higher learning whose theoretical discourse was strongly affected by a practical orientation.¹¹ As learned study became tied to the practice of producing legal rulings, focus shifted to tractates that mattered and away from those that were no longer relevant. The evidence of archaic language in several extant Talmud tractates on obscure topics dovetails with geonic reports that irrelevant tractates of Talmud were not part of the regular geonic yeshiva curriculum.¹²

The Babylonian geonim were responsible for elevating the Babylonian Talmud over all other works of rabbinic literature as the primary study text of the vocational elite.¹³ Their choice of the Babylonian Talmud was no doubt motivated by the comprehensive anthological nature of this work as the most complete work of rabbinic literature. The fact that the Talmud's language was Babylonian Aramaic and that there was a clear cultural connection with the named rabbis in its pages must have also contributed to this choice.¹⁴

The first strong utilization of the dichotomy of Halakhah and Aggadah transpired in the geonic context.¹⁵ As part of their attempt to turn the Bavli into a usable work of Jewish law, the geonim focused their curriculum away from the material they considered nonnormative. They then dismissed normative arguments drawn from that allegedly nonnormative discourse by saying: "we do not learn from the Aggadah."[16] By the end of the geonic period, there was a strong hermeneutic division imposed upon rabbinic texts that expected readers to establish prior to reading a given text whether it was Halakhah or Aggadah.[17] Though these geonic readers assumed they were identifying an important essential difference within the Talmud, those differences are nowhere marked within the Talmud. The very fact that one must say "we do not learn from the Aggadah" demonstrates that were it not for the hermeneutic restrictions imposed on the legal discourse on the basis of this separation it would be possible to find normative precedents within texts classified as Aggadah. It is important to stress that in its original utilization in the geonic period, the dichotomy functions as an exclusionary gesture, eliminating the irrelevant Aggadah from the important normative conversation of Halakhah.[18] Even if one were to insist upon Halakhah/Aggadah as an essential dichotomy in the literature (albeit one that still seeks positive definition), it would still be the case that the distinction is most important for the way it prevents legal readers from including Aggadah in their purview. In this sense, the dichotomy has been most significant as a hermeneutic rather than an essential division.

Already in the geonic period there were some who wished to formalize the essential division of the Talmud into two corpora by producing a Talmud composed entirely of Halakhah. The geonic codes—*Halakōt Pĕsûqōt* and *Halakōt Gĕdōlōt*—and Alfasi's post-geonic *Hilkōt Rabbātî* are law codes that make the Talmud a usable document for the project of delineating a clear and decisive rabbinic law. All three of these codes lean so heavily on the Talmud for their language and organization that it is easy to confuse such texts—especially in manuscript fragments—for the Talmud itself.[19] Though these codes cleave closely to the Talmud in content and form, they differ from the Talmud insofar as they strive to eliminate Aggadah. The success of this enterprise can be seen within those cultures that replaced the Talmud with *Hilkōt Rabbātî* as their primary curricular text.[20]

The rise of the printing press in the fifteenth century led to the production of two separate works—'*Aggadōt Hatalmûd* and *'Ēyn Ya'aqōb*—that invert the process of code production and create an aggadic digest of the Talmud. That it took five hundred years for this to happen further testifies to the inferior position of Aggadah among the rabbinic intellectual elite. By the mid-fifteenth century C.E. it is fair to say that the Talmud had become a divided text, separated into two separate Talmuds—one of Halakhah and one of Aggadah.

Some prior scholars have challenged the separation of Halakhah and Aggadah. Most prominent among this group is Haim Nahman Bialik, the leading Zionist poet, who penned an essay called "*Halakhah* and *Aggadah*" in 1917.[21] Bialik wrote within a Zionist environment in which the reinvention of aggadic stories as nationalistic folklore coalesced with the rejection of traditionalism to promote Judaism without Halakhah. Bialik's essay attempts to recover some notion of Halakhah by highlighting the degree to which Halakhah and Aggadah reflect complementary rather than competing discourses. Though Bialik challenges the regnant worldview that splits Halakhah and Aggadah into different discursive worlds, he does not challenge the fact that Halakhah and Aggadah are separable essential entities. In this sense, Bialik reifies the dichotomy of two distinct essential types of rabbinic text in order to argue that the two are generically distinct manifestations of a single cultural ideal—one being the fulfillment of the other.[22]

Something similar happens within Daniel Boyarin's *Carnal Israel*, a work that has been transformative for the study of both rabbinic literature and culture. Boyarin employs the language of New Historicism to bring the separate discourses of Halakhah and Aggadah in line with each other by recognizing that both are literary expressions of rabbinic culture and can productively be read together.[23] Several scholars have followed Boyarin's lead in their own discrete studies of rabbinic topics, employing halakhic texts in the reading of aggadic ones and vice versa. Despite the success of these readings, such work continues to maintain Halakhah and Aggadah as substantive essential descriptions of textual identity and, in so doing, reifies the dichotomy as an inherent one within rabbinic literature. A similar phenomenon has been noted in the purportedly interdisciplinary work that falls under the "law and literature" rubric; it has been noted that a close analysis of this work demonstrates that the disciplines are reified as separate disciplines even as scholars transgress disciplinary boundaries to poach the territory of another discipline.[24]

The reification of Halakhah and Aggadah as separate essential entities is problematic because the hermeneutics associated with the dichotomy generally value Halakhah over Aggadah. Some works of recent scholarship have tried to overcome this difficulty by deliberately flipping the scales to value Aggadah. This move generally involves transforming the Aggadah into a normative analogue to Halakhah. Yehudah Brandes's *'Aggadâ Lĕ-Maʿaśeh* literally normalizes the Aggadah.[25] Yair Lorberbaum's *Ṣelem 'Elōhîm* turns to the language of legal positivism to make the Aggadah the "second order rules" of Halakhah's "first order rules."[26] Though these works deconstruct the dichotomy, the first step of their process is an adherence to the self-evident nature of the inherent description of a given rabbinic text as either Halakhah or Aggadah.

When it comes to talmudic legal narrative, though, we are dealing with a text whose essence challenges the confidence one has in the ability to sort rabbinic texts into two categories. This chapter focuses on the following tale of lovesickness that appears in both Talmuds in a legal context:

> Rab[27] Judah [ca. 230–ca. 290 C.E.] said in the name of Rab[28] [ca. 200–ca. 260 C.E.]
> [There is] a story of a man who placed his eyes on a woman and his heart filled with black bile.[29]
> And they [came[30] and] asked the doctors,
> and [the doctors] said, "he has no treatment unless she has intercourse [with him]."
> The sages said, "Let him die, but she will not have intercourse with him."
> "She should stand before him naked,"
> "Let him die, but she will not stand before him naked."
> "She should converse with him from behind a barrier,"
> "Let him die, but she will not converse with him from behind a barrier."[31]

In this story doctors diagnose a man with fatal lovesickness; rabbis tell the man that he must die rather than engage in the acts necessary for a cure. This story is recorded in *Halakōt Gĕdōlōt*,[32] and Alfasi's *Hilkōt Rabbātî* (two halakhic digests of the Talmud) and in *'Aggadōt Hatalmûd* and *'Êyn Ya'aqōb* (two aggadic digests). Thus even according to those who understand Halakhah and Aggadah as an essential division, there is a duality to legal narrative that defies easy categorization. One of the reasons this legal narrative is difficult to categorize is that the Halakhah/Aggadah dichotomy has accumulated a considerable number of additional resonances.

As mentioned above, scholars have generally followed Sĕ'adîyâ Gāōn's definition of the dichotomy such that "Halakhah" references all legal texts and "Aggadah" references everything else. But this definitional issue does not fully describe the extent to which the hermeneutic dichotomy of Halakhah and Aggadah has come to be meaningful.

Since the geonic period, the dichotomy of Halakhah and Aggadah has privileged halakhic discourse over aggadic. From that time Halakhah has been the central curricular activity of the vocational scholar, the centerpiece of a yeshiva education. Aggadah was relegated to the more popular sermon. This divide between Halakhah and Aggadah as, respectively, scholarly and popular discourses, can be demonstrated by returning to the aggadic digests *'Aggadōt Hatalmûd* and *'Ēyn Ya'aqōb*. The earliest extant versions of these books are printed editions (not manuscripts), and it is as print editions consumed by a popular audience that they make their mark. Like Yiddish literature, aggadic materials were culturally gendered female inasmuch as the culturally elite male (rabbinic scholar) was expected to engage Halakhah.[33] The later *Tzena Rena* targeted the female population with a heavy dose of Aggadah.[34]

With the rise of Wissenschaft des Judentums, the dichotomy between Halakhah and Aggadah received an even more significant overlay of rational and irrational. The preference of the geonim was now ratified by rationalist Wissenschaft scholars who were often ashamed of the fanciful and unrigorous Aggadah.[35] The Wissenschaft division of the works of midrash into the imprecisely named *Midreshei Halakhah* and *Midreshei Aggadah* is a further mark of the transformation of a dichotomy of interpretation into a dichotomy of essential rabbinic texts.[36] Though Wissenschaft scholars worked on both Halakhah and Aggadah, they often treated midrashic works composed largely of nonlegal materials more for external form than for internal content.[37]

As part of a trend in literary and cultural studies toward the hitherto marginal, the last few decades have seen the emergence of a rigorous study of Aggadah alongside continued scholarly work on Halakhah. Upheavals in the formerly logocentric rational world have led to a revaluation of midrash as both a literature and a method of interpretation. Yonah Fraenkel's rediscovery of rabbinic stories as literary classics has led to a burgeoning cottage industry of work on rabbinic narrative.[38] Even as Aggadah has been propped up in the last thirty years, efforts in this direction have led to a further reification, this time in methodological terms, of the essential dichotomy. Though scholars of rabbinic Halakhah share linguistic, philological, and lower critical tools with each other, the higher critical work done in these two fields is distinct. Scholars of Halakhah work within an updated traditional framework primarily interested in tracking the multiplicity of different halakhic opinions and locating each such opinion on a historical timeline. Scholars of Aggadah, meanwhile, are more closely engaged with contemporary academic conversations in literary and cultural theory.

With this deeper understanding of the multiple registers at play in the Halakhah/Aggadah dichotomy, I turn now to the lovesickness story. The story of the dying lovesick man is one in which the protagonist approaches the rabbinic authorities for a legal ruling. Since the story explicitly implicates the law, it is not surprising that it is cited in the early halakhic codes. The reason why the story also appears in *'Ēyn Ya'aqōb* and *'Aggadōt Hatalmûd* is that by the sixteenth century narrative was also treated as a positive characteristic of Aggadah. The identification of narrative with Aggadah did not stop in the sixteenth century. Scholars today sometimes translate *Aggadah* as "narrative." Though a technical utilization of Sĕ'adîâ Gāōn's negative definition of "Aggadah" would presumably categorize the story of the lovesick man as Halakhah, the accretion of narrative as a positive descriptor of Aggadah creates the possibility to claim this material as Aggadah.

The designation of the lovesickness story as Halakhah or Aggadah determines whether the text is treated as rigorous or whimsical, scholastic or avocational, curricular or extracurricular, rational or irrational. In the world of contemporary scholarship, the designation of this text as Halakhah invites an attempt to, for example, historically situate the legal arguments of the text within the evolutionary timeline of Jewish law; the designation of this text as Aggadah invites an analysis of the story as narrative utilizing the theoretical techniques of New Criticism or New Historicism. The reading that follows will resist designating the story as either Halakhah or Aggadah and utilize the regnant critical methodologies of both to explore the story's meaning.

Yonah Fraenkel's Halakhah Test

Scholarship on rabbinic narrative owes an oft unrecognized debt to Yonah Fraenkel. Since he began his project in the 1970s, Fraenkel has successfully transformed rabbinic narratives from poor historiographic eyewitnesses to much studied literary short stories. The pressure against Fraenkel's project sometimes produces, within Fraenkel's writing, a dogmatic oppositional stance: rabbinic stories are not historiography,[39] they are not folklore,[40] and they cannot be read with external context. These oppositions often make Fraenkel a straw man for work that has followed his own and is willing to accept a greater degree of complexity on these binary questions.[41]

Much of Fraenkel's work is engaged in a polemic with the default practice of traditional and critical rabbinics to value Halakhah and devalue Aggadah. In his work on rabbinic narrative, Fraenkel is quick to point out that rabbinic texts are not divided based on this dichotomy and that the social practices of the *beit midrash* (house of study) in which rabbinic texts were produced were no different for one text or the other.[42] Fraenkel insists that the rabbis who produced halakhic *sugyot* are identical to the ones who produced rabbinic narrative, and that the production of each transpired side by side in the study hall.[43]

A recent collection of Fraenkel's essays includes a new work on the relationship between Halakhah and Aggadah vis-à-vis rabbinic legal narrative.[44] Fraenkel begins with the impossible task of producing a positive test to determine whether a specific text is Halakhah. Fraenkel posits that a halakhic text has three defining characteristics: a legal scenario, a prescriptive rule, and a justification. Fraenkel knows that many mainstream rabbinic legal texts ordinarily classified as Halakhah do not provide their justifications; he therefore allows that the justification of a halakhic text might only be implied. Using this test, Fraenkel shows that when an aggadic text is written in the form of a mishnah, one can tell that it is aggadic if it is missing either a concrete legal scenario or a normative prescription for such a scenario. This exercise in differentiating between halakhic and aggadic texts presumes that these are essential and consistent categories within rabbinic literature. Fraenkel here affirms the traditional understanding of Halakhah and Aggadah as essentially different texts.

Despite their essential differences, Fraenkel continues, halakhic and aggadic texts are placed side by side within rabbinic works that do not care to separate them.[45] Moreover, there are legal narratives with the artful structural design of the aggadic narratives that Fraenkel typically celebrates as New Critical high art, but that operate entirely within the halakhic discourse of scenario, prescription, and justification. The compositional purpose of such legal narratives, Fraenkel argues, must transcend their normative content, since otherwise they would have been written as statutes. Often such stories are written as stories because their literary message transcends the letter of the law, implicating higher ethical or cultural standards than the formal rules require. Fraenkel concludes his treatment of such narratives by noting that some legal narratives have been read either as dry halakhic formal treatments or as richer aggadic narratives.

In his approach to the legal narrative, Fraenkel reflects much of what this book comes to resist. Fraenkel's test requires a legal scenario and a normative rule. These requirements are not accidental; they are the raw materials of a statute. Fraenkel thus defines a rabbinic text as Halakhah if and only if it can be formulated as a statute. In his celebration of the artfulness of certain legal narratives, Fraenkel posits that the narrative form is chosen for this material in order to articulate something that cannot be expressed in statutory form. While I agree with the end result of this line of thinking, I submit that this is the clearest indicator of the hierarchy that makes the legal statute the default and judges legal narratives deviant. It is on the basis of this default that Fraenkel reads several artful legal narratives to be expressing extralegal ideas (like extremely ethical behavior). Without delving into Fraenkel's examples, I posit that one could use those very stories to create a *nomos* in which Fraenkel's "extralegal" ideas are part and parcel of the fabric of law.

Fraenkel notes that some stories have been read as either Halakhah or Aggadah. This fact alone buttresses the idea that the world of rabbinic literary stories was one in which these two discourses were intertwined, as Fraenkel writes. But it also highlights the degree to which Halakhah and Aggadah are hermeneutic lenses one employs in reading rabbinic stories and that legal narratives need not be read within the limited purview of one or the other.

There is no interest here in singling out Fraenkel. His is simply the most explicit and articulate presentation of the expectations that readers presume within the study of Halakhah. Readers read Halakhah with the presumption of finding a legal statute or a simple hypothetical. This was true even before the discourse of Halakhah was firmly solidified by the geonim. As we will see, the lovesick man story presents a problem for amoraic and post-amoraic interpreters who struggle with the fact that the narrative does not fit with the other more typical texts that comprise legal precedent.

The story of the lovesick man is found in both Talmuds. A comparative table highlights the degree of similarity in the two versions of the story (see Table 2.1).

Though the Bavli version is more elaborately developed than its Yerushalmi counterpart, there is no doubting that these two texts tell the same story.[46] In both, a lovesick man is prohibited by rabbinic authority from some encounter with the woman who is the object of his lovesick affliction. The rhetoric of the two stories includes the rabbinic voice speaking in a hortatory jussive mood and a repetition of the question with a suggested modification to the initially suggested encounter.

The two extant Talmuds are often noted for their differences; in the case of

Table 2.1. The Lovesick Man

Palestinian Talmud ʿAbôdâ Zārâ 2:2, 40d = Šabbāt 14:4, 14d	Babylonian Talmud Sanhedrîn 75a
Like one man who loved a woman in the days of R. ʾElʿāzār and became dangerously ill. They came and asked [R. ʾElʿāzār] "Is she permitted to pass before him so that he may live?"[47] He said "let him die and this not be so." "Should he hear her voice and not die?" He said "let him die and this not be so."	[There is] a story of a man who placed his eyes on a woman and his heart filled with black bile. And they [came and] asked the doctors, and [the doctors] said, "he has no treatment unless she has intercourse [with him]." The sages said, "Let him die, but she will not have intercourse with him." "She should stand before him naked," "Let him die, but she will not stand before him naked." "She should converse with him from behind a barrier," "Let him die, but she will not converse with him from behind a barrier."

this legal narrative I would like first to focus on their similarities before noting their differences. Both Talmuds are manufactured in the form of a collage in which primary sources are juxtaposed with one another in textual conversations called *sugyot*. Both Talmuds are interesting texts of interpretation because the reader encounters some of their texts within a framework in which they are already being interpreted: tannaitic texts are interpreted by amoraim and amoraic ones by the anonymous voices of the respective narrators of these works. The comparative table of the lovesick man narratives above cites the narratives themselves, absent their interpretive frameworks. In both Talmuds this lovesickness narrative is interpreted by both named amoraim and the unattributed voices that frame the respective talmudic conversations.

The interpretation of the legal narrative of lovesickness in both Talmuds is driven primarily by the need to make this story cohere with a set of precedents that do not demand the actions recommended by the story's rabbinic authority. As was noted above in Chapter 1, this drive for coherence constitutes the energy behind many if not most talmudic *sugyot*. Though *sugyot* collect disparate material on a given subject, this material is not haphazardly laid out but presented in a linear fashion through a series of questions and answers. This give-and-take is often animated by the attempt to keep a certain form of conceptual consistency within its subject matter by insisting on canonical coherence. When the subject matter of a *sugya* is a normative legal issue, the *sugya* will typically juxtapose texts with slightly different formulations and create a well-nuanced coherent conceptualization of the subject matter. And, of course, if a *sugya* contains two canonically equal texts that directly contradict each other, the *sugya* takes on the responsibility of distinguishing such texts from each other.

Both Talmuds situate the lovesickness narrative within *sugyot* that discuss a fatal choice of death versus sin. The Palestinian Talmud situates its discussion of cardinal sin within the Mishnaic context of the fatal crimes of Sabbath violation and idolatry; the Babylonian Talmud situates a very similar discussion in the context of vigilante justice. The two Talmuds cite a similar source regarding the three cardinal sins for which Judaism asks one to accept death over violation (see Table 2.2).

Table 2.2. Three Cardinal Sins

Palestinian Talmud	*Babylonian Talmud*
Rab Jacob in the name of Rab Yôḥānān [said they] may be cured with all [forbidden things] except those of idolatry, illicit sex, and murder.	Rab Yôḥānān said in the name of Rab Simeon ben Yĕhôṣādāq, "They tallied and concluded in the attic of the house of Nitzeh in Lod [that] all prohibitions in the Torah, if they say to a person, 'violate and you will not be killed' he should violate and not be killed except for [the prohibitions of] idolatry, illicit sex, and murder."

Despite their different basic texts, both of these agree on the fundamental list of cardinal sins.[48] Only murder, idolatry, and illicit sex are weighty enough to mandate the preference for death over violation. The upshot is that in a situation of either medical or political coercion, one should choose to violate a prohibition unless it rises to the level of one of these cardinal sins.

The tale of lovesickness is not a tale of proposed idolatry or murder, but it is, seemingly, a tale of illicit sex. It is worth noting that the minor differences in the original story in the two Talmuds are statutorily significant. The linguistic ambiguity of the Palestinian version makes it possible that that text never claims that actual coitus is necessary to effect a cure. But even were we to focus on the Bavli version of the story and presume that coitus is suggested as an initial medical prescription, such an act might not rise to the level of "illicit sex" as rendered in the statute. The term "illicit sex" of the statute might refer specifically not simply to unlicensed sex but to taboo sex. Though there is some debate on this in rabbinic literature, the illicit sex of the statute is generally understood as sex explicitly prohibited in the Bible: that is, homosexual sex and heterosexual sex between a man and an immediate relative or between a man and a married woman not his wife. Even if the scenario were one involving a biblically taboo sexual relationship, the suggestion in both stories of nonphysical encounters as prescribed cures makes the prohibitive declaration surprising; the story's rabbis suggest that they would rather someone die than be permitted a blind encounter with someone to whom he is not married.

The original lovesickness story absent editorial commentary does not describe the man's obsessional crush as a married woman. Since such information is decidedly relevant for legal thinkers, the absence of this information would seem to lean toward an understanding that the story's female protagonist is unmarried, and the story's rabbinic authority prohibits her anyway. Further evidence for such a reading is marshaled from a story whose textual transmission has left us with only one version written in rabbinic Hebrew: the story of Nātān Ṣûṣîtā. The only arguably rabbinic version of this story is found at Rashi Sanhedrîn 31a where the story opens:

[There is] a story about a man who placed his eyes on a woman and his heart filled with bile.
    And she was a married woman. [Emphasis mine.][49]

The Nātān Ṣûṣîtā story follows its opening line with a statement regarding the woman's marital status. The direct linguistic connection between the Nātān Ṣûṣîtā story and the lovesickness man has led some tradents to accidentally combine the two.[50] Given their remarkable linguistic similarity, the absence of a statement regarding the woman's marital status in the lovesick man story further suggests that the writer of this story either intended an unmarried woman or was not working within a milieu in which that question mattered.

If the woman is unmarried, there is little room to define the story's encounter as a cardinal sin. This would mean that the story demands a level of commitment that transcends the commitment demanded by legal precedent. Both Talmuds open their treatment of the story by focusing on the narrow issue of the woman's marital status (see Table 2.3).

Table 2.3. The Early Amoraim

Palestinian Talmud	Babylonian Talmud
What happened? Rab Jacob bar 'Îddî and Rab Isaac bar Naḥmān. One said she was married, and the other said she was unmarried.	Rab Jacob bar 'Îddî and Rab Samuel[51] bar Naḥmēnî disagreed about it. One said she was married, and the other said she was unmarried.

In this debate of early amoraim, one scholar chooses to confine the meaning of the story based on the need to make the story cohere with the statute, but the other scholar is willing to accept the possibility that the woman was unmarried and the story still advocates death over violation, expanding the commitment demanded by the cardinal sin statute.

The view that claims that the female protagonist of the story was unmarried can be understood as embracing a dialogical understanding of the narrative that recognizes the competing forces within the scenario that mitigate against a formalistic legal calculation. The story includes nothing of the woman's desire or repulsion at the prospect of this encounter, and it provides little of the sociological, political, and psychological context in which to evaluate a rabbinic prohibition. But even without that explicit information, one of the early amoraim is willing to accept the premise that the story's woman is unmarried, and that the rabbinic authority demands the choice of death beyond the scope of the formal legal rule.

The lovesickness story is a narrative text with normative consequences beyond the scope of nonnarrative legal precedent. There are other narratives with normative ramifications that are characterized as Aggadah. For example, the legend at Bavli Gîṭṭîn 57b of four hundred Jerusalem youths who commit suicide by jumping into the sea so as not to be prostituted can also be read (even in Fraenkel's definition of a halakhic text) as prescriptively normative. In fact, some medieval tosafists use this story to buttress a claim that one could actively martyr oneself.[52] Historians of medieval Ashkenaz have been debating the issue of the tosafist use of this and other aggadic texts for normative purposes. The debate has questioned neither the general dichotomy of Halakhah/Aggadah itself nor the particular narrative genre of some of the texts that are the basis for this debate. While the issue is different for post-geonic medieval commentators than for the Bavli itself, the assumptions a reader brings regarding the potential meaning of a text, especially on the normative level, are of paramount significance for his or her reading.

Neither Talmud rests comfortably with the early amoraic conflict regarding the marital status of the female protagonist despite the fact that two amoraim of equal age are generally permitted to argue with each other. Rather, both Talmuds are energized by the problem of the lovesickness narrative's ill fit with precedent, a difficulty exacerbated by an amoraic view that embraces the full normative potential of the story. To use the language of Bakhtin referenced above, the lovesickness narrative is a dialogical text that reflects a lived reality, while the normative framework of talmudic legal precedent is a monological apparatus that cannot tolerate a deviant canonical text, even if that text is authorized by an amora. Because of the drive for monological legal coherence—consistency within all cases of a single unified legal system—both Talmuds question the amoraic view that the woman was unmarried, since such a view cannot cohere with the statutory convention that demands death only in the case of the three cardinal sins (see Table 2.4).

Table 2.4. The Talmuds' Question

Palestinian Talmud	Babylonian Talmud
It is fine for the one who said she was married. But according to the one who said she was unmarried, What about Bar Kōḥa Nagrā who loved a woman in the days of R. 'Elʿāzar and [R. 'Elʿāzār] permitted him?	For the one who said she was married the story works well, but for the one who said she was unmarried, What is this all about?

The two texts diverge slightly in this question, with the Palestinian Talmud raising an objection from an identical scenario in which the same rabbinic authority produced an opposite ruling and the Babylonian Talmud presuming that the statutory basis for the question is self-evident.

The question in the Palestinian Talmud comes from a parallel but opposite legal narrative. While rabbinic narratives are not generally considered reliable as historiographic witnesses, this narrative is almost blatantly ahistorical. One might accept as a coincidence the fact that the identical scenario of a lovesick dying patient came before R. 'Elʿāzar. It is more difficult to accept such a coincidence when the figure in the story is given the allegorical name Bar Kōḥa Nagrā. The name literally translates as "the one with the strength to hollow out." The phallic semantics of such a name are too obvious to plumb, as is the fact that the name is related to the function of the character in this narrative.[53] R. ʾElʿāzār literally permits "the one with the strength to hollow out" in this narrative. Rather than taking the story as a historical possibility, I presume that the redactor of this *sugya* needed a way to challenge the view of the unmarried amora and did so by claiming a tannaitic contradiction with another legal narrative. By the time the editor of the Bavli *sugya* treated this material, there was no longer the need to create a fictitious tannaitic source; the Bavli's *stam* merely challenges the amora's notion that she was unmarried on its face by asking, "what is this all about?"

The two Talmuds ask different questions that are the same at bottom. Both are animated by a desire to confine the normative consequences of the legal narrative and ask for a justification. The answers to this question continue to operate within a legal framework that presumes to singularly control practice. At this point, though, owing to their differing periods of compositional gestation, the two Talmuds diverge (see Table 2.5).

Table 2.5. The Anonymous Editor of the Palestinian Talmud and Late Babylonian Amoraim

Palestinian Talmud	Babylonian Talmud
(a) In one case she was unmarried and in the other she was married. (b) And even if she was unmarried in both cases, you can explain that he placed his eyes on her before she was married. (c) Some want to say she was a woman of stature and wouldn't listen to him, and everything he would do, he would do in prohibition.	(a) Rab Pāpā [ca. 320–ca. 380 C.E.] said because of family shame (b) Rab ʾAḥā son of Rab ʾĪqā[54] [ca. 320–ca. 380 C.E.] said so that the daughters of Israel should not be prostituted for illicit sex

The anonymous voice of the Palestinian Talmud offers three answers to its question of the two contradictory scenarios of R. ʾElʿāzār. I will demonstrate that all three of these answers are problematic and that the problematic nature of these answers testifies to the inherent difficulty of the predicament of reading the original legal narrative of lovesickness within a monological legal frame that will account both for the normative behavior of the rabbinic authority in the story and its opposite.

The Palestinian Talmud's anonymous voice suggests first that the first of R. ʾElʿāzār's petitioners was in love with a *married woman* (prohibited because of cardinal sin) and the second with an *unmarried woman* (permitted because not cardinal sin). But this entire question was asked within the viewpoint of the aforementioned early amora who claims that the first petitioner was lovesick over an *unmarried woman*—"It is fine for the one who said [the first one] was married. But according to the one who said she was unmarried . . .*"? How then can the answer presume that the first petitioner was *married*?

The second answer offered by the anonymous text is that both scenarios were ones in which the obsessional crush was developed on an unmarried woman, but that in the case of prohibition, the woman in question had been married in the interim and their relationship resultantly rises to the level of biblically prohibited illicit sex. This answer is a clever talmudic way of turning the amora who claimed that the woman in the story was unmarried into the view that claims that she was; there is no evidence within the amoraic debate to suggest that the woman whose crush generated a prohibited ruling from R. ʾElʿāzār was now married. Though this answer is plausible, it relies on the type of distinction that the Talmuds themselves regularly recognize as forced.

The anonymous voice's third answer suggests that the woman in question was unmarried, but also uninterested. Furthermore, she was a woman of stature who would comport herself in such a way that she would never willingly submit to the lovesick man's requests. Thus "everything he would do, he would do in prohibition." Though the "prohibition" is not clear, we can presume that rape is intended. Since she is unwilling and he very willing, R. ʾElʿāzār had to choose between death and rape; the Bavli *sugya* of vigilante justice asserts that in such a case the choice is death.[55] But even if this reading of "prohibition" as rape is accurate, the story in both Talmuds includes the possibility of a nonphysical sexual encounter that is also prohibited by the rabbinic authority. While it makes sense that R. ʾElʿāzār would choose death over rape, it is less compelling that he would make that choice in a scenario in which the lovesick man forces the woman he desires to converse. In short, the Palestinian Talmud offers three unattributed answers to its core question and none of them is fully satisfying.

The Bavli cites two amoraic answers to the question regarding the amora who claims that the woman in the story is unmarried.

(a) Rab Pāppā said because of family shame
(b) Rab ʾAḥā son of Rab ʾĪqqā said so that the daughters of Israel should not be prostituted for illicit sex

Both Rab Pāppā and Rab 'Aḥā son of Rab 'Îqqā move outside the formal discourse of legal rules to explain the position of the story's rabbis. Rab Pāppā imagines the rabbinic prohibition as emerging from the sociological reality of family shame. While technically the rabbis are obligated by the rules of law to allow the couple one of the prescribed encounters, the sociological reality of family shame vis-à-vis the woman's participation forces the rabbis to prohibit such an encounter. Rab 'Aḥā son of Rab 'Îqqā finds the basis for the rabbinic position not in family shame, but in the political consequences of a permissive ruling and the damaging message such an act would communicate regarding the value of women.

One can read these two opinions through several lenses. I am drawn to the way these amoraic answers respond to the fundamental incoherence of the legal narrative with precedential statutes. When faced with this incoherence, these amoraim presume that the narrative is deviant and that its deviance must be explained through recourse to some discourse beyond the legal rules. But what is interesting in this move beyond the legal discourse is that the move itself is performed in the service of that discourse. By turning to family shame or the societal valuing of women as normative factors, these amoraim are able to maintain the framework of an all-encompassing cultural system of legal rules. The deviant legal narrative is simply expelled from the framework of legal rules, and its normative information is explained as deriving from an external discourse. The external discourse does not challenge the authority of the system of legal rules or the individuals who operate that system; in fact, the turn to external data is precisely a move to buttress the internal monological worldview of the system of legal rules.[56]

One can make a similar claim about the final answer in the Palestinian Talmud. That answer introduces the issue of the woman's agency and stature to produce new grounds for rabbinic prohibition, but even within this new terrain the answer is offered on shaky grounds. Rather than empower the woman's agency as a significant force on its own, the anonymous answer limits such agency to a woman of stature and values that agency only because it connects with the matrix of legal precedent in a new way, with the prohibition of rape.

Though the Palestinian Talmud did not undergo the kind of massive redaction, stylization, and editing that the so-called *stammaim* performed on the Babylonian Talmud, it too has an anonymous editorial voice and occasionally shows signs of editorial structuring. In this instance, these features engage in the project of producing coherence out of the statutorily deviant lovesickness narrative.

The three answers offered by the anonymous voice of the Palestinian Talmud to the fundamental question of incoherence were cited above. As outlined above, those answers are either inconsistent with the framework of the question or insufficient to address the full scope of the question. In addition to those anonymously voiced "solutions," the anonymous editorial voice of the Palestinian Talmud uses editorial license to frame the lovesickness narrative in ways designed to ameliorate the problem.

One of the ways the redactor of the Palestinian Talmud frames the lovesickness narrative is by situating it within a structural framework that challenges the completeness of the statutory presentation of the law of the three cardinal sins. The Palestinian Talmud follows its citation of the initial statutory ban on being cured via the three cardinal sins with an expansion of the definition of each of these sins: the idolatry discussion expands the sin of idolatry to include unrequested or unintentional usage of idolatrous objects; the murder discussion expands the notion of murder to include nonmurderous brigandage; the discussion about illicit sex expands its cardinal sin by invoking the story of the lovesick man. In this way, the larger structure of the *sugya* suggests that the normative material present in the lovesickness narrative is an anomaly that the statutory framework can absorb.

Despite this larger structure, the anonymous voice of the Palestinian Talmud is still uncomfortable with the lovesickness narrative, a legal text that expands the definition of its cardinal sin in two directions. The lovesickness narrative stretches the definition of an illicit sexual relationship beyond the boundaries of biblically prohibited taboo, and it expands the definition of a sex act beyond coitus to include a visual or aural encounter. While the expansions of the sins of idolatry and murder are acceptable to the anonymous voice of the Palestinian Talmud, the expansion in the context of illicit sex is not. A strong indication of the uneasiness of the Palestinian Talmud's anonymous voice was already evident in the above-cited anonymous answers to the incoherence of the lovesickness narrative with other precedent. Even more glaring, though, is the way the anonymous voice of the Palestinian Talmud frames its introduction of the lovesickness story: "And not only when he said to him, 'bring me[57] [for sexual intercourse] a *married* woman,' but even to listen to her voice."

While the core lovesickness story does not describe the marital status of its female protagonist, we have seen above that this status is the subject of an early amoraic debate that is the basis for the discussion in both Talmuds of this story. By prefacing its presentation of the lovesickness narrative with the claim that the woman in the story is married, the anonymous voice of the Palestinian Talmud biases the reader before the reader has even read the story. As with its anonymous answers, this seems to be part of the anonymous voice's strategy to effectively eliminate the position that the woman in the story is unmarried. This would limit the story's expansion of the statutory law to the realm of the definition of the act, an expansion that closely parallels both the idolatry and the murder expansions.

The Palestinian Talmud's treatment of the lovesickness narrative demonstrates that even an expansionist mode of legal analysis that considers expanding the statutory framework in light of the legal ruling faces difficulties when it encounters a legal narrative like the lovesickness story. Below I will elaborate a theory of the story's purposes, but for now it is sufficient to note that the story is a poor fit with other legal texts on the same topic. The early amoraic debate makes it clear that though the dominant voice of the Talmuds is one that privileges other materials over narrative and attempts to adjust the narrative to fit with legal precedent because of the talmudic agenda of producing a coherent and unified body of law, there are other rabbinic voices that are willing to read the narratives as they are.

The *Stam*

To traditional students of the Babylonian Talmud, the Bavli's anonymous voice is nearly invisible. Though the anonymous warp and woof of talmudic question and answer is ubiquitous on every Bavli page, this material is treated by traditional readers as if it is necessary but supplemental—the unnoticed air that allows the attributed statements and rationale of named tannaim and amoraim to breathe. The anonymous voice of the Bavli is only (and rarely) attributed agency within traditional talmudic commentaries if such agency resolves a difficult exegetical problem. In traditional exegesis, the *stam ha-Talmûd* is a poor stepchild—remembered rarely and only for blame.

Contemporary critical scholarship on the Bavli, by contrast, is heavily invested in the *stam*. Since the groundbreaking work of Shamma Friedman and David Weiss Halivni, the importance of the *stam* in constructing, interpreting, indeed authoring the talmudic *sugya* has now become the focus of various different types of scholarship.[58] Research on talmudic Halakhah and Aggadah now begins with an assumption of evolution from the amoraic to the stammaitic periods, and historians are in the process of revising all of the observations that were made before the import of the *stam* was properly noted.[59] Relatively little has been written about the *stam* from a literary perspective.[60]

While readers of the Bavli, like readers of any work of literature, presume the existence of an author, the search for an actual author is complicated by the cloudiness of Bavli's composition history.[61] Traditionally, the Bavli has been considered a record of rabbinic conversations produced naturally by the conversations themselves; like minutes of an intergenerational meeting, the Bavli is thought to have been recorded by an eyewitness whose literary impact on this material was akin to that of a voice recorder.[62] The rediscovery of the *stam* and its importance for talmudic composition has now replaced that traditional notion of the unimportant recorder as author with the view of the *stam* as author.

The *stam* is a different author than one with which contemporary readers are familiar. Though the finished product is markedly influenced by the *stam*'s comments, the *stam* inherited much of its composition from prior writers; a good measure of this is Yaakov Zussman's assertion that Yerushalmi Nĕzîqîn is the pre-amoraic composition that the *stam* modified into Bavli Nĕzîqîn.[63] The *stam*, furthermore, does not mask this interaction with prior received material; rather, the *stam* marks the disjunction with language that allows contemporary scholars the ability to distinguish between original source and amoraic comment. Thus on every page one encounters the *stam* as a writer who is also a reader. The *stam* interprets the early materials by introducing them, interpreting them, and commenting upon them. On every *daf* (page) the *stam* is engaged in the process of interpretation that is part of the process of Bavli authorship.

The *stam* is not the first interpreter within the Talmud. The pre-*stam* Talmud already contains amoraic interpretations of tannaim or tannaitic interpretations of the Bible. The whole enterprise of the Talmud is interpretive. But as the putative author of the Bavli, the *stam* is different from other authors because its exercise is explicitly and unapologetically interpretive. While the discussion in the Palestinian Talmud ends with its three anonymous answers that parallel those of Rab Pāppā and Rab 'Aḥā son of Rab 'Îqqā in the Babylonian Talmud, the Babylonian Talmud here takes its most interesting twist as the *stam* puzzles over another aspect of the rabbinic prohibition—the seeming *eagerness* of the anonymous rabbis to prohibit without considering alternatives:

So let him marry her?
That would not settle his mind because of R. Isaac.
For R. Isaac said from the day of the destruction of the Temple,
> the flavor of intercourse was taken and given to sinners as it
> is written (Proverbs 9:17), "Stolen waters are sweet and bread
> eaten furtively is tasty." (Bavli Sanhedrin 75a)

The *stam* here wonders why the sages did not suggest that the man and woman marry each other. To answer this question, the *stam* marshals a bizarre and psychologically rich source—a tannaitic statement of R. Isaac that explains that permissible sex (within the context of marriage) is not as pleasurable as forbidden sex. The man's lovesickness can only be cured, it appears, through illicit sex. The story's rabbinic authority, this answer presumes, could not suggest marriage since the scenario is obviously one in which the patient requires the full pleasure of forbidden sex.

R. Isaac's statement is posed as an answer to the suggestion of marriage. But there is a sense in which the statement answers the fundamental question about the incoherence of this legal narrative. It turns out that the story's sages who prohibit various cures do so because their permission would remove the palliative properties necessary for the cure, which stem from the taboo. In this light, the sages' behavior loses the prescriptive force of legal precedent, reflecting their own separation from the core register of sexual pleasure as palliation.

There is an uncanny quality to R. Isaac's statement and its employment here that will receive further treatment below. At this point, I return to the original story to attempt to discover a dialogical context that is at once more appropriate to its compositional context and to a complex understanding of its poetics. With the proper dialogical contextualization of the core legal narrative in hand, I will then return to the *stam*'s resolution in R. Isaac to note the ways in which this answer is the only one within the talmudic corpus that punctures the hermetic frame of halakhic rules to permit the emergence of a multidiscursive dialogical understanding.

The Thickness of Lovesickness

The story of the lovesick man, like the biblical example of primogeniture in Genesis and Deuteronomy treated in the previous chapter, expresses a fundamental incoherence between the ruling of the judge(s) in the story and the rule on the books. Since illicit nonincestuous heterosexual sex is defined everywhere as sexual intercourse between a man and a married woman, at least two of the proposed interactions do not meet the threshold of that definition and therefore should not rise to the level of prohibition. As with Cover's biblical example, the clash is not between the legal narrative and some external legal statute or precedent. Rather, the story constitutes the rule in the process of subverting it as part of a deliberate narrative strategy. In transitioning the possibility of the sexual encounter from intercourse to a gaze and, finally, to a disembodied voice, the story downgrades the severity of the sin in order to increase the reader's expectation that leniency is forthcoming. The story itself creates a gap between the expectation of an applied legal rule and the prohibition that defies those expectations. Like the Genesis narratives, this is a narrative that employs incoherence as a deliberate strategy whose purpose is broader than the mere specification of a legal ruling.

This deliberate inversion of the rule within the narrative is part of what makes the narrative more than a mere description of a sequence. As the previous chapter noted, narrative theorists suggest that what makes a narrative "tellable" is the way in which it breaches an implied canonicity. With legal narratives, the implied canonicity is often related to the precedent established by other legal texts. When the discourse becomes dominated by the expectation that law looks like those other legal texts, the end result is the persistent impression that the legal narrative is in need of a resolution to make it cohere with the dominant precedent.

In the context of the lovesickness narrative, most of the talmudic interpreters assign the legal narrative secondary status, privileging instead the system of legal precedent. Only the approach of the Palestinian Talmud's editor allows the story to take a primary position vis-à-vis the rules, and even then, only to a point. By expanding the rules to accommodate the story, the Palestinian Talmud gives the story a rightful place in the legal system. But even this approach has its limitations, as the editor's repeated attempts to marry off the female character, even according to the view that she was unmarried, demonstrate an inability to allow the story free rein to define legal precedent.

A reading of the story that ignores or brackets the legal rules encourages an understanding of the story as engaging the law in a metalegal mode, in the process of constituting legal authority. The story of a struggle between doctors and rabbis over the dying body of a lovesick man is a myth of power that attempts to assert rabbinic unilateral control on normative behavior. This story is an ill fit with legal precedent precisely because its purpose is to create the framework of authority in which such precedent generally operates. The story's deviation from the norm—its breach of canonicity—is designed to highlight that rabbis have power *beyond* the rules of law.

The hortatory formula "let him die ... let him die ... let him die" seems perversely enthusiastic. It is this strange enthusiasm, in fact, that prompts the *stam*'s question regarding marriage: why do these rabbis embrace the possibility of death without exhausting all permissible options? But if the story is a myth of rabbinic power, then the enthusiasm of the hortatory formula is understandable as a display of rabbinic confidence in the authority to control the man's fate.

Perhaps the strongest argument for understanding the story in this metalegal way as a myth of rabbinic power is the insertion of the term "black bile" in the version of the story found in the Babylonian Talmud. The Babylonian Talmud describes the man's lovesickness using the phrase *heʿelâ libbô ṭînā*. A literal rendering is "his heart raised *ṭînā*." The word *ṭînā* has traditionally been translated metaphorically as "heaviness of the heart." But the phrase can be understood not as a metaphor, but as a physiological diagnosis. Though the general definition of *ṭînā* is "cement, or clay,"[64] the term is used by *Targûm Zĕkaryâ* (10:5) to translate the word *ṭîṭ*, or "tar."[65] *Ṭînā* thus can refer to a black oozing substance.[66] For two thousand years, diseases were explained through a theory of bodily humors associated with Hippocrates (fifth century B.C.E.).[67] One of the four humors was the Greek term μέλαινα χολή, or black bile, a term that is the basis of the English "melancholia."[68] When this humor is in abundance, a patient becomes lovesick. The story offers an understanding of lovesickness not just as an intense emotional state, but also—by invoking the term *ṭînā*—as a clinical diagnosis rendered in physiological terms.

Lovesickness is a frequent motif of Greco-Roman literature, where the typical cure for such a condition is a sexual encounter between the forlorn lover and his or her beloved.[69] In several such accounts, the disease is diagnosed by a doctor, who is unable to effect a cure because the relationship between the melancholic and his or her object of obsession is barred by social taboo—a woman in love with her son, or a son in love with his father's wife.[70] Scholars have pointed out examples of rabbinic stories that borrow Greco-Roman motifs and tale types, and the story of the lovesick man should be considered another such example.[71]

Lovesick desire is also a common motif in biblical and rabbinic literature. In the biblical canon, it fuels the poetry of Song of Songs and the 2 Samuel 13 account of Amnon's rape of Tamar. Rabbinic folktales of lovesickness include

stories that are structurally similar to the talmudic lovesickness narrative—
the historical legend of the man who steals his teacher's wife at Gîṭṭîn 58a
and the aforementioned Nātān Ṣûṣîtā account which celebrates the hero's
self-control.[72]

Most tales of lovesick desire end with a climactic encounter. The Greek
lovesickness stories and the biblical and rabbinic parallels end with either
the cure of sexual congress or with the victim's death for lack of a cure. The
talmudic narrative of the lovesick man fails to narrate desire's conclusion. The
dying man's state of desire is perpetual, terminated neither by consummation nor by death. While the story certainly implies the man's death, such a
death takes place offstage. The climactic scene of the lovesickness story is the
struggle between rabbis and doctors over the dying man. This fact, combined
with the story's rhetoric and its context in rabbinic literature, determines that
the story's rabbis are its heroes. While the story is animated explicitly by the
man's desire for his obsessional crush, it is implicitly driven by the storyteller's
desire for rabbinic authority.

The argument becomes stronger if one connects this story with other stories about dying for the law.[73] Both talmudic *sugyot* are primary addresses
in rabbinic literature for the question of choosing life over law. The dying
lovesick man is a story that uses the choice of death as a way of establishing cultural norms. This reading of the lovesickness tale as something of a
rabbinic martyrology is echoed within the Palestinian Talmud, in a parallel
legal narrative that immediately follows the *sugya*'s three-part expansion of
the cardinal sins.

> A story about R. 'El'āzār Ben Dāmā that a snake bit him.
> And Jacob the man of Qĕpar Sama came to cure him in the name
> of Jesus the son of Pandera,[74] and R. Ishmael refused to allow him.
> [R. 'El'āzār] said to [R. Ishmael]: "I can bring a proof that he may
> heal me," but he did not suffice to cite his proof, until Ben Dāmā died.
> R. Ishmael said to [R. 'El'āzār Ben Dāmā]: "fortunate are you, Ben
> Dāmā, for you left the world in peace, and you did not violate the
> fence of the sages as it is written (Ecclesiastes 10:8), 'he who breaches
> a stone fence will be bitten by a snake.'"[75]

In this story of competition over a dying body, two rabbis clash over the
permissibility of a Christian cure. Though R. 'El'āzār wants the cure and
claims to have an argument that justifies its use, R. Ishmael does not allow

it. The unambiguous nature of R. Ishmael's desire for R. 'El'āzār's death—indeed his *enthusiasm* for it—is certified by the former's reaction to the latter's death: you are *fortunate* for dying so as not to violate the fence of the sages. The statement is explicit about the root of the prohibition that demands R. 'El'āzār's life—it is the sages who erect the fence, not the law that forces the sages' hands.[76] As in the lovesickness story, there is here an explicit rabbinic desire for authority beyond the law.

The etymological evidence from the word *ṭînā* suggests that this story might benefit from an understanding of Greco-Roman cultural context.[77] The literary context of the Greco-Roman world and its tropological utilization of lovesickness buttresses the metalegal reading of the lovesickness story as a myth of rabbinic authority beyond the law. Lovesickness—both actual and literary—was often the site of cultural contestation and the arena for assertion of authority in the Greco-Roman world. Mary Wack's summary of Jackie Pigeaud's study of lovesickness is eerily apt for locating the plot of this talmudic story within a dialogical context: "The disease of love, which afflicts both the body and the spirit of a patient caught in a matrix of social and ethical relationships, lay in a cultural zone intersected by the discourses of medicine, literature, natural philosophy, mysticism, pastoral theology and didactic literature. . . . In this site of contestation *priest and physician* vied for professional territory" (emphasis mine).[78]

The talmudic story's competition between rabbis and doctors is typical of Greco-Roman culture and the ideal setting for Greco-Roman battles for authority. In its rabbinic setting, this legal tale of lovesickness in which rabbis clash with doctors is the quintessential site for rabbinic writers to authorize their own power—to establish legal decisions as a tool of their own power and to establish themselves as ultimate cultural authorities. One understanding of Bakhtin's notion of the dialogical is a dialogue of different separate semiotic systems or discourses. The legal narrative suggests just such a dialogue—between medicine and rabbinic law—over its dying lovesick man. Pigeaud's research claims that the inherently dialogical context of lovesickness made it the typical site in which each discourse would attempt to monologically control meaning. The storyteller uses this dialogical context to create a metalegal myth that justifies the monological power of law. The problem of interpretation emerges when interpreters attempt to force its metalegal action into the framework of legal rules.

To read the story thickly, then, is to recognize the lovesick tale as a unique site for establishing authority—for imposing singular authority within an inherently dialogical context. The purpose of the narrative is its breach of canonicity and the way it suggests rabbinic control of a complex world. Because of the way its own poetics intentionally play with the expectations of law in order to establish authority beyond the law, the story does not fit easily with legal precedent. It is this ill fit that is palpable within all of the talmudic interpretations. Only the *stam*'s final interpretation is truly appropriate for this material.

Temple Destruction, Sexual Dysfunction, and Rabbinic Anxiety

The inherent incoherence of legal narrative motivates the *stam* to leave the confines of legal discourse and seek a psychological resolution in R. Isaac's statement about sexual pleasure. For those who like to think of Halakhah/Aggadah as an inherent dichotomy of rabbinic texts, the *stam*'s conclusion to the *sugya* seems an abrupt and uncharacteristic shift from halakhic discourse to aggadic discourse. Fraenkel's test would mark R. Isaac's psychohistorical observation as decidedly aggadic. To appreciate the meaning of this text one has to explore layers of meaning: the layer of the text itself and the layer of its usage in this context as a means of resolving a legal narrative with other legal precedent.

The *stam*'s concluding remarks follow the late amoraic statements (of Rab Pāppā and Rab 'Aḥā) that justify the rabbinic prohibition through either family shame or moral social policy. The problem with both of these justifications is that the story's avid hortatory rhetoric ("let him die") does not reflect the rabbis' struggle to balance legal positions against public policy; the hortatory language implies a swiftness that such a struggle belies. The *stam* formulates this question through a challenge to the rabbis' thoroughness: if the rabbis care about this man at all, why do they not suggest that the lovestruck couple marry? The force of the question critiques the late amoraic answers and threatens to return the question to the earlier stage in the *sugya* when the explicit question posed was the challenge to the "unmarried amora" to justify the rabbis' position within the law. Only an answer that can satisfactorily explain why the rabbis were so quick to demand death without offering any alternatives will satisfy. At this point, the *stam* cites the observation of the tanna R. Isaac:

So let him marry her?

That would not settle his mind because of R. Isaac.

For R. Isaac said from the day of the destruction of the Temple the flavor of intercourse was taken and given to sinners as it is written, "Stolen waters are sweet and bread eaten furtively is tasty." (Proverbs 9:17).[79]

R. Isaac's statement is the type of text that Fraenkel's test would characterize as Aggadah because it possesses neither a legal scenario nor a normative rule. It is a descriptive rather than a prescriptive text, and its descriptive framework might be theology, history, psychology, or some combination of the three. Within a thicker legal hermeneutic, though, it is possible for R. Isaac's statement to have significance for a dialogical legal narrative discourse that incorporates psychology, history, and theology in its purview.

R. Isaac's statement connects a new economy of sexual pleasure with the day the Temple was destroyed. In this economy, the sexual pleasure of righteous people is not only diminished by the Temple's destruction but transferred to sinners. R. Isaac employs a formula ("from the day...the...") that appears elsewhere in rabbinic literature. As a text type, this formula broadcasts a sense of rabbinic powerlessness in the world. In this sense, the formula is the polar opposite of a myth of rabbinic power.

Several examples of the formula employed by R. Isaac appear in the ninth chapter of Mishnah Sôṭâ and its associated Tosefta passage, a set of rabbinic historiographic texts. In these historical expressions of lamentation over important individuals and institutions, several figures employ this formula that connects a change in the natural order with a traumatic event. The one closest to R. Isaac's statement is the following:

> R. Simeon ben Gamĕlîēl said in the name of R. Joshua,[80] "From the day the Temple was destroyed, there is no day that is not cursed, dew will not fall beneficently and the flavor of fruit is taken."
>
> R. Yôsî said, "Even the fat of fruit is taken."

R. Joshua (cited by R. Simeon ben Gamĕlîēl) laments the destruction of the Temple by describing changes in the natural world that originated with the destruction: the dew does not fall beneficently and the flavor of the fruit is taken.[81] R. Yôsî is not satisfied with this description and adds that the fat of fruit is taken.[82]

The formula that connects a specific historical event with the absence or discontinuity of a phenomenon amplifies the symbolic power of the event, turning that single historical moment into a representation of all that is perceived wrong in society. In psychoanalytic terms, the destruction of the Temple is transformed from loss to lack, such that the prehistory of the event stands like primordial or Edenic time—as the period in which everything was good—while the posthistory or real time is pathological. This melancholic conversion of trauma from profound loss into symbolic lack enables the symbolization of the destruction of the Temple. In this way, rabbinic writers transform the Temple into a symbol whose absence is the most powerful presence within religious life. This is in keeping with the entirety of the rabbinic project of replacing the loss of the Temple; the loss is translated into an absence that is the foundation for rabbinic Judaism.

R. Isaac's statement is more provocative than the example from Mishnah Sôṭâ because it claims that sexual pleasure was transformed by the Temple's destruction. In contemporary eyes, it is impossible to ignore the psychoanalytic undertones of such a claim: R. Isaac diagnoses his law-abiding contemporaries as incapable of *jouissance*, the French term often used by psychoanalysts to connote sexual pleasure or the sexual component of pleasure. What catches the reader's attention is the claim that rabbis and other law-abiding Jews were rendered figuratively impotent by the destruction of the Temple.

The destruction of the Second Temple was a traumatic loss for the Jewish community and for individual Jews. To the extent that tannaitic sources get close enough to that historical event, we would expect to find evidence of the impact of that loss. In the case of this formula, and particularly R. Isaac's utilization of the form, the destruction of the Second Temple serves as a sinkhole for rabbinic anxiety. As the loss of the Second Temple metamorphoses from historical memory to ritualized mourning, the Temple begins to represent rabbinic primordial time, the paradise whose return is essential to rabbinic theology. The historical distance allows for fantasies of rabbinic authority in the Second Temple and during its period. R. Isaac's use of the formula is a means of lamenting a rabbinic power that never was by suggesting that during the Temple's existence the natural order worked differently and saints received the *jouissance* of sinners.[83]

R. Isaac's statement reflects an anxiety about the rabbinic project within a world that does not externally match the fantasy of halakhic control. Within an environment in which Halakhah has no currency, it is difficult to be a rabbi. In such a world, the normative values of rabbinic Halakhah are not mirrored in the larger culture. Under such conditions, the constructed and contingent nature of the halakhic *nomos* is obvious to all. But by connecting this chaotic world to the destruction of the Temple, R. Isaac establishes the chaotic antihalakhic reality as a theoretical anomaly. It is only within the topsy-turvy world that halakhic order is not established.

The *stam* mobilizes R. Isaac's statement because its articulation of a disjuncture between reality and the normative discourse of legal rules mirrors the disconnect that inheres within the legal narrative; just as the legal narrative reflects normative behavior that cannot be explained via precedent so the postdestruction realities of R. Isaac's declaration reflect practices that do not cohere with legal authority. But the connection of these two rabbinic texts—the use of one highly affected text to read another—radically transforms the story's message. I argued above that "The Lovesick Man" is inherently a Greco-Roman tale whose purpose is the construction of rabbinic power beyond the discourse of rules that ordinarily functions as the rabbi's tool of power. By connecting the story with R. Isaac, the *stam* turns the rabbis of the legal narrative (and rabbis in general) into an impotent group who must remain bystanders within their chaotic world. The *stam*'s approach concedes the incoherence of legal narrative within the discourse of legal rules by confining the details of legal narrative to a theoretically anomalous period of time: the postdestruction period.

Though the application of R. Isaac to the narrative is not true to the narrative's own assertion of rabbinic power, there is another sense in which the *stam*'s connection of the two uncanny texts is insightful. Where the story's poetic strategy is an assertion of rabbinic power and R. Isaac's mourning performance is a description of rabbinic impotence, both texts can be understood as reactions to rabbinic anxiety. Power and impotence are not necessarily opposing realities, but opposing directional strategies to the same problem.[84] Faced with anxiety about their own marginalization, rabbis could either attempt to assert power or explain its absence. While neither strategy is uniquely effective, both admit to a world broader and more complex than the normative world articulated within the narrow confines of talmudic and post-talmudic legal rules discourse. That discourse encourages a legal hermeticism that pretends that its own authority is already and unassailably established.[85] But in all legal systems, and certainly in the stateless rabbinic version, the practices of legislation, adjudication, and enforcement are inherent assertions of authority. Within such a world, it is often beneficial for the system to assume its own authority.

Within the normative world, the discourse of legal rules is a language spoken and understood by adherents and interpreters. But it is neither the only such language nor the only one capable of justifying or mandating behavior. If only for this reason, rules of law are always connected to the exercises of power that authorize and enforce them. Those exercises of power are negotiations among cultural languages within which legal meaning is broadly constructed. Both the legal narrative of the lovesick man and the statement of R. Isaac shine a light on these negotiations of rabbinic power and contextualize the discourse of law, allowing the reader to see the ways in which legal meaning is inscribed within the multivoiced *nomos* and the way in which the behavioral mandates of legal rules can only be actualized through negotiations of power.

The story of the lovesick man is a legal narrative whose parallel treatment in the two Talmuds reflects the problems that emerge when a deliberately antinomian story is read within a discourse that seeks to flatten it into a legal rule and make that rule cohere with the other rules of legal precedent. Only the *stam*'s final reading of the story actually expands the discourse of reading to imagine that the matrix of legal rules is insufficient to the task. The *stam*'s bizarre psychological denouement allows the story to function in the multidiscursive ways in which it was originally designed. The *stam*'s strange reading gains texture from an understanding of the extent to which the story can function (and was originally intended to function) as a myth of rabbinic power beyond the legal discourse. By recognizing the Greco-Roman context of lovesickness stories as sites for staging claims to authority, one can understand how the original story might be read in a broader context and how the narrow legal discourse of amoraic and post-amoraic readers struggles because of its inability to read it that way. In attending to legal narrative and the treatment of legal narrative I have demonstrated the limitations of a narrow discourse of legal reading and the potential advantages to broadening that reading. By widening the discourse and taking the interpretation of the narrative as part of this literary object, one gains insight into rabbinic anxieties about authority that are reflected within both the original story and its interpretation.

A narrative that plays with the expectations of halakhic rules in order to stage a metahalakhic claim for rabbinic power does not sit comfortably within an essential division of Halakhah and Aggadah as two different types of rabbinic texts. Neither do other legal narratives whose breach of canonicity draws energy from cultural discourses other than that of legal rules. Nor for that matter do those famous talmudic legends like "The Oven of Aknā'ī" that play fast and loose with legal materials for metalegal purposes. Recognizing that the dichotomy of Halakhah/Aggadah is most powerful in the way it structures readings within discursive conventions leads one to question the dichotomy's universal application and its benefit as a heuristic tool.

Chapter 3

A Touch of the Rabbinic Real: Rabbis and Outsiders

The existence of the Babylonian Talmud, a massive anthological work attentive to periodization and scholarly citation, is an incredible boon for historiographers of late antiquity. And yet, scholars sometimes bemoan the absence of other data from the period. The imbalance between the Babylonian Talmud's extensive source material on a wide variety of intellectual and social issues and an archaeological field that has produced little beyond magic bowls is striking and presents a unique environment for the symbiosis of literary and historiographic work. In this and the next two chapters I take note of the significance of the genre of talmudic legal narrative within rabbinic historiography and introduce a set of readings that will further the use of such texts for historiographic purposes while slightly tweaking the manner in which such work is conducted.

When using the Bavli as a historiographic source, there was once a tendency to gravitate toward extensive rabbinic narratives and to accept, almost entirely, the details of such narratives as historical evidence.[1] Such histories, which I will label traditional, build their own historical narratives around those inherited from Bavli stories.[2] This traditional historiography is somewhat unsurprising; since rabbinic narratives often present themselves in historiographic form and narrate the lives of named rabbinic protagonists, they lend themselves to adaptation within historical metanarratives. Traditional histories tend to employ rabbinic narratives fairly naively, accepting miraculous fantasy as historical fact and presuming the stories to be eyewitness accounts that simply translate transpired events into historical narrative.

The beginnings of Jewish tudies within a rationalist milieu led to the development of what I will call "rationalist histories."[3] Rationalist histories are still drawn to narrative sources, but discard certain fantastic stories in toto or discount fantastic elements, either eliminating fantastic details or treating them as metaphors for more reasonable referents.

At the height of rationalist historiography, biography was in vogue. Scholarly biographers assembled all of the narratives featuring an individual rabbi alongside statements attributed to the same scholar and crafted social and intellectual biographies.[4] One of Jacob Neusner's many paradigm-shifting contributions to rabbinics has been his critique of rationalist historiography and rabbinic biography. Ironically, Neusner knew the rationalist milieu so well since his own initial scholarly work was a rationalist biography of Rabban Yôḥānān ben Zakka'y and a rationalist history of the Jews of Babylonia.[5] Through his many writings, Neusner has ushered in a period of skeptical rabbinic historiography in which rabbinic texts are suspect unless they can be corroborated by external data.

One of the effects of Neusner's influence on rabbinic historiography has been a shift in the scholarly perception of the status of the rabbis responsible for producing rabbinic literature. Where traditional histories once presumed the rabbis to speak for all Jews and took rabbinic anecdotes and legal frameworks as descriptive of a world in which the rabbis were the social, religious, and political elite in Jewish society in both Palestine and Babylonia, skeptical histories now presume the rabbis to have been somewhat marginal within their own societies politically, socially and even religiously.[6]

This new understanding of the rabbis as a marginal social group is particularly well drawn in the context of rabbinic Palestine, where the skeptical turn has been significantly aided by the existence of nonrabbinic, non-Jewish, and archaeological external sources. It is fair to say that Neusner's critique of rationalist historiography has led to a sea change in the use of rabbinic sources for historiographic purposes; where once nonrabbinic sources were interpreted on the basis of rabbinic ones, the opposite now obtains.[7]

Because of the paucity of external evidence in Babylonia, the Babylonian context is a bit thornier. While Neusner's critique of rabbinic narratives as historiographic sources is still largely relevant, the claim of significant gaps in time between narrator and event is not as strong when speaking of stories about amoraic Babylonia. Additionally, because there are few external sources from which to paint historical metanarratives, scholars continue to feel the magnetic pull of the Bavli's massive archive.[8] Even after the skeptical turn within rabbinic historiography, Babylonian rabbinic history is largely written on the basis of passages in the Talmud. For scholars of rabbinic

Babylonia there is, necessarily, greater overlap in source material and method among historiographers and literary scholars than among scholars of rabbinic Palestine.

One of the most important histories of rabbinic Babylonia is Neusner's *History of the Jews of Babylonia*. In this work, written in a rationalist mode with hints of skepticism, the father of the skeptical turn attempts to process Bavli materials in a historiographically responsible way. Neusner articulates a methodology for treating Bavli sources as historiography. This methodology weights Bavli genres differently. Court case narratives—stories about amoraic trials that are a large subset of talmudic legal narratives—are considered exceptionally reliable: "These reports never tax one's credulity, and never appear not to conform to the known conditions of everyday life. Strikingly, they almost *never* include the kinds of miracle-stories we have considered above [discussed in Neusner's *History*], and they rarely lead to the supposition that someone is telling a story for some clearly identifiable, ulterior motive, so that we may doubt the details of the story itself."[9]

Neusner's assessment of these legal narratives as credible historical witnesses stems from an implied contrast with extensive aggadic stories that often include supernatural aspects and are located within explicitly moralistic talmudic *sugyot*. Neusner is not alone in his reliance on such sources. Both Isaiah Gafni and David Goodblatt, two contemporary Babylonian historiographers, rely heavily on such stories either individually or in the aggregate.[10] For readers conditioned by fantastic Bavli Aggadah, talmudic legal narratives seem simply to present events as they were.

Despite the historiographers' unanimity about the reliability of talmudic legal narratives, my focus on tellability pushes me toward skepticism in handling these sources. I argued in Chapter 1 that talmudic legal narratives are worthy of being narrated because they are tellable; the deviant and unexpected qualities of legal narrative that often make such narrative a difficult fit with legal statutes are the reasons such narratives are interesting and entertaining. The more tellable a narrative, the more likely it is that its composer did significant work to produce it as a narrative. Narratives do not write themselves; they are produced by a narrator who molds events into a narrative frame. This is best expressed by Hayden White in his critique of the notion that any historiography simply finds narratives within history: "no given set of casually recorded historical events can in itself constitute a story; the most it might offer to the historian are story *elements*. The events are *made* into a story by the suppression or subordination of certain of them and the highlighting of others, by characterization, motific repetition, variation of tone and point of view . . . in short, all of the techniques that we would normally expect to find in the emplotment of a novel or a play."[11]

Following White, I treat talmudic legal narratives as sources for historiography with reservations. One of the elements of careful treatment is an approach that incorporates the hermeneutics of suspicion to highlight the tendentious nature of texts that have hitherto been considered reportage even by the most skeptical of historians. It is my presumption that these stories are doing cultural work, reflecting the mind-set of authors who have framed these narratives. Even though these narratives are often written within rigid conventions, they are hardly as simple as they appear. Attending to their complexity allows for insight into the power dynamics operative in amoraic and stammaitic Babylonia.

This and the following two chapters offer a rabbinic textual anthropology. In successive chapters the book treats three of the most important personal relationships in rabbinic culture: the relationships of rabbi/nonrabbi, rabbi/student, and rabbi/rabbi. Each chapter focuses on a Bavli *sugya* that strongly integrates legal narrative sources; these sources are unique textual nuggets expandable because of the way they compress the conflicts of semiotic systems that compose culture. As such, these legal narratives encourage thick descriptions that enrich historiographic understandings of rabbinic Babylonia in the late amoraic and stammaitic periods.

While the issue of the marginal political, social, and religious status of the rabbis in Palestine is well discussed, comparatively little work has been done on the rabbis in Babylonia.[12] In his *History* Neusner argues, largely on the basis of court case narratives, that the Babylonian amoraim had a degree of established institutional authority and jurisdiction over both rabbinic and nonrabbinic Jews.[13] As judges, public teachers, and market arbitrators, Neusner claims, the Babylonian rabbis exercised formal authority. In this and subsequent chapters I will complicate this claim by returning to the same text types, reading against the grain to show the degree to which Babylonian rabbinic authority was palpably unstable. Though Neusner seems correct in the claim that the rabbis had some formal authority, theirs was not a confident authority, but one that required—in the most immediate of social encounters—continuous constitution, manipulation, and performance. The readings below allow skeptical historiography to remain skeptical within its historical work by thickening our description of the realities of Babylonian rabbinic culture.

Historiographers often approach the Talmud's archive with a set of a priori questions about static realities of rabbinic society. Primary historical interest lies with large-scale political institutions and economic data. Scholars comb through the Talmud looking for scattered acontextual clues to the relationships between the Jewish community and Persian authorities, for indicators of the form and function of the economy and for a sense of the bureaucratic operation of the Jewish community. With the rise of skeptical historiography, though, scholars are increasingly realizing the ways in which the scholar's expectations of communal institutional structure have been structuring the research and imagining a more stable rabbinic institutional world than existed.[14] Part of the problem is that talmudic texts are poorly designed as an archive for the kinds of institutional questions historians ask. These texts are often poor sources of stable facts about rabbinic cultural life, but they are terrific witnesses to the social dynamics of that life. Talmudic texts provide an aggregate picture of life in the rabbinic world by communicating, reflecting, and projecting various individual rabbinic lives. The heightened sense of the rabbinic individual—author, character, and redactor—is ideal for focusing on the social dynamics of rabbinic life inasmuch as it captures the individual's situation within those dynamics. The format of a talmudic *sugya* that incorporates disparate individual pieces into a larger unit allows for the construction of a vivid picture of the fissures and stabilities of individuals in rabbinic culture.

These chapters are structured around core talmudic *sugyot* that are themselves unified by legal subject. These *sugyot* are the products of multiple contributors: tannaim, amoraim, and the *stam*. The focus of these readings is the Babylonian amoraim and the *stam*. In highlighting the underlying tension points and foci for these Babylonian rabbis, I aim to produce an aggregated picture of the social dynamics of amoraic and stammaitic Babylonia. Where possible, as in the case of the educational setting, I will distinguish between the amoraic and stammaitic contexts. But the goal here is not to so distinguish, but to follow the texts and allow them to shed light on the mundane everyday social dynamics of rabbinic Babylonia.[15]

To Stand Up or Be Upstanding: Ethics and Culture in Courtroom Rituals

The major genres of rabbinic literature—midrash, mishnah, and talmud—originated in rabbinic educational practices. Extant works of midrash are literary versions of a hermeneutic activity in which the tannaim and amoraim engaged. Though we have a single definitive Mishnah, the existence of other mishnah-style works indicates that mishnah production was a common intellectual practice in rabbinic Palestine.[16] The existence of two Talmuds with the same type of text indicates that these strange texts mimic the intellectual conversation of a rabbinic study hall.

Amoraic courtroom narrative is a textual genre with a corollary in social practice. Courtroom narrative is a type of legal narrative that purports to record trials that transpired within amoraic courts.[17] Though it is hard to establish with any certainty that a given courtroom narrative is historically reliable, the aggregate of such narratives presents a picture of amoraim as judges that is hard to deny; it is also likely that many such stories are as reliable as any historiographic narratives. The evidence of courtroom narratives presumes that the amoraim responsible for many of the Talmud's theoretical legal positions also adjudicated actual cases. As a practice, such legal proceedings appear to have interrupted the generally theoretical discourse of the amoraic study hall, allowing the practical and real to intrude in ways that made that theoretical discourse meaningful, powerful, and relevant. As a genre of literature, courtroom narratives (and legal narratives more generally) have the ability to similarly allow reality to intrude upon otherwise theoretical ruminations. While I have noted above the ways in which the legal discourse perceives legal narratives as incoherent in negative ways (in the sense of not fitting with the matrix of legal precedent), legal narrative can also challenge the legal discourse by presenting a connection with the realities of lived life.

This chapter follows the trajectory of a single talmudic *sugya* whose topic is participant posture in the amoraic courtroom. This seemingly trivial issue is the site of an important discussion about the encounter of rabbinic and nonrabbinic Jews in amoraic Babylonia. This encounter engenders a talmudic discussion that balances the formal requirements of biblical law, norms of social etiquette, and both social and judicial ethics regarding the other. Courtroom narratives import the external realities of the rabbinic cultural world into the internal space of the study hall.

Schematic of *Sugya*

This chapter's primary source text is an extensive talmudic *sugya* at Šĕbûʿôt 30a–b. Schematically, the *sugya* develops out of a single *baraita* that narrates a tannaitic debate over the postures that courtroom participants must assume. This initial tannaitic debate embodies a dichotomy between a formal commitment to posture requirements as legally mandated rituals and ambivalence to such formal mandates if they do not emerge from the ethics of equal judgment in the courtroom. The *sugya* explores both the formalist and the ethical avenues within a meandering discourse that treats one and then the other before interweaving the two. The formalist and ethical conversations intersect within the *sugya*'s consideration of a court scenario in which rabbinic and nonrabbinic Jews face off as opponents. Such a scenario is treated by both statutes and courtroom narratives. For purposes of presentation, this chapter veers slightly from the original talmudic organization of the material for the sake of clarity; the arguments work equally well within the original talmudic arrangement.

Opening *Baraita*: Tannaim Debate Courtroom Posture

The talmudic discussion of courtroom posture opens with a *baraita* featuring a debate between the anonymous majority and R. Judah:

> Our Rabbis taught:
> "And the two men will stand up" (Deuteronomy 19:17).
> It is a *commandment* [emphasis mine] that the litigants stand.[18]
> R. Judah said, "I have heard that if the court wishes to seat them[19]
>   they seat [them].
> "[But][20] one should not stand and one sit, one speaks all of his needs
>   while they[21] say to the other, 'shorten your words.'"

The anonymous majority interprets Deuteronomy 19:17 as producing a legal imperative for litigants to stand in the courtroom. R. Judah disagrees with the imperative, citing an unattributed tradition (using the rhetoric of rumor) to say that a court has discretion. Though the court has such discretion, R. Judah insists that it only be exercised in the service of judicial equity to seat both litigants. The issue of litigant posture is comparable to the procedural content of the trial; both must be completely equitable.

The above-cited version of R. Judah's statement in the *baraita* is a translation of this *baraita* as recorded in the Vatican 140 manuscript of Šĕbûʿôt; I chose this version because its concise language is lower critically, closest to the original text of the Talmud. An addition that appears in other versions is helpful as commentary to the *baraita*. All other talmudic text witnesses of this *baraita* and its Tosefta parallel insert a two-word Hebrew phrase prior to

R. Judah's second clause. These sources add the words: "but what is prohibited?" These words introduce a way of characterizing R. Judah's position as an approach to law. The insertion creates a contrast between the *mandate* that litigants must stand in the courtroom simply because the Bible says so and a *prohibition* that insists that no one be asked to stand if the opposing party is invited to sit. The insertion highlights the extent to which R. Judah considers courtroom posture a scenario ripe for prohibition rather than mandate. It picks up on the latent way in which R. Judah's rumor tradition dismisses the anonymous majority's formal commandment and suggests that this dismissal is grounded in a desire to legislate in the service of ethics rather than as a commitment to a biblical verb ("and they will stand"). While it would be something of a stretch to extend this single example into an idea that the historical R. Judah rejects a degree of halakhic positivism—that is, the position that law is authoritative because it is posited but not because it represents something ethical or moral—it is helpful to introduce into this discussion the idea that a legal thinker might dismiss issues like posture as legal grammar. The fact that some might be inclined to dismiss courtroom posture as content-empty is important considering the lengths to which the ensuing Bavli discussion refuses to accept R. Judah's position on its own terms.

The *sugya* cites two early Babylonian amoraim who insist, each after his own fashion, that R. Judah's notion of discretion is limited and that there is unanimous tannaitic support for mandatory courtroom posture:

> 'Ûllā [ca. 230–ca. 290 C.E.] said [that] the argument [between the anonymous majority requiring standing and R. Judah's position that both can sit] is about litigants, but regarding witnesses it is unanimous that [the witnesses are] standing as it says "And they will stand" (Deuteronomy 19:17)

> Rab Hûnā[22] [ca. 230–ca. 290 C.E.] said the argument[23] [between the anonymous majority requiring standing and R. Judah's position that both can sit] refers to the time of deliberations, but at the time of the conclusion of justice it is unanimous that [the litigants are] standing and the judges [are] sitting, as it says, "Moshe sat to judge the people and the people stood"[24] (Exodus 18:13).

'Ûllā confines R. Judah's optional ruling to litigants, while asserting that R. Judah would mandate the standing posture of witnesses on the basis of the *baraita*'s biblical proof texts. ʿÛllā's contemporary, Rab Hûnā, confines R. Judah on the basis of courtroom procedural time: R. Judah's discretionary position refers to court deliberations not to the period of the verdict; even R. Judah concedes that litigants stand during the ruling. Rab Hûnā cites an additional biblical proof text from the story of Moses' adjudication to buttress this interpretation of R. Judah.

While one could understand the positions of ʿÛllā and Rab Hûnā as discrete units, with each amora insisting upon their positions vis-à-vis R. Judah in light of specifically cited midrashic inferences, it is intriguing to note their joint interest in confining the position of R. Judah and insisting on maintaining some measure of the *baraita*'s postural mandate. Why do these amoraim insist on such distorting readings of R. Judah? I will digress briefly to two other Bavli sources that contextualize the significance of relative posture in rabbinic Babylonia.

Rabbinic interpretations of the Bible famously conflate biblical time with their own. The rabbis have been described as "living in biblical time."[25] Retold biblical stories are often wonderful opportunities for noting the ways in which rabbinic culture updates the classics to reflect its own milieu. A story found at Sanhedrîn 101b transforms the most fundamental divide in Jewish history—the division into the separate monarchies of Israel and Judea during the reign of Solomon's son Rehoboam—into a clash over relative posture. The biblical story of the division of Solomon's united monarchy into the northern Israelite and the southern Judean monarchies describes Jeroboam's creation of two new temples at Bêt ʾĒl and Dān. The biblical text speaks of Jeroboam's fear that holiday pilgrimages to Jerusalem would prompt nostalgia for the united monarchy that would result in Jeroboam's political demise. Rab Naḥmān (ca. 260–ca. 320 C.E.) reimagines Jeroboam as a participant in rabbinic discourse:

> Rab Naḥmān said, "The haughtiness of Jeroboam caused his removal from the world [to come],[26] as it is written: 'Now the kingdom will return to the house of David if this people will go up to make sacrifices in God's house in Jerusalem. And the heart of the people will return to their master, Rehoboam, king of Judah, and they will kill me and return to Rehoboam, king of Judah' (1 Kings 12:27).
>
> "[Jeroboam] said, 'we learn that "sitting in the sanctuary is limited to Davidic kings alone." When they will see that [Rehoboam][27] sits and I am standing, they will say, "this one is the king, and this one is the servant," but if I stand, he [understand "I"] will be a rebel against

the monarchy and they will kill him [understand "me"] and go after [Rehoboam].'

"Immediately, 'the king took counsel and made two golden calves and said to them, "it is too much for you to go up to Jerusalem; here is your God Israel who took you out of Egypt."[28] And he put one in Bêt 'El and one he put in Dān'" (1 Kings 12:28).

Rab Naḥmān transforms Jeroboam's biblical fear of nostalgia into the fear of the legal reality of the non-Davidic king in the temple. As a good rabbinic Jew, Jeroboam would not brook the rule that only Davidic kings may sit in the temple, and the relative postural difference would result in the immediate identification of Rehoboam as true king and Jeroboam as usurper.[29] To avoid this outcome, Jeroboam creates two idolatrous competing temples so as not to lose political power.

The story imagines Jeroboam as loyal to rabbinic postural norms governing Temple practice. Jeroboam's commitment to these postural norms turns him toward idolatory! The rewrite enables the realization that postural rituals—the relative postures demanded by cultural norms—are important within Babylonian rabbinic culture. The story demonstrates that such postures are highly visible symbols whose content has the power to crown or depose a king. It is remarkable that the basis for the positive rule of temple seating practice is unquestioned; its inviolability can account even for the creation of idolatrous temples. The Babylonian amoraic rewrite of this biblical story in light of the postural requirements demonstrates the extent to which hierarchy was a central concern for the Babylonian rabbi and the degree to which postural positions regularly staged hierarchical divisions.

The Babylonian Christian writer Aphrahat (ca. 270–ca. 345 C.E.) provides evidence of a contemporaneous Babylonian obsession with visible hierarchy. In a stinging critique of contemporaries, Aphrahat accuses them of substituting hierarchical focus for genuine religious devotion: "It is rare in our times to find someone asking, 'Who is it that fears God?' Rather [the question is], 'Who is the oldest for the laying on of hands?' And when they say, 'Such and such is the oldest,' they say to him, 'You may recline at the head of the table.'"[30]

Aphrahat is bothered that his contemporaries show more concern for hierarchy than for religious meaning. The second clause indicates en passant that hierarchy is deliberately connected to performance and visibility. The establishment of a hierarchy based on age is directly implicated in the staging of this hierarchy through table seating rituals.

Standing on Ceremony: Qîddûšîn 32b–33b

A series of stories at Bavli Qîddûšîn 32b–33b furthers the image of visible hierarchy as a specific symptom of amoraic Babylonia. Qîddûšîn 32b–33b transitions from a mishnah about the respect owed biological parents to a discussion of the respect owed to intellectual mentors. Though a parent may decline deferential treatment, the Talmud avers, various rabbinic authorities consider whether rabbis are similarly entitled to decline such respect. This discussion includes a set of narratives in which rabbis decline deferential treatment. Each of these narratives is the story of a rabbi marrying off a child and deliberately demeaning himself as the host of a wedding reception. There are three such narratives in this *sugya*. The first is a *baraita* with tannaitic protagonists paralleled in other works of rabbinic literature; the distinct modifications heighten the sense that Babylonian rabbis were particularly invested in public displays of hierarchical respect. The second and third are identical stories told about different Babylonian amoraim that will also highlight the special standing of postural respect in amoraic and stammaitic Babylonia.

In the first story, R. Gamĕliēl hosts three of his tannaitic colleagues at the reception for his son's wedding:

> A story of R. 'Elî'ezer, R. Joshua, and R. Ṣādôq who were reclining in the wedding house of the son of R. Gamĕliēl, and R. Gamĕliēl was standing and pouring them drinks.
>
> [R. Gamĕliēl] gave a cup to R. 'Elî'ezer and he did not take it, he gave it to R. Joshua and he took it.
>
> R. 'Elî'ezer said to [R. Joshua], "What is this, Joshua? We are sitting and R. Gamĕliēl stands and serves us?"
>
> [R. Joshua] said to him, "we know of a greater one than he who served—Abraham was the greatest of his generation and the verse says about him (Genesis 18:8), 'and he stood over them.'
>
> "And perhaps you all will argue that they appeared as angels to him? They appeared to him only as Arabs.
>
> "And should we not have R. Gamĕliēl the son of Rabbî serving us?"
>
> R. Ṣādôq said to them, *"for how long will you set aside the honor of God and busy yourself with the honor of the creations?* [Emphasis mine.]
>
> "The Holy One, blessed be He, energizes winds and raises clouds,[31]

causes rain to fall and the ground to grow, and sets the table before every individual, and we should not have R. Gamĕlîēl stand and serve us drinks?"

R. Gamĕlîēl declines his hierarchical position and lowers himself to stand while serving his seated colleagues/underlings. R. Gamĕlîēl willingly serves as a steward at his son's wedding. The other rabbis debate whether they can permit R. Gamĕlîēl to serve them in this manner. R. 'Elî'ezer declines service, while R. Joshua accepts it. R. 'Elî'ezer challenges R. Joshua's acceptance, and both R. Joshua and R. Ṣādôq produce paradigms that permit this acceptance.

In the tannaitic version found in *Mĕkîltā Dĕ-Rabbî Šim'ôn bar Yôḥa'y*, the arguments of R. Joshua and R. Ṣādôq structurally parallel each other.[32] R. Ṣādôq argues midrashically that God serves a world full of idolators much like Abraham served a threesome of perceived idolators. The Bavli version alters R. Ṣādôq's argument, deleting the midrashic references in order to place R. Ṣādôq as a rhetorical critique of the entire conversation about R. Gamĕlîēl's deference. R. Ṣādôq now says, "for how long will you set aside the honor of God and busy yourself with the honor of the creations?" Though this critique of the entire discussion is undermined by R. Ṣādôq's involvement in the discussion, the rhetoric inserted into R. Ṣādôq's attribution reflects a storyteller's discomfort with the obsessive focus on hierarchy.[33] The rewriting of R. Ṣādôq makes this tanna sound like Aphrahat.

The *sugya* follows the R. Gamĕlîēl story with two stories—about Rābā (ca. 290–ca. 350 C.E.) and Rab Pāppā respectively—that structurally mimic the tannaitic narrative:

Rābā was pouring drinks at the wedding home of his son.

[Rābā] poured a drink for Rab Pāppā and Rab Hûnā son of Rab Joshua [ca. 320–ca. 380 C.E.] and they rose before him, for Rab Merî and Rab Pinḥās son of Rab Ḥîsdā and they did not rise before him.

[Rābā] took offense and asked, "Are these rabbis rabbis and these rabbis not rabbis?"

Rab Pāppā was pouring drinks at the wedding home of his son 'Abbā Mar.

[Rab Pāppā] poured a drink for R. Isaac son of R. Judah and he did not rise before him.

[Rab Pāppā] took offense.

Rabbinic texts have a fondness for multiple tellings of the same story, and the biographical proximity of Rābā and Rab Pāppā and their frequent confusion is well documented.[34] In each of these stories, the rabbinic protagonist celebrates his son's wedding by pouring drinks for lesser rabbinic figures. The first story uses the names of its protagonists to magnify the insult to Rābā. Rab Pāppā and Rab Hûnā son of Rab Joshua are well known and prominent disciples of Rābā while Rab Merî and Rab Pinḥās son of Rab Ḥîsdā are rarely mentioned in the Bavli. While the well-known prominent disciples show deference by standing, the lesser-known figures insult Rābā by refusing to stand. In a similar vein, Rab Isaac son of Rab Judah who does not stand for Rab Pāppā in the second story is also fairly unknown.[35]

Two major differences emerge from a specific comparison of the tannaitic story of R. Gamĕlîēl with these amoraic stories of Rābā and Rab Pāppā. In the tannaitic version it is a third party (R. 'Elî'ezer) who takes offense on behalf of the distinguished individual and suggests that the others show respect to R. Gamĕlîēl by declining the wine service. The reader is not told R. Gamĕlîēl's position, but his action indicates a willingness to decline his own deference. In the Rābā and Rab Pāppā stories, the two rabbis who decline their own respect by serving wine at their sons' respective weddings are the *same* individuals who take offense when their guests do not stand. This *ambivalence* about declining one's honor adds to the picture developed from the alteration of R. Ṣādôq's reasoning, lending the impression that Babylonian rabbis took displays of hierarchical respect seriously and were emotionally invested in them.

The second major difference between the stories is that the necessary sign of respect in the amoraic stories is postural—the rabbinic underlings do not *stand* for their superiors. From a compositional standpoint, this may be dismissed as a neater way to construct a story in which respect is both declined and demanded, but one could also argue that these stories evidence a particular Babylonian proclivity to postural positions as a way of demonstrating hierarchy through a semiotics of power.[36]

Returning to the Šĕbû'ôt *sugya* about courtroom posture, there is now a basis for understanding why R. Judah's rejection of a biblical mandate to stand in the courtroom was not acceptable to 'Ûllā and Rab Hûnā. Relative posture was an active semiotic language in which the Babylonian rabbis were quite fluent; in such an environment, one has a hard time dismissing postures as legal grammar.

Unethical Rabbis

The Šěbûʿôt *sugya*'s original *baraita* introduced both the formal requirement for standing in the courtroom and the fear that discretion could lead to unethical breeches of judicial equity. With somewhat typical talmudic free play, the *sugya* leaves the discussion of mandatory posture to focus on a discussion of judicial equity.[37] Biblical law is very clear about judicial equity. Leviticus 19:15 reads, "You shall not render an unfair decision: do not favor the poor or show deference to the rich; judge your kinsman fairly." R. Judah's insistence on the equality of court posture is of a piece with the ethical tone of biblical law.

Within the *sugya*'s analysis of the ethical content of R. Judah's position in the *baraita*, the *sugya* cites a statute and paired legal narrative that challenge basic judicial ethics of rabbinic jurisprudence.

> Rab Joseph[38] [ca. 260–ca. 320 C.E.] taught[39]:
> "Judge your kinsman fairly" (Leviticus 19:15).
> With the one who is with you in Torah and mitzvoth endeavor to judge him well.[40]

Though midrashic readings often perpetrate violence on the biblical texts they read, there is hardly greater violence than Rab Joseph's reading that turns a biblical verse into its semantic opposite. The biblical verse demands that judgment be equitable; the midrashic reading calls for inequity in judgment. Rab Joseph draws on the strangeness of the word ʿamîtekā (your fellow) and chooses to read this word as an abbreviation: ʿim šeʾîtěkā (the one who is with you). The general term including all is parochially altered to mean "one who is like you."[41] A text that asked for equity now demands imbalance—favoritism toward the insider.

The term invoked by Rab Joseph—"the one with you in Torah and mitzvoth"—is not an oft-used term for differentiating rabbinic insiders and outsiders. It appears in one other talmudic source, a similar amoraic midrash at Bābā Měṣîʿā 59a that limits the protection of price gouging to "the one with you in Torah and mitzvoth" through a similarly acrostic reading of the biblical text. The nonstandard nature of this term is helpful, for it provides us not only with a boundary but with context; it is as much definition as term. Rab Joseph asks for equitable judgment of those who stand for the rabbinic program of Torah and mitzvoth. An outsider, we may extrapolate, is one who either violates commandments (as understood by the rabbis) or fails to sufficiently represent Torah. While a Torah-studying rabbi is clearly protected from such a designation, who else is included on the inside? A rabbi's wife? The merchant whom the rabbi engages in commerce? One who marries his or her daughter to a rabbi?

Rab Joseph's narrow interpretation of "kinsman" (and the parallel interpretation of "kinsman" in Bābā Měṣîʿā 59a) challenges one's picture of rabbinic ethics. It is hard to accept the testimony of these witnesses that rabbinic law is designed to lean toward the rabbis. And yet, Rab Joseph's statement is buttressed by an analogous remark attributed to his colleague Rābā at Šabbāt 119a:

> Let it be taken from me [oath language]
>   if when a ṣûrbā mērabbānān came before me for judgment, I would not lay my head on the face of the pillow so long as I had not turned it over for his benefit.

In other words, Rābā claims that he would not sleep until he had figured out a way to decide the case for the ṣûrbā mērabbānān. Bracketing the translation of ṣûrbā mērabbānān momentarily, Rābā's statement bears in form and content the imprint of reality; the oath language of the form lends an aura of credibility here, and the statement claims this tilting of justice as a regular practice. Rābā's assertion is not challenged by the *stam* at Šabbāt 119a; another assertion that follows Rābā's suggests a different judicial ethic:

> Mar bar Rab 'Asî [ca. 380–ca. 440 C.E.] said, "I am ineligible to judge
>   all ṣûrbā mērabbānān.
> "For what reason?"
> "For I love them as my own body and a man is unable to see an
>   obligation against himself."

Mar bar Rab 'Asî shares Rābā's predilection but, sensing the ethical dilemma, recuses himself from such cases.[42] Rābā, on the other hand, is perfectly satisfied with perverting judicial equity for the sake of a rabbinic insider.

Returning to the Šěbûʿôt passage, Rab Joseph articulates a theoretical position to judge insiders equitably but not to extend judicial equity to those outside the rabbinic program of Torah and mitzvoth. The Talmud follows Rab Joseph's hypothetical statute with a courtroom narrative that connects Rab Joseph's theory with his practice:

78   Chapter 3

> 'Ullā[43] had a court case before Rab Naḥmān.
> Rab Joseph sent to [Rab Naḥmān saying] "'Ullā[44] is "with you in Torah and mitzvoth."

The story does not detail the particulars of 'Ullā's legal matter nor identify 'Ullā's opponent in the case. One can assume that the case is civil rather than criminal and that 'Ullā's opponent is a rabbinic outsider. The story is silent about Rab Naḥmān's response, leaving the reader to assume that the rabbi acted as his colleague requested. Were one to consider the relationship between this extremely terse narrative and Rab Joseph's statute, one could even construct a genealogy whereby the story begets the midrashic statute. The proximity of statute and story invites the reader to consider the purpose of this narrative. Unlike legal narratives that stand in conflict with the matrix of legal precedent, this story functions as an exemplum that buttresses the theoretical statute. The story lends the statute an air of reality, underlining the problematic teaching by insisting upon its actionability.

The *stam* is troubled by the problematic ethics of Rab Joseph's position, either theoretically or practically. It is the narrative, though, that provides space for interpretive transformation.

> Why[45] did he send [this message]?
> That he should favor[46] [him]?[47]
> He then said to begin [with][48] his business.
> Alternatively, for discretionary judgment.

The *stam* employs a rhetorical question ("Why did he send this message?") as a way of establishing an initial interpretation of the story and setting up a reinterpretation. By presenting the simple reading of the story through the rhetorical question, the *stam* signals its plan to subvert this initial interpretation. Rather than understanding Rab Joseph's letter as requesting judicial favoritism, the *stam* interprets procedural advantages that might not be unethical. While the story clearly aims to buttress Rab Joseph's statutory preference for insiders through a connection to a real event, the *stam* interprets that event to suppress the radical insider ethics that it seems to implicate. While it is tempting to suggest that the *stam's* is always a more strongly ethical take on earlier sources, I do not believe this to be the case. Rather, the *stam* is motivated by a desire to rein in outlandish behavior in favor of a more balanced presentation. In this case, the outlier is Rab Joseph's unethical program and the *stam* controls this by reinterpreting the narrative's implications. In the ensuing passage, the *sugya* marries its discussion of mandatory courtroom posture with this strand of rabbinic judicial ethics, reconnecting the two pieces of R. Judah's comment in the *baraita* within a discussion of amoraic trials that pit rabbis against nonrabbis.

The *Mêmrôt* of Rabbâ bar Rab Hûnā

The *sugya* continues by citing several theoretical *mêmrôt* (amoraic apodictic statements or statutes) attributed to a single amora, Rabbâ bar Rab Hûnā. Text critics have argued that such *mêmrā* collections were likely joined into literary units before their utilization in talmudic *sugyot*.[49] Assuming that such was the case here, the original source, uninterrupted by other materials that the redactor uses to interrupt the statutes would have read as follows:

1. Rabbâ bar Rab Hûnā [ca. 260–ca. 320 C.E.] said [when] a *ṣûrbā mērabbānān* and an am haarez oppose each other at trial we seat them [both].[50]
   And if they will not sit, we contend[51] with the *ṣûrbā mērabbānān*, while with the am haarez we do not contend.[52] . . .
2. Rabbâ bar Rab Hûnā said [when] a *ṣûrbā mērabbānān*[53] and an am haarez oppose [each other][54] at trial, the *ṣûrbā mērabbānān* should not sit down [before the judge][55] before [the am haarez does] because it looks like [the judge] is arranging [the *ṣûrbā mērabbānān*'s] judgment. . . .
3. And Rabbâ bar Rab Hûnā said if a certain *ṣûrbā mērabbānān* knew testimony but it was degrading to him to go to the house of judges[56] who are less than he to testify before it, he should not go.

These three statements are a small set of texts concerned with the status of the *ṣûrbā mērabbānān* in the amoraic courtroom. The term "*ṣûrbā mērabbānān*" does not have static meaning. It sometimes refers to the most prominent amora, sometimes deliberately to the student rabbis of an amora, and sometimes to all members of the rabbinic community.[57] In the above citation to Šabbāt 119a and Rābā and Mar bar Rab ʾAšî's judicial predilection toward this figure, the term's meaning is ambiguous.

The term "am haarez" was once understood as a static term referring to a specific social group.[58] Recently Stephen Wald has shown that the term is fluid, which explains how it functions as the semantic opposite of a member of either the purities elite (*ḥābēr*) or the intellectual elite (*ḥakām*) in tannaitic literature.[59] Both Wald and Jeffrey Rubenstein have noted the way in which rhetoric about the am haarez is increasingly strident in late amoraic and stammaitic layers of the Talmud.[60] I believe that the fluidity of the term am haarez and the strident rhetoric point to a Babylonian rabbinic cultural anxiety over place. Passages about the am haarez teach about the self-identity of rabbinic writers because the project of constructing otherness (especially in the face of an imagined static other) always projects self-identity.[61]

In the context of Rabbâ bar Rab Hûnâ's *mêmrôt*, *ṣûrbā mērabbānān* and am haarez function as semantic opposites. The *ṣûrbā mērabbānān* here is any member of rabbinic society and the am haarez is any outsider. In this way, the division between insider and outsider echoes that of Rab Joseph's "with you in Torah and mitzvoth." The usage of *ṣûrbā mērabbānān* and am haarez as opposites clarifies the polarization of inside and outside that some have connected quite specifically to the late amoraic period in Babylonia while inviting the reader to pressure the dividing line between the two camps.[62] Though ultimately this text can teach more about rabbinic perceptions of self and other, it is also likely the closest one comes to information about nonrabbinic Jews.

Mêmrā 1

Rabbâ's first *mêmrā* plans an elaborate choreography for insider/outsider litigation. The setting puts general requirements of respectful posture, courtroom postural requirements, and procedural equity in conflict with one another. Since the rabbinic judge is a peer, a case that pits rabbinic Jew against nonrabbinic Jew creates friction automatically: if the rabbinic Jew sits in parallel with the rabbinic judge, there is unequal posture with the nonrabbinic Jew, which is good for cultural positioning but bad for justice. But if the rabbinic Jew stands alongside the nonrabbinic Jew, the disparity of level between the rabbinic litigant and the rabbinic judge communicates cultural disrespect. While ordinarily both litigants (following the majority position of the *baraita*) are asked to stand in the courtroom, Rabbâ claims that both litigants are seated in *ṣûrbā mērabbānān*/am haarez litigation. If the litigants, however, refuse to be seated, the court compels the rabbi to sit, while allowing the am haarez to stand. Though the end result creates the very inequitable situation targeted by R. Judah in the *baraita* ("one should *not* have one standing and the other sitting . . ."), it does so as the volition of the respectful outsider, not the court's mandate.

Rabbâ's *mêmrā* balances the competing claims of the different discourses, but it ultimately prefers cultural respect for rabbis to both courtroom postural requirements and ethics. The default practice of standing is superseded at the outset because of the social requirement that greater rabbis not stand before lesser colleagues; though the seating is an ethically balanced a priori commitment, if cultural deference leads to inequitable posture, this is acceptable according to the statute.

Mêmrā 2

Having posited in the initial statute that the litigants in insider/outsider litigation are both seated, Rabbâ insists in his second *mêmrā* that the *ṣûrbā mērabbānān* not take that seat before the arrival of the am haarez, since such a scenario has the appearance of judicial impropriety. Though I have to this point excluded the *stam*'s commentary on Rabbâ's *mêmrôt*, it is helpful here to cite the *stam*'s limitation to the second *mêmrā* because it provides cultural context: "We only say this if [the *ṣûrbā mērabbānān*] does not have a regular time slot [to learn with the judge], but if he has a regular time slot, there is nothing for us in it."[63]

The *stam* limits Rabbâ's *mêmrā* to allow for the possibility that the litigant is a regular student/colleague of the judge. This alerts the reader to the fact that the courtroom and the *beit midrash* were a single space wherein a regular participant in the *beit midrash* would have held (forgiving the pun) home court advantage.

In his 1975 monograph *Rabbinic Instruction in Sasanian Babylonia*, David Goodblatt challenges the traditional and rationalist historiographic presumption that amoraic study was conducted in large institutional yeshivas. Though initially resisted by rationalist historiographers, Goodblatt's work has now been universally accepted, especially since Jeffrey Rubenstein demonstrated that the few Bavli texts that reflect institutions are stammaitic.[64] The period of the *stammaim* coincided with a rise in Babylonian institutionalization that culminated in the geonic period with the attachment to Abbasid political power.[65] Goodblatt's insight encourages one to read amoraic court case narratives in light of amoraic disciple circles—small groups of students clustered around charismatic authorities in the local synagogue or even the scholar's home.[66] Unlike the geonic yeshiva, which contemporaneous literary sources sometimes analogize to the Sanhedrîn as a national judicial institution with a strong institutional claim to legal authority, the amoraic study hall was a local court whose sole claim to legal authority was the charisma of its lone judge.[67]

While research on the exilarch has claimed that the exilarch had some political authority in amoraic Babylonia, it is not clear how much and what kind of relationship the exilarch had with individual rabbis.[68] Sometimes the relationship seems supportive and sometimes it seems antagonistic. The Talmud testifies to the function of amoraim as judges, but it is difficult to ascertain either the frequency of such adjudications or the penalty for non-compliance with an amoraic ruling. The sources indicate that judicial authority was local.[69]

The court case in the amoraic *beit midrash* was a deconstructive moment that collapsed the inside/outside binary. In this place of theoretical study, the law came to practical life. At the same time, the practical adjudication did not negate the pedagogical scene: the students who sat before their teachers in the theoretical classroom were instantly transformed into clerks and judges in training as their teachers became judges.[70]

The penetration of real-life scenarios into its confines animated the *beit midrash*, injecting its theoretical study with an occasional dose of reality. That reality both justified the theoretical study and functioned as a control for it. The purpose of theoretical study, the court case suggested, was the practice; fine distinctions of idealized theoretical study could be tested in this practical environment.

Like the larger genres of rabbinic writing, the literary forms that compose the Talmud map onto some of the different activities that transpired in the study hall. *Mêmrôt* represent teacher's lectures, while the discursive reasoning represents the give-and-take of the interactive study hall in which students, teachers, and their respective colleagues fleshed out topical issues. The court case narrative as a literary form interrupts the theoretical discourse of the study hall with a measure of reality.

Amoraic court cases drew litigants from among study hall regulars and nonrabbinic Jews. The penetration of the class outsider into the *beit midrash* creates a moment in which the inside space becomes a performative one in which rabbinic authority is asserted and constituted. The amoraic court case was an opportunity to perform and constitute the relationship of outsiders to the rabbinic program. Imagine the levels of inequity such a courtroom represented for the am haarez. The dual function of the *beit midrash* as vocational study hall and courtroom afforded comfort to those who regularly studied there and discomfiture to those who arrived for adjudication alone. The rabbinic Jew was comfortable in the ideational space of Torah within which the adjudication would transpire, but also with the physical architecture of the *beit midrash*. While many insiders were undoubtedly unlearned members of rabbinic society, some were likely participants in the study hall's majority discourse of theoretical study. In some cases, the litigant who was a master teacher might find adjudication within a space he otherwise dominated as a lecturer. Discomfort must have been the norm for the am haarez.

The multiple roles of the *beit midrash*—the way it shifted from theoretical laboratory to courtroom—add another level to our understanding of the general Babylonian interest in postural positions. Alongside the Babylonian awareness of the power of postural symbols to crown kings and establish rabbinic hierarchy, these symbols were also importantly employed in the creation of judicial space. Since the architecture of the Babylonian amoraic *beit midrash* did not specifically demarcate the activities performed in the *beit midrash*'s confines, postures were necessary to establish the court as a court.

The scenario of rabbinic insider and outsider as opposing litigants creates a conflict of postural semiotics that is arguably more conflicted than the conflict of formal legal requirements. While on the formal level the conflict between courtroom equity, rabbinic hierarchical postural customs and the mandates of courtroom posture lends itself, perhaps, to some form of compromise (making the posture of the rabbinic outsider optional, for example), the semiotic significance of these postures demonstrates the extent to which compromise is out of the question since the very postures that crown a rabbinic insider also undermine the authority of the courtroom that epitomizes the rabbinic project. In other words, the semiotic ramifications of two competing postural requirements create an inner rabbinic conflict: can one show the requisite cultural respect for rabbis while maintaining the authority of rabbinic law?

Mêmrā 3

Rabbâ's third *mêmrā* does not pit the *ṣûrbā mērabbānān* against the am haarez, but imagines a case in which a rabbinic witness considers a certain court case beneath his dignity because the judges are his hierarchical inferiors.

> And Rabbâ bar Rab Hûnā said if a certain *ṣûrbā mērabbānān* knew testimony but it was degrading to him to go to the house of judges who are less than he to testify before it, he should not go.

The Mishnaic context in which this discussion is located is the "oath of testimony," an oath the rabbis derive from the Bible whose purpose is to compel testimony from reluctant eyewitnesses. Since a litigant can subpoena a suspected witness to swear before God that he does not know anything material to the case, the law would seem to be invested in the notion that eyewitnesses testify to what they know. It is surprising, then, that Rabbâ can state simply that the rabbinic insider who feels superior to the court in which a case is being tried can choose not to appear in that court.

Troubled by the implication of the *mêmrā*, the *stam* first justifies it by connecting it to another similar amoraic text about the return of lost objects and then confines both texts to limit their damage:

> Rab Šîšā bar Rab ʾÎddî [ca. 320–ca. 380 C.E.] said we also have learned [something similar] in a mishnah: "if he found a bag or box, if it is not his routine to pick it up, he should not pick it up."

By connecting refusal to testify with refusal to return a found object (also the subject of a specific biblical imperative), the *stam* draws support for flouting an explicit biblical rule. Then the *stam* limits both:

> And this is true regarding monetary [matters], but for [moral] prohibitions "There is no wisdom and no insight and counsel to counter God": Wherever there is desecration [of God] we do not grant honor to the rabbi.

Even the *stam* is unsatisfied with the connection to the found object and modifies Rabbâ's *mêmrā* by limiting it to monetary affairs: in cases of moral prohibitions, though, the rabbi is second to God. The limitation does not undermine the focus on hierarchy; it uses that hierarchy to limit ethical damage.

There is little reason to presume the *stam*'s modification as Rabbâ's intent. This is a typical moment of stammaitic editorializing in order to confine the problematic contours of a source text. While earlier chapters focused on this characteristic of the *stam*'s response to legal narrative, it is a phenomenon that is by no means limited to such original sources. The *stam* is disturbed enough by the clash between Rabbâ's *mêmrā* and the general principles of Jewish law to attempt to control some of the damage.

All three of Rabbâ bar Rab Hûnaʾs *mêmrôt* share the feel of balancing commitments. Each hypothetical imagines a scenario in which the jurisprudential scene is loaded with conflicting obligations—cultural norms of postural deference, procedural rules of the courtroom, ethical principles of jurisprudence, and moral obligations demanded by the Bible. In two of the three cases (relative posture and eyewitness testimony) Rabbâ offers a compromise that recognizes the conflict before coming down on behalf of the paramount importance of deference for the rabbis and their program.

The analytic philosopher Gilbert Ryle coined the phrase "thick description" within an essay entitled "The Thinking of Thoughts: What Is 'Le Penseur' Doing?"[71] The French phrase in the title refers to Auguste Rodin's famous sculpture *The Thinker*; Ryle's essay explores a textured understanding of what the subject of the sculpture is doing when he seems lost in thought. In order to explain the fact that the simple act of thinking can be complex, Ryle invokes the example of a winking eye. Imagining a young schoolboy as possessing the shutting lid, Ryle first explores the basic difference (voluntary/involuntary) of twitches and winks before moving on to the semiotic potentials of winks (communicating, parodying, pretending to parody, and so on).

Clifford Geertz made Ryle's phrase the title of a famous essay about the need for anthropologists to become more interpretive.[72] The essay has become so famous that the term is often attributed to Geertz rather than Ryle. Stephen Greenblatt has written a literary scholar's appreciation of Geertz for scholars of literature, entitled "A Touch of the Real."[73] The eponymous idea of Greenblatt's essay and his development of it in conversation with Ryle and Geertz are helpful for introducing the *sugya*'s legal narratives.

Greenblatt argues that the pivotal difference between Ryle and Geertz is the type of argument they respectively register. In introducing his own grounds for argument, Geertz critiques Ryle's hypothetical wink: "Like so many of the little stories Oxford philosophers like to make up for themselves, all this winking, fake-winking, burlesque-fake-winking, rehearsed-burlesque-fake-winking may seem a bit artificial."[74]

In place of the artificial wink, Geertz offers "a not untypical excerpt" from his field journal: a story in which a local Jew negotiates sheep theft, murder, tribal conflict, and modernization within a colonial Morocco that is politically controlled by the French but under de facto tribal rule.[75] Greenblatt argues that the story subverts the philosopher's systematic methodology and calls into question the feasibility of ever describing a culture systematically.[76] Furthermore, the story's strangeness provokes an intense curiosity that is a necessary condition for cultural interpretation. Pushing the comparison of Ryle and Geertz further, Greenblatt asserts that while thickness for Ryle inheres in the narrative surroundings of the action being discussed (the context for winking or the reason for pumping bicycle tires), in Geertz's writing "thickness begins to slide almost imperceptibly from the description to the thing being described."[77] Thickness is not just about the framing of an interpretation, but it inheres in the object of study itself. Some texts are inherently thicker than others.[78] "Geertz's . . . excerpt from his fieldnotes is a complex narrative in which the motivating intentions seem intrinsic. . . . In practice . . . certain constructions of cultural reality appear compressed and hence expandable."[79] It is this sense in which certain texts appear intrinsically to compress cultural dynamics and allow for expansive interpretation that Greenblatt refers to as "the touch of the real."

Within the talmudic passage, the three *mêmrôt* of Rabbâ bar Rab Hûnâ are akin to the philosopher's hypothetical in that they can be described thickly by providing, as I have done, the narrative context that includes the conflict of laws that is central to their propositions. But the legal narratives about this topic provide a touch of the real inasmuch as they invite the reader's curiosity about complex cultural dynamics and encourage expansive interpretation. Like Geertz's Moroccan Jew story, legal narratives are expandable nuggets that "can widen out into enormous complexities of social experience."[80]

Three Legal Narratives

Three legal narratives are interspersed among the three *mêmrôt* of Rabbâ bar Rab Hûnâ, each contextualizing Rabbâ's idealized notions with a narrated episode. As discussed above, Rabbâ's final *mêmrā* licenses a rabbinic eyewitness to fail to report and testify. One of the narratives responds to this *mêmrā*:

> Rab Yêmar [ca. 350–ca. 410 C.E.] knew testimony about Mar Zûtrā [ca. 350–ca. 410 C.E.].
> [Rab Yêmar] came before 'Amêmar [ca. 350–ca. 410 C.E.].[81]
> ['Amêmar] seated [Rab Yêmar][82]

Since Rab Yêmar need not have reported to 'Amêmar's court, 'Amêmar defers to this rabbi and allows him to testify seated. The *sugya* had earlier established some leeway for litigant posture; until this point, though, we have seen nothing permitting witnesses to testify while seated. Elsewhere in the Talmud the *stam* asserts that testimony offered while seated is *inadmissible*.[83] The story's record of leniency vis-à-vis this postural requirement is noteworthy.

An additional talmudic text that again employs the trope of courtroom posture as a central measure of political authority can also help contextualize this short story of Rab Yêmar. Sanhedrîn 19a narrates a clash between the Hasmonean king Alexander Jannaeus (Yann'ay in the Bavli) and the proto-rabbinic hero Simeon ben Šeṭaḥ. In this famous story of speaking truth to power, Simeon ben Šeṭaḥ demands that a seated King Yann'ay stand during the proceedings. When Yann'ay asks Simeon's colleagues if they agree with this demand, the other judges cower out of royal fear and are struck down and killed by an angel after Simeon calls forth the wrath of God. This story famously parallels a similar story in Josephus and a comparison permits the identification of certain specifically Babylonian features. One of the features of the story introduced within the Babylonian version is the special focus on courtroom postures as determinative of judicial and political authority. The story is a Babylonian rabbinic fantasy that insists on the postural stature of rabbis above kings. And yet, within the same culture that narrates a story of a sovereign forced to stand during someone else's testimony, a rabbi is permitted to sit while testifying.

The *stam* is troubled by the difficult fit of Rab Yêmar's story amid the preceding legal discussion about the mandatory postures of witnesses: "But[84] 'Ûllā said the argument [in the *baraita* between the anonymous position and R. Judah about posture in the courtroom] was only about litigants, but regarding the witnesses *everyone agrees* that they must stand?"

The *stam* questions 'Amêmar's actions on the basis of the unanimous statutory position that witnesses must always stand. The *stam* answers its own question: "We say[85] this is a [biblical] positive commandment and this is a [biblical] positive commandment, but the positive commandment of honoring Torah takes precedence."

I noted above that two of Rabbâ's *mêmrôt* balance their commitments firmly in the direction of rabbinic deference. One of those was the *mêmrā* determining that Rab Yêmar need not arrive in court to testify in the first place. The narrative developed that *mêmrā* further by having rabbinic deference extend to the seating of witnesses. The *stam*'s answer makes Rabbâ's motivations in his *mêmrôt* explicit: when there is a conflict between commitments, the commitment to rabbinic honor takes priority. In order to do this, the *stam* imagines each of its commitments as originating in a biblical positive commandment. The postural requirements of the courtroom are the result of positive commandments and so are the requirements to honor Torah through the rabbis who possess and disseminate it. No explanation is offered for the choice of honoring Torah as preeminent.

One of the other legal narratives interspersed among Rabbâ bar Rab Hûnā's *mêmrôt* brings to life his first *mêmrā*—the one that seats both litigants but gives the rabbinic outsider the option of standing—and in so doing demonstrates the difficulty of the line this *mêmrā* draws:

> Rab bar Šěbā[86] [ca. 320–ca. 380 C.E.] had a court case before Rab Pāppā.[87]
> [Rab Pāppā] seated both of them.
> The court agent came and kicked [the am haarez][88] and made him stand.[89]

In placing this narrative immediately after Rabbâ bar Rab Hûnā's statement, the *stam* highlights the difficulty of actualizing the kind of theoretical compromise that Rabbâ advocates. The *stam* struggles to make the story cohere with its adjacent precedent:

> But how could he do this? The [opponent's] arguments were being silenced?
> [The am haarez] certainly said [to himself], "[Rab Pāppā][90] seated us [both]; the [court][91] agent is not appeased[92] by me."

The *stam* questions the narrative from the ethical demand for equality in the courtroom that was evident in the words of R. Judah in the opening *baraita* of this *sugya*. Though Rab Joseph explicitly denied this ethical imperative vis-à-vis amme haarez, Rabbâ's *mêmrā* clearly rejects Rab Joseph's principle and struggles to juggle all of its commitments, including the commitment to equity. For this reason, Rabbâ insists that litigants are seated but allows the nonrabbinic litigant the standing option. The story suggests that within a culture pervaded by an obsession with the hierarchy constituted by relative postures with respect to other Jews, it is not always possible to draw a fine distinction and make standing optional. The outcome of the story is worse than either making the rabbinic litigant stand or licensing inequality by creating a law that seats the rabbinic litigant but not his opponent. In the story, the violence of the court bailiff uses court power to enforce rabbinic hierarchy. There is little likelihood that a rabbinic outsider could feel in such a situation as if he or she were getting an equal hearing. The *stam* attempts to resolve this within the theoretical plane, imagining a rabbinic outsider so skilled in rabbinic dialectic that he could make the distinction between the actions of the bailiff and the objectivity of the court. The outsider would somehow maintain that Rab Pāppā as judge was neither aware of nor the force behind the unequal treatment. The *stam*'s[93] efforts to confine the legal narrative and contain its damage are disappointing to the reader because one of the advantages of the story's "touch of the real" is its critique of the type of compromise offered by Rabbâ in his *mêmrâ*.

The Goose

One of the three legal narratives interspersed among Rabbâ bar Rab Hûnâ's *mêmrôt* functions, like Geertz's story of the Moroccan Jew, as a compressed tale that holds all of the cultural conflict of the *sugya*'s competing semiotic systems (anthropology, formal biblical law, and ethical behavior) in a manner that defies the *stam*'s general dynamic that molds legal narrative to a statutory framework. In this legal narrative, the demands of competing normative systems literally weigh down the rabbinic protagonist, Rab Naḥmān.

> Rab Hûnā's wife[94] had a court case before Rab Naḥmān.
> [Rab Naḥmān] said [to himself], "How should I[95] act?—[if] I stand before her [in her honor], the arguments of her opponent will be silenced; [if] I do not stand before her, [it will be a breach of honor because] the wife of a *ḥābēr* is exactly like a *ḥābēr*."
>
> He said to his bailiff, "Fly a goose [at me] so that I will stand."[96]

The scenario of the narrative is again one in which a rabbinic figure opposes someone of lesser rabbinic standing in a courtroom. The story's rabbinic figure is not a rabbi or even a rabbi in training who studies in the *beit midrash*, but a rabbi's wife. Rab Naḥmān wishes to display postural deference by standing in the presence of Rab Hûnā's wife, but such a display might silence her opponent. To resolve this contradiction and satisfy both mandates, Rab Naḥmān asks his bailiff to send a goose flying in his direction. The flying goose forces Rab Naḥmān to stand, an act that satisfies the formal requirement of deference without breaching judicial equity by currying favor with one side.

The story's ethical imperative to treat litigants equally is identical to R. Judah's position on the issue in the initial *baraita* of the *sugya*. Rab Naḥmān juggles that ethical position against the need to defer to a rabbinic authority through one's posture. The rhetoric of the story presents an intriguing contrast. While the story explicitly narrates the rationale for remaining seated ("the argument . . . will be silenced"), it never explains the motivation for standing, even though the object of postural respect is not Rab Hûnā himself but his wife. The self-evidence with which postural deference is narrated is demonstrative of the basic and pervasive quality of deference for rabbis within rabbinic culture.

Rab Naḥmān explains the extension of rabbinic postural norms to Rab Hûnā's wife by saying that "the wife of a *ḥābēr* is like a *ḥābēr*." I mentioned above that the term *ḥābēr* in tannaitic literature for someone who commits to purities regulations is the semantic opposite of *ʿam hāʾāreṣ*. Though the *ḥābērîm* ceased to exist as a separate group within the tannaitic period, the term *ḥābēr* lives on in the post-tannaitic literature, where it functions as a synonym for the other group that opposes the amme haarez in tannaitic literature—the scholars.

The term "the wife of a *ḥābēr* is like a *ḥābēr*" appears at ʿAbôdâ Zārâ 39a within the context of a discussion of the purities status of items that emerge from a household after the death of its patriarch. It is employed there, quite sensibly, within the context of purities or other analogous objects whose reliability depends upon their provenance. This passage about courtroom posture borrows the logical extension of a patriarch's credibility to his household for use in the context of deference. Presumably, the practice of standing for the rabbi's wife was culturally self-evident and the use of this term is a weak justification for the practice. Even so, the borrowing of the purities discourse in which *ḥābēr* is employed suggests a Babylonian self-understanding of the rabbinic community as purities fellowship wherein rabbis, rabbinic disciples, and their households are included to the exclusion of others.

Rab Naḥmān produces a novel solution. By having the bailiff send a goose his way, Rab Naḥmān is convinced he can simultaneously stand for Rab Hûnā's wife and appear equitable. Rab Naḥmān imagines Rab Hûnā's opponent as a Babylonian Jew who reads postural signs very closely, understanding within them the power to crown and depose aristocracy. By bringing a goose into the equation, Rab Naḥmān detaches the physical signifier (standing) from its signified (respect for Rab Hûnā's wife). The absurdity of Rab Naḥmān's solution turns this moment into farce. The detachment of signifier from signified not only makes the posture's message of respect unreadable to the opponent, it renders it unreadable to anyone. Though Rab Naḥmān appeared to weigh the need to respect the rabbi's wife against the ethical value of judicial equality, in actuality Rab Naḥmān wants to make sure that he is not *caught* sitting in her presence. At issue is not respect, but the formal requirement of its display.

Only a formalistic understanding of the norm could generate such a farcical "resolution."

Proper understanding of the importance of courtroom postures as rituals that determine the space of adjudication in a multipurpose study hall/courtroom allows us to further develop the depth of this farce. The introduction of the goose into the courtroom complicates the message of Rab Naḥmān's posture, turning the significant fact of his posture into the mechanical reflex in response to a startling event. But the introduction of the goose also undermines the gravitas of authority that courtroom postures are designed to implement. Within this serious space of adjudication created by the rituals that constitute this space as a courtroom, the reader encounters a moment of physical comedy.[97]

Judging is like a juggling act in which the judge tries to keep multiple balls in the air simultaneously; at the end of the juggling act, the judge is forced to drop one ball in favor of the others. Rab Naḥmān's attempt to resist the choice of judgment in resolving his conflicting mandates is a moment of true crisis before the law. While humorous as farce, the decision to bring a goose into the courtroom is also tragic because it demonstrates the dangers of a judge who is unwilling to choose and bear responsibility for that choice.

Though Rab Naḥmān did not articulate his dilemma as a formalistic one—choosing between two positive postural commands—the *stam* frames its reading of the story formalistically, noting that Rab Naḥmān's dilemma should have been animated not just by the clash of cultural practice and ethical value but also by the formal requirement for judges to sit during adjudication. One of the curious ironies of the story of Rab Hûnā's wife is that it comes in the *sugya* directly on the heels of Rab Hûnā's reading of R. Judah in which Rab Hûnā establishes that there is unanimity to the notion that judges must sit. It is no doubt for the purpose of this irony that the woman in the story who forces Rab Naḥmān out of his judicial chair is Rab Hûnā's own wife. The *stam* has little appreciation for this irony, instead demanding that Rab Naḥmān's practice in the story cohere with Rab Hûnā's established unanimous position.

> But was it not just said that[98] at the time of the conclusion of justice it is unanimous that [the witnesses are] standing and the judges [are] sitting?
>
> He sits as one who is tying his shoes and says "So-and-so you are exonerated and so-and-so you are obligated."

The *stam* answers its own question with another farcical scenario. To resolve the contradiction between Rab Hûnā's earlier declaration that all agree that the judges must sit at the close of judgment and the story of Rab Naḥmān, the *stam* suggests a physical compromise between standing and sitting: a crouch.

While Rab Naḥmān's solution severs the postural symbol from its signified, the *stam* offers a solution that splits hairs in an attempt to fulfill all mandates. The basis for the *stam*'s position is the *stam*'s formalistic reading of the problem as a conflict of three biblical positive commandments. The postures are signifiers with no signifieds and one might conceive of a single position (the crouch) that can work as a lowest common denominator of both sitting and standing. Even more than Rab Naḥmān, the *stam* empties the postural requirements of their meaning, thinking of postures as the fulfillment of biblical positive commands. In the *stam*'s interpretation, the story of Rab Naḥmān completes the devolution of the *sugya* from R. Judah's initial desire to insist on ethical meanings rather than formal postures to an exclusively formalistic take on these postures.

One can resist the *stam* and read the goose narrative as an intentional farce that magnifies, through absurdities, the limits of formalistic understandings of the law. The story of Rab Hûnā's wife becomes, like the story of the Moroccan sheep-stealing, an epitomic example of cultural thickness because of the intrinsically overdetermined nature of its plot. To read such a story thickly one needs to contextualize formalistic understandings of the law against the political and social narratives in which those formal positions function. One can imagine the inner conflict of Rab Naḥmān in entirely nonformal terms by recognizing the backdrop of each cultural norm. To wit, a native of rabbinic culture is bodily aware of the expectation to display deference for one's betters even as the demands of creating space for judgment insist on a set of rigid courtroom postures. Even more centrally, the rabbinic insider would find the postural yin/yang animated by ambivalence over equity toward the nonrabbi: though there was undoubtedly some expression of ethical ideals, there also existed decidedly unethical impulses.

The *sugya* of courtroom posture is a *sugya* animated by the kinds of conflicting demands that provoked Geertz to define culture as a web "comprised of the semiotic systems man himself has spun."[99] From the initial *baraita* that introduces the conflict between formal legal requirements and ethically derived rules, between the mandates of biblical verbs and the prohibitions that emerge from the Bible's morality, the *sugya* is about conflicting value systems more than conflicting individual values. As the *sugya* unfolds, it adds the ambivalent attitudes of rabbinic insiders toward their outsider brethren and demonstrates the extent to which rabbinic insiders regularly constituted their own prestige and hierarchical advantage using the only tool possible—rabbinic law. The rare instance of an amoraic courtroom provoked both theoretical largesse (think of the impulse of Rabbâ bar Rab Hûnā) and practical imbalance (Rab Joseph and others of his ilk). The legal narratives interspersed along the way bring the hypothetical discussion back to contemporaneous rabbinic cultural life, challenging the comfortable compromises of the theoretical study hall by forcing that space to become a living courtroom. Though the discourse of the *stam* (and some of the amoraim) cannot but attend to legal conflicts as conflicts of formal rules, legal narratives invite the reader to see such formalism as reductionistic and missing the point. If one understands postures as creating gravitas, doing the cultural work of separating classes and forging a strong judicial ethics, there is no room to see geese and crouches as "solutions" to conflicting mandates.

Epilogue: Maimonides

In his code of Jewish law, *Mishneh Torah*, Maimonides addresses the legal issue of courtroom postures. Sanhedrîn chapter 21:2 states that litigants *should* stand in the courtroom, but allows the court leeway to seat them. Witnesses, on the other hand, are legally required to stand. Immediately following this statute, Maimonides writes: "All Jewish tribunals since after the Talmud have become accustomed that in all sessions they seat both litigants and they seat the witnesses in order to avoid argument, *for we do not have the energy to ensure strict enforcement of these religious (ritual) laws*" (emphasis mine).

Though the preceding rule clearly states that the rule of law requires witnesses to stand and allows individual courts to compel litigants to stand, this text records the practice of post-talmudic courts not to follow this requirement. These post-talmudic tribunals routinely seated both litigants and witnesses in order to avoid argument.

The earliest source for this counterstatutory procedural practice is a geonic responsum attributed to Rav Hai Gāôn in which the author speculates that the basis for the counterprecedential activity is an unattested legal tradition.[100] The responsum further hypothesizes that the practice arose to prevent arguments over hierarchical standing in the wake of the Talmud's claim (in the above-cited legal narrative) that rabbis may testify while seated.

In his comparative work on Jewish and Islamic law, Gideon Libson offers a compelling historical hypothesis: that the Jewish practice of seating litigants and witnesses was influenced by the Islamic legal practice of seating the litigants.[101] Though Islamic law does not specify the posture of witnesses, Libson assumes that the practice of seating the litigants in Islamic tribunals resulted in the practice of seating both litigants and witnesses in Jewish tribunals.

Libson's argument suggests that cultural practice is responsible for the nonstatutory legal behavior. The practice of seating witnesses can be described as a communal custom. The status of the antistatutory custom in Jewish law is complex. Though no mechanism exists for determining the strength of such a custom, there is a notion, developed primarily within the Palestinian Talmud, that a custom can annul a statutory rule: *minhāg měbaṭēl halakhah*.[102] This rhetorical notion is a mechanism through which the legal discourse permits itself to consider living custom a competing authoritative voice within the theoretical discussion. It is a means through which that theoretical legal discourse can manage the threat that messy life poses to the clarity of theoretical legal constructs.[103]

It is noteworthy that neither Rav Hai in his responsum nor Maimonides in his code reach for the *minhāg měbaṭēl halakhah* mechanism. Rather, Rav Hai presumes the existence of a missing or lost tradition—a text that must exist to justify the deviant practice. Maimonides takes a different tack. The man whose magnum opus establishes every detail of halakhic observance uncharacteristically writes: "we do not have the energy to ensure strict enforcement of these religious (ritual) laws." Maimonides is here motivated by a dismissive attitude toward the formal postures of courtroom procedure. While he includes their legal requirements within his code, he dismisses them as procedural grammar, not worthy of significant energies of enforcement.

Medieval and early modern Jewish communal customs have much in common with talmudic legal narratives. Both entities are perceived deviant within a world dominated by a sense of law as textual precedent. Each importantly connects the theoretical discourse of Jewish law with the worldly realities which that discourse claims to structure and control. Both the legal narrative and deviant communal custom testify to the larger world that might contextualize rabbinic law as one of several claimants to normative control.

In his dismissal of courtroom mandatory postures, one catches the inner philosopher peeking through Maimonides' legal writing. Much as R. Judah before him, Maimonides dismisses courtroom postures because they are morally empty. The tanna R. Judah and the medieval Maimonides share a disinterest in such postures, bookending a talmudic *sugya* obsessed with them. The lack of interest in tannaitic Palestine and medieval Egypt heightens awareness of the degree to which amoraic Babylonia *is* exercised by the issue of courtroom postures. For the Babylonian amoraim, courtroom postures were not merely technical, even biblical, requirements, but rituals that constituted rabbinic social importance by creating a boundary between insiders and outsiders and that transformed small study halls into proper courtrooms. These rituals were the ways in which rabbinic insiders struggled to balance their ethical commitments to judicial equity against the unique opportunity to constitute and communicate rabbinic authority.

Chapter 4

Social Dynamics of Pedagogy: Rabbis and Students

No relationship is more central to the fabric of rabbinic culture and its law than that of teacher and student. The pedagogical scene of student before teacher is the implicit context of all talmudic text. Readers rightly presume such a setting when they read talmudic legal discussions that present themselves as dialogues. Despite the ubiquity of texts that implicate a pedagogical environment, only a small percentage of talmudic texts lend themselves to explorations of the social dynamics of rabbinic pedagogy. This chapter takes the opportunity offered by one such text to undertake this exploration.[1]

This chapter attends to two narratives situated in the heart of a talmudic legal passage that encourage a psychological investigation of the teacher-student relationship in rabbinic Babylonia by including the emotional register within their legal conversation. As the emotional investments of teacher and students bubble to the surface, they stand as visible representatives of relational undercurrents that are regularly suppressed within talmudic legal discourse. The legal narratives about bailee liability that provoke this inquiry into teacher-student social dynamics constitute the expandable cultural nuggets to which I referred in the preceding chapter. Like a rich fieldwork narrative, these stories encourage an interpretive anthropology that unpacks their historiographic potential, providing an opportunity for dynamic depiction of cultural life rather than a static description of cultural facts. While the presumption of rabbinic historiography has generally been that teacher-student relations were stable manifestations of cultural institutions, this chapter demonstrates the local instability of these relationships and articulates their contours, explaining where the teacher-student relationship is located within rabbinic culture.

The preceding chapter referenced David Goodblatt's thesis that amoraic Babylonia was not populated by the bureaucratized and politically empowering yeshivas of later Babylonian life in the geonic period.² This discovery has untapped potential for transforming the presumptions of readers who rightly read talmudic texts as produced in pedagogic settings. Where scholars once imagined amoraim as heads of yeshivas with concomitant political authority and economic stability, now scholars must consider the smaller scale pedagogical setting of the disciple circle. Within the richer world of Palestinian rabbinic historiography, scholars are increasingly reaching a conclusion analogous to Goodblatt's, denying the existence of institutional yeshivas during the amoraic period.³ The highest level of rabbinic pedagogy—the amoraic dialogue whose literary representation appears in the Talmud—was produced in small disciple circles in which rabbis discussed their statutory declarations, midrashic inferences, and legal rationalizations with small groups of students.

In both Palestine and Babylonia there was an institution that had power by virtue of its relationship with secular authorities. The patriarch in Palestine represented the Jewish community vis-à-vis the Romans and often the patriarchy's interests overlapped with those of the rabbis.⁴ Likewise, the exilarch in Babylonia represented the Jewish community vis-à-vis the Sassanians and sometimes (less often than in Palestine) found common cause with the rabbis.⁵ While the patriarchy and exilarchate provide the strongest argument for actual rabbinic authority, in neither culture is there a strong connection between the power-giving institution and the context of pedagogy.⁶ Rabbinic education in both cultures takes place in an institutional vacuum.

The noninstitutional nature of rabbinic pedagogy becomes visible in a highly charged text at Bābā Měṣīʿā 97a, which will be examined shortly. To understand this text, one needs to understand the rabbinic legal context of bailee liability.

Bailee Liability

The section of Exodus 22 sometimes called "The Covenant Code" describes three different scenarios of liability for an object or animal that one guards, rents, or borrows (bailee liability): a person who is exonerated from liability in the event of theft, a person who is liable for theft but not for acts of God, and a person who is liable even for acts of God. Though there is clarity in the differing outcomes of the scenarios, the biblical passage is murky in its delineation of these different liability categories. One reading of the passage distinguishes the first and second bailees from each other on account of the goods being watched (greater liability for animals, lesser liability for chattel).[7] Various rabbinic sources distinguish the two scenarios by establishing that the verses of lesser liability refer to one who watches a friend's items without compensation while the verses of greater liability refer to a paid watchman.[8] By interpreting the Bible in this fashion, the rabbis understand a direct relationship between benefit and responsibility: the greater degree of benefit the bailee derives from the relationship with the object, the greater the bailee's liability.[9]

Though some rabbinic texts retain the biblical notion of three bailees, many rabbinic texts create a fourth category of bailee—the renter—whose status is roughly equivalent to the paid watchman.[10] This equivalence is unsurprising. Since both the renter and the paid watchman benefit from their respective relationships with the animal, they are more invested than the unpaid watchman; because they both have costs that outweigh their benefit, neither is as liable as the borrower who has maximal benefit and minimal cost.

Amid the rabbinic understanding of a directly proportional relationship between benefit and liability, there is a surprising aspect of the biblical law. Within the verses that describe the maximal liability of a borrower, Exodus 22:13–14 includes a liability exception for the presence of the owner: "When a man borrows [an animal] from another and it dies or is injured,[11] its owner not being with it, he must make restitution. If its owner was with it, no restitution need be made."

The double language of owner presence/absence clarifies that the borrower is only liable if the owner is absent, but exonerated if the owner is present. The text provides no rationale for the exception, but one might assume that in an agrarian society landowners would contract with animal owners to work the field with their animals; in such a case, the animal is secondary to the arrangement, like a carpenter's hammer.[12]

Rabbinic readers were bothered by the redundancy within Exodus 22. Since verse 13 says that the borrower pays when the owner is absent, the fact that the borrower does not have to pay in the owner's presence is already known. The opening clause of verse 14 is entirely redundant. One way of making sense of this redundancy is by using the extra language to create a new component of the exception. Some rabbinic readers use the extra words to introduce time as a factor to the discussion: the liability exception of owner presence only applies if the animal was borrowed either *after* the owner was borrowed or *simultaneous to* that borrowing. If the animal was borrowed first, however, then the borrower is liable.[13]

One could understand the midrashic interpretation of the verses' redundancy to work well with the rationale: if the animal was borrowed first, then the animal needs to be considered independent of its owner and not akin to a carpenter's hammer. Though it works with the rationale, the principle of contractual simultaneity/priority invites formalistic interpretations that shuck the rationale completely. Thus we find a rabbinic reader who focuses on the contractual language of the midrashic interpretation to suggest that even if the owner and animal are working in *different* fields, if they were hired simultaneously, or if the owner was hired first there is a liability exemption for their borrower.[14] In other words, the notion of owner presence has now, on the basis of the introduction of timing, metamorphosed from a focus on physical presence to a contractual presence that takes priority over physical presence. One can understand the following legal discussion at Bābā Měṣiʿā 97a in this light:

> Rābā[15] said: "A man who wishes to borrow something from his peer and yet be absolved of responsibility, should say to him, 'Give us a drink of water' (so that it constitutes a loan together with the owner's service).[16]
>
> "But if [the lender] is wise, he should answer [the borrower], 'First borrow it [17] and then I will give you a drink.'"

While earlier rabbinic readers began to mine the formalistic consequences of the notion of owner presence as "time of contract," Rābā's statement here pushes those consequences to more absurd extremes by imagining a scenario in which an individual takes advantage of the formal characteristics of law to gain exemption from liability. One who understands that the principle of contractual owner presence that does not depend on whether owner and animal are working together can create a minimalistic contract with the owner (pour me a glass of water!) and in doing so gain exoneration from liability for the loss of the animal. Rābā realizes, though, that the success of such a venture is predicated on the ignorance of the lender; a wise lender could prevent a loss of liability protection by demanding that the animal's contract have priority.

The meaning of Rābā's statement is inherently unclear. One could understand this statement as a reductio ad absurdum, which critiques contractual and temporal redefinition of owner presence. And yet, given Rābā's subsequent statement and participation in the legal discussion, it is hard to read Rābā ironically as a critique of the rabbinic revision. The reader is left taking

Rābā seriously, as play. Rābā suggests, playfully, that students of the law could have fun by exploiting absurdities; they can duel with legal sabers. The wily borrower's thrust is parried by the equally competent lender.

Although the talmudic text is a literary composition and not the record of an oral performance, the text presents itself as if it were a record of such a performance. As such, it is easy to imagine this *sugya* as a lecture offered by Rābā to his disciples. In that setting, this opening playful remark suggests the homilist's comic opening. Elsewhere in the Talmud, Rābā reports on his own tendency to open a lecture playfully: "For Rābā[18] before he commenced [his discourse] to the scholars, used to say something humorous, and the scholars were amused; after that, he sat in awe and began the discourse" (Šabbāt 30b).

This Šabbāt text creates the expectation that Rābā's lecture might turn from comedy to serious matter, and the passage meets this expectation. Immediately following his playful ad absurdum suggestion, Rābā turns to the topic of owner presence and makes the following assertion: "Rābā said: A teacher of children,[19] (a gardener),[20] a butcher, a cupper,[21] (and a town[22] scribe)[23]—all [if they lend something] while at work constitute a loan in the owner's presence."[24]

Medieval commentators to the Talmud assume that the common feature of the listed professions is public service.[25] The butcher, cupper, and children's teacher are individuals contracted by the community. Rābā asserts that these individuals who have a contractual relationship with the community are considered contracted for purposes of owner presence. Thus, if someone were to borrow an item from the butcher, the borrower would have no liability on that borrowed object. In this sense, Rābā's statement is tough on public servants. And yet, if one reads closely one can extrapolate that Rābā limits the liability exemption to the times in which these individuals are "at work."[26] In this way, Rābā moves owner presence away from contractual priority and toward simultaneous work: only when the public servants are fulfilling the terms of their contracts are they considered present for purposes of the exemption.[27] In a sense, Rābā here moves in the direction of the biblical contextual understanding of owner presence as physical, rather than contractual, presence.

Rābā's assertion about public service is met by a reply from his students: "The scholars said to Rābā,[28] 'You, Master, are in our service.' "[29] There is much going on in this simple sentence. For starters, the reply from Rābā's students confirms the sense from Šabbāt 30b that the statutory text projects the image of a transpired pedagogical event. This usage of the term "scholars" refers to a teacher's disciples.[30] The disciples here suggest to their teacher that he is in their service. As a group serviced by a single provider, the students draw an analogy between the schoolteacher and their own teacher. Rābā is not pleased with the analogy:

> He was enraged:[31]
> "You wish to deprive me of my money!" [he exclaimed].
> "On the contrary, you are in my service! For I can change you over from one tractate to another, while you cannot change me!"

Rābā hears his students' attempt to deprive him of liability protection and counters it with his own attempt to place them in his own service and exempt himself from their liability by noting his control of the topic.

Rābā's rage interrupts the rational legal discourse, adding emotional resonance to the transaction of teacher and students. Rābā is concerned that the students wish to be exempt from his liability. But clearly the rage is not about the specific suggestion of exempted liability. Rather, it is the implication of the direction of their service relationship that enrages Rābā. Rābā is insulted that his students could analogize his own position to that of the public servant. Noting their Torah currency, Rābā positions himself as the master in control of his students, not as the public servant subservient to the public.[32]

The transaction between Rābā and his students closely echoes Rābā's playful opening statement with the wily borrower and equally wily lender. The students are the wily borrowers who attempt to use their control of the legal material for their financial advantage; one could imagine a playful smirk on their faces while they assert that their master is a public servant. To extend the analogy, Rābā is akin to his own wily lender. Except that Rābā goes beyond the wily lender. Where the lender of the opening statement is content simply to parry the thrust of the borrower by pouring the glass of water after lending the animal, Rābā wishes to reverse the service relationship and place the students in a subservient role. Here, undoubtedly, Rābā's rage is relevant for one's understanding. An enraged Rābā is not content merely to smirk back at his students; Rābā hears their suggestion as mutiny and strikes back.

That Rābā's assertion that the service relationship is unidirectional is a conceptual strain can be seen from the intellectual calisthenics the medieval commentaries engage in to try and explain this position.[33] Rābā's rage enters the legal discourse and suggests within it an expansion of the notion of service that allows students to be considered employed by their teachers. In the disciple circle context, Rābā declares his own control of the disciples by claiming that he alone can change the topic from tractate to tractate.³⁴

The rhetoric of Rābā's mastery of his students because of his control of the topic is telling because of the confusion of verbal objects. Though the object that Rābā claims to change is the subject matter, the rhetoric imagines the person: "*I* can change *you* over . . . while *you* cannot change *me*." The verb "to teach" encourages this slippage by allowing for two different types of direct object: the person being taught and the material being covered. Though this confusion is natural to "teaching," in this case it is overdetermined, caused both by that confusion and by Rābā's assertion of control over his students; there is here a replication of content in form as Rābā claims to control his students through an assertion of control. A natural result of Rābā's assertion is an overenthusiastic embrace of the confusion over teaching that allows Rābā to claim control of his students themselves because he decides the subject matter of their pedagogical exchange. This moment of negotiated power calls to mind Michel Foucault's work because of the way Rābā uses knowledge literally as power: control of the subject matter becomes control of the subject.³⁵

Emotional outbursts are often overdetermined, and Rābā's is no exception. The students' attempt to place Rābā in their service offends him because he is their superior in the rabbinic hierarchy. But in their claim to his service the students manifest their own claim to being Rābā's teacher. By suggesting an unexplored possibility, the students contribute to the legal discourse; the contribution alone suggests a claim to equality. The students' claim is playful, of a piece with Rābā's opening borrower and lender. As such, the students simultaneously defy Rābā's ability to transition from the playful opening to the awestruck lecture and repeat the opening of the lecture with their own playful homiletic opening. The latter reality turns Rābā into a member of their listening audience—a student.

Though teacher/student is not a standard hendiadys, it is the type of relationship predicated on difference that deconstruction critiques. In the teaching relationship, one could say, the student is always already the teacher and vice versa. Elsewhere, the Talmud recognizes the potential in this relationship: "Rabbî³⁶ said: I have learned much [Torah]³⁷ from my teachers, and from my colleagues more than from my teachers, and from my disciples more than from them all" (Taʿanît 7a).³⁸

By conducting their own lecture and adding to Rābā's list of public servants, the students momentarily teach their teacher, a dynamic that leads to Rābā's rage and the need to reestablish his own mastery over them. The teaching context holds out the possibility that a student will surpass the teacher. Within the nonformalized institutional setting of the disciple circle established around a master, the possibility of a student's surpassing the teacher threatens to upend the entire structure or cause rifts through the creation of new disciple circles. The competitiveness of rabbinic culture and the individual rabbi's investment in hierarchy both emanate from a fundamental anxiety over relative place on the totem pole and the concomitant assignment of value on the basis of that position.[39]

Though Rābā's performance of control over his students seemingly ends the interaction, the scene is extended through the addition of a third protagonist, the Talmud's anonymous voice—the *stam*:

But it is not so.
He is in their service during the *kallâ* days, while they are in his service on other days.

Though the *stam* as an editorial voice is removed from the represented historical amoraic scene, there is evidence from the rhetoric that the *stam* is not a detached and emotionally objective reader. The language of *wĕlā hî*—"but it is not so"—is as forceful as Rābā's own counterthrust and just as rationally questionable, for the *stam* follows the forceful "but it is not so" with a compromise position that agrees to Rābā's statement by placing the students in Rābā's service for the vast majority of the year. Thus the rhetoric of "but it is not so" is stronger than the argument that follows it, an incongruity that reflects a surfeit of emotions. Unhappy with Rābā's treatment of the students within the original story, the *stam* extends the story into the stammaitic contemporary setting in order to respond to that treatment and soften the blow of Rābā's rage.

The *stam* suggests that Rābā is in his students' service during the *kallâ* days, and they are in his service the rest of the year. The term *kallâ* is one of the central talmudic terms Isaiah Gafni used to contest Goodblatt's critique of the amoraic institutional yeshiva.[40] There are several talmudic passages that employ the term *kallâ* to describe a scene of Babylonian institutional pedagogy.[41] Historiographers understand the talmudic *kallâ* on the basis of geonic utilization of the term as an important biannual series of public lectures.[42] These lectures were attended by a larger audience than the registered students of the geonic academies. The geonic *kallôt* preceded the two major holiday months, during the months of Adar and Elul.[43] Because other talmudic sources claim that intellectual preparation for Passover begins thirty days before the holiday, it is presumed that the *kallâ* during Adar concentrated on those studies.⁴⁴ This has been the traditional explanation for the mechanics of the *stam*'s compromise: during the *kallâ* days when the topic defaults to the holidays, the teacher is in the service of the students.

The debate between Gafni and Goodblatt moved toward resolution shortly after Jeffrey Rubenstein noted that the terms focused on to argue for amoraic institutions appear only in stammaitic passages in the Talmud.⁴⁵ The Stammaim are thus responsible for the traditional history generally attributed to geonic chronographers like Šĕrîrā Gaôn and Nātān Habablî. This strongly suggests, as Rubenstein argues, that the period of the Stammaim is the period in which Babylonian yeshiva institutionalization began.⁴⁶ The *stam* here invokes the *kallâ* anachronistically, pulling a discussion that originates within the disciple circle of Rābā's study hall into the nascent institutional world of the Stammaim.

According to the traditional interpretation of the *stam*'s compromise Rābā is hoist by his own petard. Where Rābā intended to control the room by descriptively reminding of his control of the subject matter, the *stam* takes such topical control prescriptively as a test of power. Transferring Rābā into the institutional light, the *stam* (perhaps unknowingly) highlights the gap between disciple circle and institution. While the noninstitutional amoraic pedagogical scene transpires within a power vacuum that encourages minute struggles to assert control, in the stammaitic world there is an institutional order that creates a balance between teacher and student that limits the naked power grab of the hierarchical superior by identifying a finite context in which even the greatest teacher is beholden to others.

Another way of understanding the stammaitic invocation of the *kallâ* is to focus not on the issue of topical control, but rather on the relationship of the academy to the larger public. The *stam* argues that on *kallâ* days the walls of the *beit midrash* become permeable, permitting the outsiders inside; on such days the teacher is in the service of the broad community. During *kallâ*, the teacher is a public servant along the lines of the elementary schoolteacher or butcher. This is ironic because for a figure like Rābā (or his parallel in stammaitic days), such days would presumably be unrivaled moments of cultural celebrity that elevate the lecturer to paramount status; the *stam*'s is an idealistic critique that reminds Rābā and the reader that the world outside is the telos for that which transpires within the theoretical laboratory of the *beit midrash*. In this understanding, the *stam* shifts from the ideational realm in which topical control is significant to the social realm in which popular reception authorizes the great rabbinic figure. The *stam* deliberately responds to Rābā's change in currency (money to Torah) by changing to yet another currency (Torah to social capital) in which the teacher serves the students.[47]

Paideia, Pedagogy, and Rābā's Anger

To this point I have described the disciple circle as noninstitutional in contrast with the institutional yeshivas of the stammaitic and geonic periods. It is important to recognize, though, that the disciple circle is differently institutional inasmuch as it operates within the continuum of the Greco-Roman educational program known as *paideia*.

Paideia is the name given to the Greco-Roman system of education that was a strong component of Hellenistic cultural colonization.[48] The term *paideia* has a semantic range that includes both an educational system and the culture whose indoctrination was enabled by that educational system.[49] This dual meaning of *paideia* makes the term reminiscent of, if not directly parallel to, the term *Torah* in rabbinic Judaism.[50] *Torah* refers both to subject matter and a cultural commitment to the study of that subject matter. When speaking of rabbinic *paideia* one speaks of the culture of Torah.

Since the work of Ben Sira, Greek and Jewish thought have often been conceptualized in opposition, creating the Athens/Jerusalem binary that has long been intellectually productive. Despite this binary, scholars are aware of a strong degree of Greco-Roman influence on the rabbinic educational program.[51] Both the structure and the mechanics of rabbinic educational life were strongly influenced by its Greek counterpart.[52]

The rabbis are often celebrated for the programmatic goal of universalized education.[53] Though one must differentiate between programmatic commitments and real world achievements, it is nevertheless significant that the rabbis understood and valued the potential benefits of universal education.[54]

Rabbinic elementary education consisted of studying the alphabet and reading the Hebrew Bible.[55] A student who became proficient in this reading could graduate to a second level of teaching that included mishnah-form and midrash-form texts and the dialectical skills necessary to parse such texts. Students who mastered these texts and forms could proceed from this setting to study in a disciple circle surrounding a leading tanna or amora. This three-tiered educational structure mirrors the Greco-Roman model of *grammatisteis, grammatikos, sophisteis/rhetor*.[56] Since biblical educational expectations do not share this three-tiered structure, it is fair to suggest that the structure of rabbinic education is derivative of *paideia*.[57]

Paideia transmitted Greek culture through a heavy diet of classical literature and the language necessary to consume such a diet; the rabbinic educational system similarly focused on language acquisition and literacy. Just as the higher levels of Greco-Roman *paideia* elevated rhetoric and, specifically, dialectic, the students of mishnah and midrash and the disciples within the disciple circles were taught to develop their own active dialectical voices.

Several rabbinic texts describe the exercises through which elementary students acquired language proficiency; these methods mirror known Hellenistic ones.[58] At the middle level of *paideia*, students developed compositional skills through a regimen of generic forms such as narrative, disputation, and *chreiai* (short biographical accounts of classical figures).[59] These forms are all attested in rabbinic literature, a fact that may indicate their use in the same manner in rabbinic culture.[60] Students of the rhetors were schooled in debate skills that allowed them to argue both sides of a philosophical dilemma; rabbinical students were similarly taught to argue for both the purity and impurity of an object or animal.[61] In fact, the importance of disputation is more than copied in rabbinic culture, whose literature is famous for raising disagreement to an art form.

While it is conventional among scholars of rabbinics to presume Roman influence in Palestine and Persian influence in Babylonia, in the case of *paideia* influence, this distinction is of little value; all of the aforementioned parallels between *paideia* and rabbinic pedagogy are equally true of Babylonian and Palestinian rabbinic cultures. Cultural influence cannot always be mapped with the same coordinates as political authority. In fact, the entire scholarly construct of "late antiquity" is meant as a corrective that separates cultural contributions from political realities, recognizing that the "Dark Ages" were some of the most fruitful intellectual years, especially for Western religion.[62] Even when bearing political history in mind, the Eastern Roman Empire lasted into the eighth century C.E. and the cultural influence of Greco-Roman culture on the Eastern world far outlived Roman political rule. When speaking of a Babylonian culture that bordered upon the Roman Empire, trading goods and people with that empire, we need not explain that cultural seepage is likely.[63]

Awareness of the background of rabbinic educational institutions in *paideia* invites an investigation of the phenomenon of hierarchical sensitivity in the parallel examples of the talmudic story and Greco-Roman *paideia* writ large. In the Greco-Roman context there is record of upper-level rhetors bristling at the encroachments of lesser pedagogues.[64] Such perceived encroachments were met with hostile insistence upon the rigid hierarchy. In the Bābā Měṣīʿā 97a passage Rābā similarly insists upon his own standing. Rābā is bothered both by the attempt to equate him with the teacher of his example and with the students' attempt to jump the divide between teacher and student, or to turn the tables and place student above teacher.[65] The story confirms the cultural parallel, while the parallel deepens one's understanding of Rābā's excessive anger.[66]

Rābā's anger testifies to his own sense of instability. This echoes the similar anxiety manifest in rabbis continually performing their hierarchical advantage over the amme haarez as discussed in Chapter 3. I argued above that am haarez is a fluid category rather than a static descriptor. I now argue that the position of master teacher at the opposite end of the spectrum is also unstable. A skeptical historiography presumes the marginal position of the rabbis and rabbinic Judaism. If one reads Babylonian rabbinic sources with skeptical eyes one finds basis for recognizing that Jews in the community had differing degrees of commitment to the rabbinic project. Within such texts one may discover that even basic inclusion within the rabbinic project (not being an am haarez) is a source of anxiety.

Consider a comparison between a Mishnaic social hierarchy and a similar Bavli one. Mishnah Sôṭâ cites R. 'Elîʿezer the Great within a series of texts that employ the formula (treated above in Chapter 2) that connects chaos with the destruction of the second temple:

> R. 'Elîʿezer the Great said, "from the day of the destruction of the temple the sages began to become schoolteachers and the schoolteachers began to become sextons and the sextons began to become amme haarez. And the amme haarez became more and more worn down." (Mishnah Sôṭâ 9:15)

The destruction of the temple lessened the prestige of all four social classes. Though amme haarez occupy the lowest rung on the ladder, they are otherwise not called out for particular opprobrium. I mentioned in Chapter 3 that the term should not be understood as a signifier for a specific social group, but as a fluid term, which in this context seems to mean "hoi polloi." Contrast this formula with a similar formula from Bavli Pĕsāḥîm 49a:

> The rabbis taught, one should sell everything he has in order to marry the daughter of a rabbi.
> If he does not find the daughter of a rabbi, he should marry the daughter of one of the greats of the generation.
> If he does not find the daughter of a great of the generation, he should marry the daughter of a head of synagogue.
> If he does not find the daughter of a head of synagogue, he should marry the daughter of a charity collector.
> If he does not find the daughter of a charity collector, he should marry the daughter of a schoolteacher.
> But he should not marry the daughter of an am haarez.

This text, located within a passage famous for its negative treatment of the am haarez, establishes the continuum of rabbinic society from the outsider (am haarez) to the cultural ideal of the rabbi.[67] The differing strata of communal positions are a hierarchy created by proximity to the ideal—the rabbi—and distance from its opposite—the am haarez. It is telling that there are six classes in this society and that the text leans toward its ultimate point—that one should not marry the daughter of an am haarez. The energy of the text suggests that its composition is animated by the need to definitively assert one's standing in the rabbinic community by resisting the possibility of being dragged into the am haarez abyss. The delineation of various titled intermediate positions between rabbi and am haarez may reflect the need to prevent falling into the am haarez category by having an alternate rigidly defined social place.

In a world in which the position of rabbi was determined by charismatic authority and the ability to attract and maintain students, distance between rabbi and am haarez could not be large enough. This helps explain the rising opprobrium directed toward the am haarez in this period: the proximity of the abyss motivates an insistence upon the greatness of the rabbinic project and the particular honor due an individual rabbi. It also adds explanatory fuel for the divide between amoraic rabbis and schoolteachers.

Notice that in the Mishnah's list the class of rabbi is proximate to the class of schoolteacher. In the Talmud's list, in contrast, the class of schoolteacher is separated from the rabbi by three intermediate classes (charity collector, head of synagogue, "great of the generation"). The net result is a distancing of rabbi and schoolteacher that makes the schoolteacher the class neighbor of the am haarez.

Rāba's need to distance himself from the schoolteacher of his example and his rage at his students finds its echo in the artificial distance between rabbi and schoolteacher in this list; the terms "great of the generation," "head of synagogue," and "charity collector" grasp for positive identifications of men who are not amme haarez.

It is significant that the classes in between the amora and the am haarez are defined by stable institutional positions within rabbinic culture. These hierarchically lower positions on the rabbinic totem pole offer institutional stability. Because of the stability of his position, the schoolteacher as a member of the secondary intelligentsia—butcher, sexton, scribe, and so on—is assured identification as a rabbinic Jew and the social and economic advantages that attach to such identification within rabbinic society.

In his work on the Palestinian tannaim, Shaye Cohen theorizes that the rabbinate emerged from a sectarian social elite movement into a bureaucratized middle-class occupation perhaps through the aegis of Rabbi Judah the Patriarch around the turn of the third century.[68] By Cohen's argument, the late Palestinian tannaim and amoraim no longer needed to come from the financial upper class. Rather, individual rabbis could attain paid positions through their success within the rabbinic cultural market. The rabbinate in Palestine, the theory goes, developed institutional economic stability.

One of the most important sources for Cohen's schematic is a story that appears both in the Palestinian Talmud and in Genesis Rabbâ in which the town of Simonias asks Rabî Judah the Patriarch to delegate a man who will teach at the primary level and the secondary level and adjudicate their cases.[69] The mention of the three levels of rabbinic instruction bespeak an inherent parallelism to the three levels of *paideia*; when necessary, a single individual sometimes fulfilled multiple pedagogical functions of *paideia*.[70] When Rabbî assigns Levi ben Sisi to the task, the latter is presented to the community and placed on an elevated pulpit before them. In this position, he is asked three theoretical issues of Jewish law. Affected by hubris, Levi is unable to answer the questions though he is intellectually more than capable, as the story establishes.

Though some of the historiographic claims to patriarchal authority that have been made on the basis of this story overreach,[71] the story suggests that Palestinian rabbis were in some cases able to make their rabbinic pedagogical activities the basis for a livelihood. Even so, it is noteworthy that rabbinic activities are only remunerated when they include elementary education. There is no evidence of a similar professionalization of upper-level rabbinic pedagogy in

Babylonia or of renowned amoraim moonlighting as elementary pedagogues. In Babylonia, it seems, one could become a remunerated professional schoolteacher or an unpaid charismatic master teacher with a disciple circle.

In the Greco-Roman paideic world, the system of education enabled the full absorption of the nouveau riche into classical culture.[72] The children of new wealth managed, through *paideia*, to belong fully to aristocratic life. In this way *paideia* came to replace the military as the vehicle for social climbing. A rabbinic insider would describe the rabbinic world as a meritocracy that similarly permitted the am haarez to climb into the rabbinic aristocracy; in both Palestine and Babylonia a position in the secondary intelligentsia simultaneously marked inclusion in the rabbinic project and the inability to become a full "rabbi." Leviticus Rabbâ 2:1[73] cites a text that testifies to the tripartite *paideia* structure, while characterizing the rabbinic project along the lines of survival of the fittest: "In the normal course of the world a thousand people enter to study Bible, and one hundred emerge, one hundred [enter to study] Mishnah, and ten emerge, ten [enter to study] Talmud and one emerges. That is what is written (Ecclesiastes 7) 'one man out of a thousand I have found.'"[74]

In this competitive environment in which the goal (at least for the minority that produce the literature) is to become an amora, the schoolteacher is sometimes considered a bulwark against amme haarez and sometimes a failed amora whose failure places him near the social camp of the am haarez. This emerges to light most vividly when the schoolteacher attempts to participate fully in rabbinic discourse. In a source that appears in three different places in the Palestinian Talmud, Rab Měnā puts Bar Šalmîyā the Teacher in his place for asking the kind of absurd question only a lowly schoolteacher would ask.[75] A similar source appears in the Bavli attributed to Rab Yann'ay and Rab Ḥanînā the Teacher.[76] Though these figures are Palestinian, I am not arguing for Babylonian uniqueness and the inclusion of such a text in the Bavli implies that the ad hominem attack on the teacher qua teacher was not foreign to the Bavli mind-set.[77] The opprobrium aimed at the schoolteacher is, in my reading, a function of resentment and envy even as it serves to put the schoolteacher in his place within the *beit midrash*.

Another Bavli text illustrates both the proximity and the distance between schoolteacher and amora. Within a complex legal discussion at Yĕbāmōt 31b, a story is told in which Rab Ḥîsdā successfully explains a legal paradox. As part of his explanation, Rab Ḥîsdā includes an account of an encounter with a prophetic Chaldean shaman:

And a Chaldean said to me, "You will be *malpānā*—a teacher."

[Rab Ḥîsdā] [ca. 230–ca. 290 C.E.] said (to himself) "if I will become a great man, I will explain (this) from my own knowledge, but if I will be a schoolteacher, I will ask it of the rabbis who enter into the synagogue."

Now (that I am a great man) I have explained it from my own knowledge.

The Chaldean prophesies that Rab Ḥîsdā will become a teacher using the term *malpānā*. This is not a common term, but the story itself indicates that it has a semantic range that includes both lower-level elementary schoolteachers and upper-level rhetor amoraim. Rab Ḥîsdā relates the prophecy to the legal paradox with which he is struggling by asserting that either he will become an amora and resolve the paradox on his own or he will become a schoolteacher and resolve the paradox by asking the amoraim who enter the synagogue. With this introduction Rab Ḥîsdā offers his creative interpretation. On its surface, the text argues that Rab Ḥîsdā is able to resolve the riddle because he is an amora. I prefer to argue the opposite: that the ability to resolve the legal paradox confirms (or constitutes) Rab Ḥîsdā's standing as an amora. Thus this text testifies both to the extent to which a Babylonian rabbinic Jew could understand the amora and schoolteacher to engage in comparable pedagogy and to the fact that amoraim in such a world regularly looked for confirmation of their own higher standing within the pedagogical hierarchy.

Rab Ḥîsdā wants to be a dialectician, but the term he uses is "great man."[78] *Paideia* was a lecturer's culture.[79] The lecturer was the star, and public lectures were the epitome of the culture; those lectures were not that dissimilar, though, from the rhetorical exercises that were the highest level of the *paideia* education.[80] The *kallâ* of geonic (and possibly amoraic or stammaitic) Babylonia shares this characteristic: though they were popular, they were not entirely dissimilar from the typical yeshiva curriculum. The civilization of *paideia* held up individual exemplars as classics, as much a part of the curriculum as classical literature and philosophy.[81] Both rhetors and amoraim enjoyed an intense subjectification by students who wished to copy their masters and become them, rising to the pinnacles of social glory. And yet that subjectification, Bābā Měṣîʿā 97a suggests, might motivate an imbalance, or an assertion, of power.

The interaction between Rābā and his students is charged both by their intimate relationship and by the mutual need for the teacher to be a master lecturer. Rābā's assertion implicates the notion of a public servant, including a butcher, cupper, and teacher within that list. The term for teacher in Rābā's list was originally *sôper*, a term that, like *malpānā*, has a broad semantic range that can include schoolteacher or amora (or scribe).[82] The ambiguity in the term is analogous to the ambiguity of Rab Ḥisdā's Chaldean prophecy and one could understand the students' question to Rābā quite innocently.[83]

Rābā's Shame

The scene of pedagogy, so loaded with anxiety about the position of rabbis with an unstable if elevated position of social authority, continues within the talmudic text with another parallel legal narrative on the same substantive legal concern:

> Mar[84] bar Ḥanînā[85] rented his mule[86] to Bê Ḥôzā'î.[87]
> [Mar bar Ḥanînā] went out to lift up a load with [Bê Ḥôzā'î].[88] They were negligent with it and it died.
> When they[89] came before Rābā, he obligated [Bê Ḥôzā'î] [to pay].[90]
> The Rabbis [his disciples] said to Rābā:[91]
> "But it is negligence with the owner [in service]!"
> He was ashamed.
> Eventually it was ascertained that he had gone forth to examine[92] its load.

Where the previous story took place within the confines of the theoretical study hall, this story describes the puncturing of the hall's hermetic seal as outsiders enter the space for adjudication. As explained in the preceding chapter, the court case narrative presents a "touch of the real."

The story describes a typical scenario of bailee liability. An individual or group of individuals from Bê Ḥôzā'î pays money to Mar bar Ḥanînā to rent a mule, presumably to take goods back to Bê Ḥôzā'î from Měḥôzā, Rābā's hometown. Mar bar Ḥanînā is a nice person, so he decides to assist his renters in loading the animal. The people from Bê Ḥôzā'î, however, are negligent with the mule and the mule dies. The case arrives in Rābā's courtroom (*beit midrash*) and he decides in favor of the animal's owner, ruling that Bê Ḥôzā'î must pay for the lost animal. The students, attending this court case in their *beit midrash*, question Rābā's ruling because the owner was present, and owner presence exempts the renters from liability.[93] Rābā is ashamed and exits the narrative silently without a word of explanation.

Prior readers of this passage have assumed that Rābā's shame and silence are two witnesses to an error of memory: Rābā forgot a well-established rule that owner presence exempts even a grossly negligent bailee.[94] But such a reading flattens out Rābā's shame by equating it with a legal rule. The story, by such a reading, simply states that owner presence exempts a grossly negligent bailee and could have been replaced by a statute with that express content. The complexity of legal narrative as narrative challenges the simplicity of this reading, using the poor mapping of narrative onto regulum as an invitation to read Rābā's shame more complexly as a remarkable emotional nugget of rabbinic life. Though Rābā's shame can be read simply as an instance of forgetting, both the scenario and the legal issues surrounding this case are too thorny for a simple and erroneous application of law. Deconstructive readings are arguably most compelling when they shift attention to the margins, recentralizing a reader's focus on discarded matter previously deemed ancillary. The marginalization of shame is here tantamount to the effort of ignoring narrativity itself. By focusing on shame, one can restore narrativity to the center.

The dominant reading of this passage treats shame as a marker of legal content—it is valuable inasmuch as it informs the discourse of legal rules through its commentary on the issue of bailee liability. But a consideration of the biblical and rabbinic principles of bailee liability only heightens the need to refocus on shame because the dominant legal discourse *fails* to fully account for this narrative. Consider the scenario of Mar bar Ḥanînā in light of the biblical notion of owner presence. The rationale for the biblical exemption is arguably based on the idea that the borrowing of the animal is secondary to the employment (borrowing) of its owner. The narrative of Mar bar Ḥanînā, though, does not fit with such a model since the owner is not *employed* by the renters, but *voluntarily* assists them in the loading.[95] The tannaitic reinterpretation of owner presence as a contractual principle requiring either owner priority or simultaneity is also inappropriate to the story's legal scenario: since Mar bar Ḥanînā exits to assist in the loading *after* the renters have already taken possession of the animal and begun its loading, the scenario should not be eligible for the owner presence exemption suggested by the students. Finally, if in light of Rābā's initial playful hypothetical one allows for the possibility that "contract" is used less than formally to imply any agreement between the borrower and owner over the owner's services, there is no indication within the story that Mar bar Ḥanînā offered to assist in the loading because of any request by the renters. Rather, Mar bar Ḥanînā exits to load the animal out of kindness. The story does not seem to meet the threshold of owner presence. If this threshold is not met, it is difficult to understand why Rābā acquiesces to his students' suggestion, as if there were no point in arguing his own ruling.

Continuing along the same lines, the matter of law that is at issue in the scenario of this narrative is more complex than the simple issue implied by those readers who read Rābā's blunder as an error of memory. To understand this complexity and again challenge the simple reading by creating room for Rābā's ruling one must return to the above discussion of the categories of bailee liability. Mishnah Bābā Měṣîʿā 7:9 (= Šěbûʿôt 8:1) offers a sliding scale as the paradigm for bailee liability.

> There are four bailees: an unpaid watchman, a borrower, a paid watchman, and a renter.
>
> - An unpaid watchman swears for everything [and does not have to pay anything].
> - A borrower pays everything.
> - A paid watchman or a renter swears concerning an animal that was injured, [one that was] taken captive, or [one that was] dead; but pays for loss or theft.

The Mishnah asserts four types of bailee: the unpaid watchman who watches without compensation, the borrower, the paid watchman, and the renter. Within its liability analysis, the Mishnah establishes that the paid watchman and the renter have the same liability, so there are only three liability rules (see Table 4.1). These rules connect liability to benefit: the borrower who has all benefit with no cost is liable even for acts of God while the unpaid watchman pays for nothing. The paid watchman and renter, whose benefit is offset by their costs, are liable for loss or theft but not liable for acts of God.

Table 4.1. Bailee Liability According to the Mishnah

Type of bailee	Circumstance of loss	
	FORCE MAJEURE	ORDINARY LOSS/THEFT
Borrower	Liable	Liable
Renter/paid watchman	Not liable	Liable
Unpaid watchman	Not liable	Not liable

To understand the legal situation of the Mar bar Ḥanînā story I will insert within the Mishnah's neat liability table two different competing exceptions—gross negligence and owner presence. If a bailee is guilty of "gross negligence," he or she is liable even when the default rules of liability exonerate.⁹⁶ By contrast, if the owner is present, all bailees are relieved of liability even when the rules obligate.⁹⁷ If one updates the Mishnah's table to reflect the two extreme exceptions of gross negligence and owner presence, the new exceptions stand as opposing extreme columns (see Table 4.2).

Table 4.2. Exceptions to Bailee Liability

Type of bailee	Circumstance of loss			
	OWNER PRESENCE	FORCE MAJEURE	ORDINARY LOSS/THEFT	GROSS NEGLIGENCE
Borrower	Not liable	Liable	Liable	Liable
Renter	Not liable	Not liable	Liable	Liable
Unpaid watchman	Not liable	Not liable	Not liable	Liable

In light of Table 4.2, one can understand the complexity of the issue of law that arrived in Rābā's courtroom. Mar bar Ḥanînā rented his animal to Bê Ḥôzā'î. That relationship brought with it limited liability: liability for ordinary loss/theft but exemption for force majeure. Two factors complicate this limited liability. The text says that the people from Bê Ḥôzā'î were grossly negligent, and that Mar bar Ḥanînā, the owner, was present. In this situation both special factors obtain, and the matter of law being discussed is whether gross negligence outweighs owner presence or vice versa.⁹⁸

Both Talmuds cite an explicit debate regarding the conflict of gross negligence and owner presence. I cite here the Bavli's debate both because it is more explicit, and because it appears a mere two pages before the Mar bar Ḥanînā narrative at Bābā Měṣî'ā 95a:

Resolved: Gross negligence in the owner['s presence].
Rab 'Aḥā [ca. 350–ca. 410 C.E.] and Rabînā [ca. 350–ca. 410 C.E.]
    debated it;
one said [the bailee] is liable and one said [the bailee] is exempt.⁹⁹

As is common in this type of formulation, the Talmud records a debate between two named amoraim without attributing either position to a specific name. The Palestinian Talmud's debate is attributed to amoraim who lived before Rābā, while the Bavli's debate is attributed to amoraim who lived after him.[100] Since scholars both before and after Rābā debate the very issue of law that erupts in Rābā's courtroom, how can one accept a reading that presumes Rābā's shame as the response to a simple error of application?

The existence of amoraic debate on the very issue of the story's law is not lost on the *stam*, who questions the story's veracity on this basis and ultimately rewrites the story:

> Now, on the view that for negligence with the owner in service there is no responsibility, it is well; [for that reason he was ashamed.][101]
>
> But on the view that one is liable [for negligence in the presence of an owner],[102] why was he ashamed?
>
> They were not negligent with it, but it was stolen and it died a natural death in the thief's house; and they[103] came before Rābā, and he obligated them.
>
> [Thereupon] the Rabbis said to Rābā: But it was theft with the owner [in service]! He was ashamed.
>
> Eventually it was ascertained that he had gone forth to examine its load.

Referring to the debate between Rab 'Aḥā and Rabînā without mentioning names, the *stam* notes that the story makes sense according to the view that a bailee is exempt in a case of simultaneous gross negligence and owner presence. But if one asserts, as either Rab 'Aḥā or Rabînā did, that one *is* liable in such a case, Rābā's shame makes no sense. In light of this problem of interpretation, the *stam* rewrites the story so that Rābā's shame works for both positions. Instead of a case of gross negligence, it was a case of ordinary theft complicated by the animal's death at the thief's home. While a renter would ordinarily be exempt for natural death (force majeure), since that death transpired in the thief's home, the renter is liable for the animal's loss through theft, not through natural death. Rābā therefore rules that the people of Bê Ḥôzā'î are liable. The students correct Rābā by noting that owner presence is a factor, and Rābā is ashamed.

The rewritten story implicates a much simpler legal mistake since it does not pit owner presence against gross negligence; Rābā's ruling is now an obvious blunder. Rābā's shame is more sensible according to the rewrite because the law is unequivocally on the side of his students. And yet, even within a skeptical historiography that questions the historiographic veracity of all rabbinic narrative, this explicit rewrite is remarkable. The *stam* treats the legal narrative as it would any other legal text, ignoring its claim to reality and reinterpreting it in order to resolve its legal contradiction. The *stam*'s renarration makes the legal issue less complex in order to accommodate the simplicity of its own understanding of Rābā's shame as a mere act of forgetting. This is akin to what we saw in Chapter 2 in the talmudic movement to interpret the lovesickness story in light of legal precedent and change the details of the story to ensure coherence. Once again, I turn to the original narrative and its complex legal issue to understand shame as determined by a number of factors that emerge from a fuller understanding of Rābā's interaction with this legal issue.

The basis for my rereading of Rābā's shame is a pattern established from Rābā's opinions on bailee liability within other talmudic discussions. Throughout the Talmud, Rābā challenges the Mishnaic sliding scale of bailee liability and requires a greater degree of fault for every category of bailee. Rābā exonerates a borrower if the animal dies (force majeure) in the course of ordinary work, though this exoneration goes against rabbinic understandings of explicit biblical law.[104] When called upon to adjudicate an unambiguous case involving the ordinary loss of a shepherd—a paid watchman—Rābā exonerates the shepherd against the objections of his amoraic contemporaries because the loss did not stem from any unwarranted activity; this position goes against the explicit position of the above mishnah and its bailee liability categories.[105] Within the case of a grossly negligent unpaid watchman, Rābā disagrees with his colleague 'Abayê and will not obligate if the gross negligence is not directly responsible for the animal's death: though the opening of the barn door that allows the animal to walk into dangerous terrain is a textbook example of gross negligence, Rābā will not obligate the watchman when the animal dies of natural causes in the dangerous terrain.[106]

Rābā's three innovations all exempt a bailee from liability because of an absence of direct fault. In moving toward a fault-based notion of liability, Rābā sets a higher bar for bailee liability than the Mishnah, ruling more frequently on behalf of the bailee and against the owner even where the Mishnah and its categorical strict liability would have established liability for the bailee.

Mar bar Ḥanīnā v. Bê Ḥôzāʾî is within the same category as the case of the shepherd whom Rābā exonerated because the shepherd had performed no

Table 4.3. Rābāʾs Innovations to the Rules for Bailee Liability

Type of bailee	Circumstance of loss						
	OWNER PRESENCE	FORCE MAJEURE	FIRST INNOVATION: FORCE MAJEURE BECAUSE OF WORK	ORDINARY LOSS/ THEFT	SECOND INNOVATION: ORDINARY LOSS/THEFT, NO UNWARRANTED ACTIVITY	GROSS NEGLIGENCE	THIRD INNOVATION: GROSS NEGLIGENCE UNRELATED TO LOSS
Borrower	Not liable	Liable	Not liable	Liable		Liable	
Renter/paid watchman	Not liable	Not liable		Liable	Not liable	Liable	
Unpaid watchman	Not liable	Not liable		Not liable		Liable	Not liable

unwarranted activity—no fault. When Rābā hears of Bê Ḥôzāʾîʾs gross negligence, he immediately obligates, since his own liability model is predicated on tying liability to fault. But in this case there is an exempting factor: owner presence. Rābā is not ashamed because owner presence always predominates; rather, Rābā is ashamed because he did not consider the question of owner presence and the opportunity that that exemption offered for deciding on behalf of the bailee. Rābāʾs shame is caused by a realization of a lost opportunity to decide on behalf of the bailee.

This reading of shame is predicated on recognition of the pattern in Rābāʾs bailee rulings as reflecting a bias. One way of understanding Rābāʾs proclivity toward increased fault is on the basis of the fact that in Babylonian rabbinic culture the bailee was generally the economically weaker party.[107] Rābā repeatedly resists formal rules of liability because he empathizes with the shepherd's economic situation. Rābā is ashamed before his students, I would suggest, because they have determined a way to side with the economically weaker party—a way to remain true to the rationale that motivates the movement toward greater fault within bailee liability. Rābā is ashamed because he did not consider all the options as his students did, because his own move toward fault within liability blinded him to the rationale that animated that move, because his students outperform him and because the outperformance suggests Rābāʾs own antiquation.

In the first story Rābā objects to his students' attempt to subject him, turning the tables on them and declaring his mastery over them. Rābā's slinking off in shame in the second story is a nearly opposite result. Rābā's shame does not merely determine that the students' perception of the law is correct, but that their perspective on the pedagogical relationship has merit. In a way this story is akin to the *stam*'s compromise because both respond to Rābā's attempt to assert mastery over his students. The storyteller of this story, like the *stam*'s interjection within the earlier narrative, responds to Rābā's attempt to control his students by narrating a moment in which the teacher is beholden to students.[108] The earlier narrative suggests that need and service go hand in hand—that if the students need Rābā, they are in his service. In this second narrative, the students still serve their teacher, but it is Rābā who needs them. This second story complicates the earlier story's simple approach to pedagogy as service by highlighting the two-way nature of the pedagogical relationship.

In describing Rābā's shame, the text says that he was shamed, but eventually it was determined that Mar bar Ḥanînā had gone out to inspect the load. The text is divided against itself, saying simultaneously that Rābā was shamed by his error and that Rābā's ruling was no error at all. The facts of the case, the narrator informs, eventually emerge and match Rābā's initially erroneous or too-quick ruling. This textual move, while seemingly exciting, is actually formulaic. The pattern of "he was ashamed, eventually it was ascertained" is a trope, appearing several times in the Talmud.[109]

The formula merits attention as a trope. This formula is employed whenever a narrative shames an amora. The purpose of the formula is to prevent the stigma of shame from attaching to the amora's legacy. In this sense, the formula parallels the formulaic invocation of the narrative of the donkey of Pinĕḥās ben Ya'îr who was miraculously prevented from prohibiting the Sabbath to argue that God does not let the righteous fall prey to sin or error.[110] Both formulas resuscitate the legacy of the rabbinic protagonist by reinterpreting the narrative so that the protagonist can unknowingly walk with God and truth. In both cases, however, the formula signals its opposite: that the stories to which they are appended demonstrate an amora in sin or error. Furthermore, these formulas attempt to paper over the strong cultural impulse to narrate such stories. Though the hagiographic attitude toward rabbis does not prevent the narration of stories that paint rabbis in a relatively bad light, it does cause writers to include formulas that mitigate such behaviors by turning their protagonists into infallible holy men.[111]

The formulaic resuscitation of Rābā's reputation says that eventually it was ascertained that Mar bar Ḥanînā went out to inspect the loading. This reevaluation of Mar bar Ḥanînā's intent eliminates the story from the exemption of owner presence since Mar bar Ḥanînā did not assist in loading. Leaving aside the violence this reevaluation does to the original story, the reinterpretation highlights the extent to which there is room within the scenario for Rābā to maintain his ruling even after the students' suggestion. The reevaluation employs an extremely formalistic notion of physical presence that implies that the "owner presence" exemption requires an owner *working* alongside the animal; this notion (that is neither the biblical nor the rabbinic models discussed above) asserts that if the owner is physically present but not working, no exemption exists. The ill fit of this resolution with the norms of owner presence established in this pericope and elsewhere stands as another ungrammaticality that encourages literary analysis.

While the tropaic nature of Rābā's shameful interaction with his students argues against a refocus on shame, the redactor's skillful juxtaposition of two stories about Rābā's emotional interactions with his students over the same issue of law demands not to be overlooked. The first narrative transpires in the theoretical classroom and finds Rābā asserting control over a group of students who are well taught and think themselves ready to begin teaching their own lectures. Their teacher is not ready for that to happen and puts them in their place as lowly students in order to establish his own standing in society. This move reflects the hard-won charismatic authority of Babylonian amoraim in a nonbureaucratized rabbinate. The *stam* intervenes in the story to locate the very enterprise of intensive rabbinic study within a larger discourse of the institutional *kallâ*, an anachronistic move that aims to marginalize Rābā's own authority through appeal to the more powerful and authorizing community. The second narrative transpires in the classroom now transformed into a courtroom. The change in activity signals a change in the function of its actors. The role of the students is more marginal to the activity of adjudication since they are neither judges nor witnesses in the proceedings. Even in this setting, the story claims, they are not absent, but make themselves relevant and important to their teacher. In suggesting "owner presence" within this scenario, the students turn the courtroom back into a classroom and demonstrate to their teacher that they have learned well to consider all issues and demand that he do the same. This move contextualizes the theoretical classroom and its activity within the actions of the courtroom and its larger discourse of adjudication. Rābā's shame is here a corrective apology for his anger, recognition imposed by the story's narrator on Rābā that the students are necessary and important for him even if they are in his service. In fact, it is in their capacity as servants to their master that they are most helpful; they can see things to which their teacher has been blinded.

Chapter 5

Torah as Cultural Capital: Rabbis and Rabbis

In his book *The Rules of Art*, Pierre Bourdieu models a method of literary analysis that employs his own socioeconomic framework of analyzing culture to read Flaubert's novel *Sentimental Education*.[1] The novel is structured around the life of Frédéric Moreau and several friends and set in nineteenth-century Paris. Many critics have understood Frédéric as a proxy for his creator, and literary analysis of *Sentimental Education* is dominated by historicist readings that map the novel onto Flaubert's autobiography. *The Rules of Art*, by contrast, employs the novel as a window onto nineteenth-century Parisian sociology. The book opens with each of its central characters possessing disparate quantities of different forms of capital (political, financial, social), and each character is motivated by his or her construal of success as the assimilation of great quantities of one or more forms of capital. By using the characters' own constructions of these separate fields of capital, Bourdieu can evaluate each character's own sense of success. The novel thus enables an internal sociological analysis. The novel provides "all the tools necessary for its own sociological analysis: the structure of the book, which a *strictly internal* reading brings to light, that is, the structure of the social space in which the adventures of Frédéric unfold, proves to be at the same time the structure of the social space in which its author himself was situated."[2]

Bourdieu's literary approach offers an alternative historicism that allows the critic to plumb the novel for the social space it constructs, using the outcome of that probing to construct a sociology of the author's cultural context. Bourdieu claims that *Sentimental Education* possesses a prophetic awareness of sociological structure, an awareness veiled until the sociological critic unveils it.[3] In Bourdieu's understanding, the textual unconscious preserves sociological structures. The critic's job is to uncover these structures through a strictly internal reading of the literature.

Bourdieu's model of internal literary sociology is enticing for the study of Babylonian rabbinic sociology because in the case of Babylonian rabbinic Judaism the absence of significant data on the rabbis external to the Talmud makes internal sociology the only possible sociology. The following pages employ Bourdieu's technique and theoretical insights in reading Bābā Batrā 20b–22a as a cryptogram that provides its own key, using these texts to describe the parallel fields of Torah and commerce. The results of this internal sociology are an awareness of the internal hierarchies of the rabbinic world and the struggle of individual rabbis to assert a personal authority over other Jews, even rabbinic ones.

The Rules of the *Sugya* as Art

The novel and the *sugya* are dissimilar genres of writing. The nineteenth-century novel is an explicitly fictional work written by a single author within a strict modern convention. The Bavli *sugya* is an ancient work that derives from a protracted process of oral composition involving multiple authors in different locations and historical periods within a loose ancient convention.

It is hard to describe the structure of a typical Bavli *sugya* because there is no single model. Though one can find patterns in *sugya* construction, the sense one generally gets from a Bavli *sugya* is of random free association, the natural result of a process of rabbinic transmission recorded in literary form. Talmud critics have taken advantage of this general assumption to surprise their readers by discovering intentionality within the composition of *sugyot*; any order or authorial arrangement is a revelation.[4]

The stammaitic revolution of the last three decades has made readers aware of the import that the later rabbinic authorities had not only in interpreting earlier materials but also in structuring them.[5] Redactors of Bavli passages are increasingly shown to have a point of view and to structure their materials accordingly. Though the direction of much of this scholarship is oriented toward descriptions of the evolution of ideas, it also can enable and has enabled aesthetic redaction criticism.[6]

The earliest work on the role of these redactors as authors of Bavli passages focused on the collage-like discursive conversations that combine attributed statements, interpretation, and anonymous argumentation. More recent work has focused on lengthy Bavli narratives and story cycles.[7] The compositional approach to narrative has created an analogy between the collage-like *sugya* and the extensive narrative: both are the products of a strong-handed late redactor who draws upon a significant body of inherited material to create the redacted text.

While it is undeniably the case that both the discursive conversation and the extensive narrative bear the heavy imprints of their redactors, the two genres project a different attitude toward the earlier material that they mold into final form. The discursive conversation molds prior materials within a structure largely inherited from earlier amoraic discussions or even an earlier redaction. The inherited material is marked as such by the practice of attribution to named authorities. The extensive narrative, by contrast, masks its debt to earlier materials, in effect plagiarizing from other rabbinic sources, both narrative and nonnarrative alike. This difference indicates that the storytellers responsible for extensive Bavli narrative were motivated by storytelling and an aesthetic interest to produce a highly readable finished text.

Until this point, this book has focused on relatively terse Bavli legal narratives. These narratives are sources incorporated within discursive conversations and earlier chapters have considered the relationship between such narratives and their redactional frames. This chapter examines an extensive Bavli passage that includes both an extensive discursive conversation that incorporates legal narratives of this type as well as some nonnormative narratives (what others would term Aggadah) and two extensive narratives characterized by redactional activity. This chapter analyzes all of these forms but builds toward its reading of one of the extensive narratives, a story that magnetically draws in the normative, cultural, and literary themes of the larger passage.

Literary approaches to the study of rabbinic narrative have moved with the currents of contemporary literary criticism from historicism to New Criticism to poststructuralism and a focus on rhetoric, power, and the hermeneutics of suspicion.[8] My own analysis aims to produce textual insights that cannot be ignored by subsequent readers even as they choose to frame their own readings in light of their own goals and subjectivities. The insight in question in this analysis is not the traditional *ḥiddûš* that resolves a thorny exegetical problem, but a way of thinking about the material that uncovers latent content. Bourdieu's approach in *The Rules of Art* serves in this chapter both as theoretical model and as framework. In this chapter, I think through Bourdieu's ideological world with its economization of sociology. Bourdieu's claim is that one can uncover the sociology of nineteenth-century France through a capital-based reading of the protagonists of *Sentimental Education*. I argue similarly that one can gain perspective on the social dynamics of Babylonian rabbinic culture through a capital-based reading of a lengthy Bavli passage about the restriction of competition within both the commercial marketplace and the parallel world of Torah *paideia*. This approach recognizes that one of the functions of Torah within the Babylonian rabbinic world is as the currency (capital) that structures competition within the rabbinic field (to use Bourdieu's term). The notion of cultural capital introduced within Bourdieu's work allows for an understanding of Torah in socioeconomic terms that provide insights into the market construction of Babylonian rabbinic sociology.

Schematic

This chapter builds toward its reading of a lengthy Bavli narrative within a Bourdieuian framework. The richness of its reading is facilitated by a foray through the larger passage that incorporates the extensive Bavli legal narrative (and several other narratives) as its coda. The interested reader is invited to open an edition of the Talmud for the full *sugya*. For purposes of presentation, though, I will treat this material schematically.

The passage this chapter comments upon stretches from Bābā Batrā 20b through Bābā Batrā 22a, over three printed talmudic pages. It is a passage famous for treating the issue of competition in the economic marketplace. The passage starts with a mishnah about nuisance law before unfolding in three sections. The first section is a discursive conversation regarding job security for schoolteachers. This initial discussion transitions to a more general discursive conversation about market protection in all fields. The third section contains seven stories: three terse one-line legal narratives and three nonnormative historical narratives with a lengthy narrative that bridges these two story cycles, pulling together the issues addressed in the discursive conversation and both the legal narrative and the nonnormative historical story cycles.

Rābā, Rab Dîmmî, and Rab Joseph on Competition

In typical talmudic fashion, the Bābā Batrā passage transitions rapidly and seemingly haphazardly from the Mishnah's discussion of rights to protest against a neighbor's activity in a shared courtyard to a discussion of education including a famous legend that a Second Temple figure named Joshua ben Gamlā initiated a system of public education.[9] Toward the end of the passage's discussion of the value of education, the text cites two debates between Rābā and Rab Dîmmî about job competition among teachers. For purpose of presentation I will reverse the order of these debates.

In one of the two debates, Rābā and Rab Dîmmî of Něhardě'āʿ argue about the criteria by which one rates one teacher better than another.

> And Rābā said, "[If there are] two schoolteachers: one is well versed but imprecise and one is precise but not well versed, we establish the one who is well versed [but imprecise]; 'mistakes undo themselves.'"
>
> Rab Dîmmî of Něhardě'āʿ said, "we establish the one who is precise but not well versed; 'a mistake once it enters has entered.'"

Rābā's statement narrates a hypothetical scene in which two applicants vie for the local schoolteacher position with different intellectual strengths (and weaknesses). Rābā asserts that the hiring should privilege quantities of knowledge rather than precision in that knowledge because the mistakes of imprecision will eventually be corrected. Rab Dîmmî of Něhardě'āʿ disagrees with Rābā's preference, claiming that precision is more important than the quantity of a teacher's knowledge since it is difficult to unlearn a mistake.[10]

In their other debate, the scenario changes from a choice of potential applicants to a situation of possible replacement:

> And Rābā said, "a teacher of children who is learned, and there is another who is more learned, we do not fire [the first one] lest he[11] become slack."
>
> Rab Dîmmî of Něhardě'āʿ said, "all the more so he [would] learn.[12] 'Scholarly envy will increase wisdom.'"

In this debate, quantitative knowledge is the sole metric of teacher quality and the newcomer is undeniably more learned than the incumbent. Rābā asserts that the initial teacher retains his position lest he become slack. Rab Dîmmî disagrees, invoking an aphorism that claims: "Scholarly envy will increase wisdom."

Source critics evaluate statements independent of their interpretive contexts. In the Talmud, this usually means separating amoraic material from the anonymous material that frames it. In this case, we must separate Rābā's initial statement from Rab Dîmmî's comment. On its own, Rābā's statement can be understood to express concern for the psychology of teachers. Rābā recognizes the importance of teachers and wants to ensure that teachers are not despondent—"we do not fire the initial teacher lest he become slack."

Rab Dîmmî's response interprets Rābā's statement before disagreeing with it. For Rab Dîmmî, Rābā is not concerned for the teachers because he values them per se; rather, Rābā is concerned for the teachers as part of his overall concern for the health of Torah education and the acquisition of knowledge capital. Rab Dîmmî understands Rābā's concerns to be utilitarian: a despondent teacher will stop studying. In order to keep teachers studying, Rab Dîmmî interprets Rābā to say their jobs have to be protected. Rab Dîmmî's response to this version of Rābā is a different analysis of teachers' psyche. A threatened teacher will learn more in order to maintain his or her position.

The difference between a source-critical understanding of Rābā as concerned for teachers and Rab Dîmmî's interpretation of Rābā as concerned for teacher knowledge is the difference between thinking about the health of the individual or the health of the field. While Rābā's statement can be understood on its own to care for the individual teacher without any utilitarian concern, Rab Dîmmî's interpretation of and disagreement with Rābā demonstrates the way Torah study is constituted as a field and the field (market) perspective is employed to value the good of the group over the needs of the individual. Rab Dîmmî's interpretation of Rābā focuses not on the teacher as an object of compassion, but on the teacher's knowledge as part of the aggregate knowledge of the group.

Though the *sugya* addresses a narrow legal issue, its approach to that issue underlines a rabbinic groupthink that is relevant for understanding how Babylonian rabbis think of their core project of Torah scholarship and education. Group achievement and group goals are elevated (at least theoretically) within Rab Dîmmî's understanding above individual impact.

Rab Dîmmî's own approach takes the group interest idea a step further. Against his own interpretation of Rābā's focus on the teacher, Rab Dîmmî asserts that the old teacher *is* replaced in favor of his better. Rab Dîmmî's market argument employs an aphorism that is blatantly capitalist: "Scholarly envy will increase wisdom." Even his own interpretation of Rābā—as valuing the teacher's knowledge for its group value—is insufficient because the system is made more efficient when competition encourages individuals to increase and hone their knowledge. Group interest outweighs individual impact completely; this group interest is the core project of Torah scholarship.

Because of an overlap in syntax and word choice, scholars have connected

Rab Dîmmî's aphorism to a parallel text in Ben Sira. Ben Sira 38:24 reads, "The wisdom of scholars will increase wisdom, and the one without a profession, he shall become wise."[13] Various passages in the book of Ben Sira implicate a parallelism between wisdom and the professions that rhetorically positions wisdom as a parallel profession. In Bourdieu's terms, we can think of wisdom as a field animated by the competition for pursuit of wisdom capital. The possibility of considering Torah as a profession and of the teacher-student relationship as an apprenticeship appears not infrequently within rabbinic literature.[14] But there is a change rendered on the aphorism as it travels from Ben Sira to Rab Dîmmî. Ben Sira's aphorism is transformed in the Babylonian context by the notion of envy as a productive goad. While in Ben Sira, the aphorism advocates choosing a life of scholarship over a profession in order to become a possessor of greater wisdom capital, in Rab Dîmmî's hands the aphorism coldly applies market competitive forces to educational life. Both texts truck in an implied parallelism between the parallel market fields of scholarship and moneymaking. While Ben Sira's aphorism encourages a separation of fields, Rab Dîmmî's aphorism invites the jealousies of the marketplace into the world of scholarship, collapsing the divide and recognizing the similarity between the professions.[15] This collapsing of the fields encourages Bourdieu's ideological framework and the recognition that Torah functioned as cultural capital at the center of tremendous competition within the sociological world of the Babylonian rabbinate. Possession of greater quantities of Torah capital translated into other modes of capital through a slippage that Bourdieu presumes automatic to any set of parallel marketplaces.[16] Despite the impossibility of quantifying knowledge or creating convincing metrics of relative quality, the hierarchy of rabbinic Babylonia was an environment in which individual scholars were sometimes ranked on the basis of their Torah wealth.

Rābā and Rab Dîmmî each offers positive justification for his rule within the context of teachers; Rābā is motivated by teacher laxity and Rab Dîmmî by increased market wisdom. A reader cannot infer from either position a default rule regarding job security *in general*. This lacuna motivates the Talmud's transition into the next subsection: a discussion of the general legal issue of market protection and economic competition.

Jewish law is (in)famous for its stringent rules restricting competition.[17] The popular perception is that Jewish law is anticapitalist because it prevents competitors from opening competing establishments. Though there have been moments in Jewish legal history in which such an understanding reigned, the talmudic discussion of the issue is subtler, based on two extreme positions and a third, compromise position. The extreme restrictive position is the assertion of Rab Hûnā that a proprietor owns his or her market and can prevent competitors from entering the protected market. Against this extreme restrictive position, the Bavli cites the view of a baraita that asserts that property grants its owners the right to open any business, even if a neighbor already runs that sort of business. To resolve this contradiction of canons, the Talmud marshals the view of a late Babylonian amora, Rab Hûnā son of Rab Joshua, who splits the difference by offering market protection to city residents from foreigners but allowing competition among residents of a city.

The Talmud offers an exception to this three-way argument.[18] Rab Joseph asserts that all three opinions—even the extremely restrictive position of Rab Hûnā—recognize the importance of education and refuse to allow any job protection in that context. Invoking the aphorism we saw above, Rab Joseph asserts that in the education market, "scholarly envy will increase wisdom."

At first glance, Rab Joseph's position seems a mere reminder of the discussion and debate between Rābā and Rab Dîmmî in the *sugya*'s previous subsection in its discussion of market protection for teachers. In other words, Rab Joseph sides with Rab Dîmmî in claiming that teachers can be replaced if better ones come along for the good of the larger societal value. The Talmud even uses the formula 'âmar mar, a formula for referencing earlier citations, in introducing Rab Joseph's aphorism. There is, however, a possible distinction between the two usages. Rab Dîmmî's position is uttered in response to Rābā's concern for the individual teacher and thus may reflect the notion that the individual teacher is more likely to learn when put in a competitive environment. Rab Joseph's assertion, by contrast, undeniably thinks of the field as a whole in imagining competition as a positive force in the field. This possible difference is not insignificant because it marks the same difference as this passage demands for the commerce and knowledge fields respectively: where the commerce field is motivated by a focus on individual (property) rights, the knowledge field is motivated by communal concerns. This is not to say that Rab Dîmmî's formulation is not market-based on the basis of communal concerns; rather, that in the aftermath of the general discussion of restricted competition, the Talmud deems it important to return and underline the fundamental difference between the fields through the mechanism of Rab Joseph's repeating the identical aphorism. Once again, this subsection addresses the tension between communal interest and individual rights and decides that the knowledge field is animated by group interest rather than individual right.

Despite the small difference in their contexts, Rab Dîmmî and Rab Joseph are normative twins. Both disagree with Rābā and claim that there is no restriction on competition for teachers. This agreement is a compositional problem: since the historical Rab Dîmmî of Něhardě'ā' was active long after Rab Joseph (and Rābā), why would the Talmud frame Rābā's position in a debate with Rab Dîmmî and not with the identical position of his (and Rābā's) predecessor Rab Joseph? I will return to this question below when I discuss the *sugya*'s lengthy legal narrative.[19]

Thus far I have examined a digest version of the passage's discursive legal conversation and its two subsections (on education and market restriction) and recognized the extent to which this material implicates a parallelism between the commercial marketplace and the field of Torah education, situating Torah's *paideia* at all levels within an economic milieu. At the same time as it constructs these two fields as parallels, the discursive conversation contains in both Rab Dîmmî and Rab Joseph a repeated argument for the special status of the field of Torah study. The cultural significance of the pursuit of Torah capital marks this field as the one requiring the advantages of laissez-faire competition rather than the rights protection of the parallel commercial marketplace. As I transition now to the passage's narratives I note the way in which the parallel fields overlap as Bourdieu predicts they must. The slippage between the two fields renders it impossible to maintain in close proximity a rule of open competition in one field with rules of restricted competition in an adjacent one.

The Narratives

The passage continues with seven consecutive narratives. These narratives can be further subdivided by form. The first three narratives are one-line legal narratives, and they are treated as part of the discursive legal conversation and framed by anonymous editorial comments. The final three narratives are not directly related to normative legal questions and are not framed or interrupted; those who employ the Halakhah/Aggadah dichotomy as an essential division would characterize these as Aggadah though they conclude a normative legal passage. In between these two sets of three stories there is a lengthy narrative that bridges the terse normative stories and the collage-like legal *sugya* with the nonnormative final three stories. Because of its centripetal position, it is helpful to read the middle story in light of both the story cycle of the three legal narratives that precede it and the story cycle of the three nonnormative stories that follow it.

The Legal Narratives

The legal narrative story cycle of three stories is composed of stories akin to ones that the book's earlier chapters have examined. These are short stories with overt normative subject matter that claim a touch of the real. The realities of competing cultural voices come across in all three cases.

The first legal narrative describes Rābā's granting special extralegal market permissions to visiting rabbis: "Rābā permitted Rab Josiah and Rab Obadiah to be established [in the local marketplace] not according to Halakhah."

Though neither Rab Obadiah nor Rab Josiah is particularly well known, Rābā sanctions their status as merchants in the local marketplace despite the theoretical precedent that restricts them. That Rābā would favor visiting rabbis is not without precedent. At Nĕdārîm 62a Rābā expressly permits rabbinical disciples to broadcast their Torah credentials upon visiting foreign destinations and demand priority service on the basis of this capital. Though Nĕdārîm 62a–b cites other sources that heap opprobrium on scholars who benefit from their scholarship, Rābā justifies his position by equating the rabbis with the priests: just as priests receive tithes on the basis of their elevated ritual status, so rabbis may trade their Torah capital.[20]

The story presumes Rābā to be the *agoranomos*, a person with political authority over the local market, and Rābā uses this authority to prefer members of the rabbinic class.[21] There is little reason to doubt the story's historiographic claim to rabbinic control; Rābā was a resident of Mĕḥôzā and in regular contact with the exilarch who would presumably have licensed Rābā's economic supervisory role. The story precludes a reader's attempt to justify Rābā's approach to the visiting rabbis within precedent by explicitly declaring that Rābā's action is *not in accordance with Halakhah*. This characterization can be understood descriptively or as a judgment, either positive or negative.[22] Rashi understands it to be positive judgment when he explains that Rābā went *beyond the letter of the law* to reward his rabbinic colleagues. The problem with this positive evaluation is that it fails to value the impact of this transcendence on competing merchants.[23] As in the earlier discussion of rabbi/outsider litigation, trading on rabbinic status comes at the cost of the outsider who loses legal equity as a result of rabbinic privilege.

Though the story declares simply that Rābā's action violates the law, the *stam* is uncomfortable with this deviance. To minimize the deviation, the *stam* frames the story within a precedential context in which the violation of the law is minimized. The *stam* appends the story to the back of a preexisting exception to the rules of market protection. Rab Naḥmān had suggested within the discursive conversation treated schematically above that the rules preventing foreigners from selling in the local market do not apply to traveling perfume salesmen whose work facilitates the communal interest of procreation. The *stam* creates a distinction within Rab Naḥmān's exception and situates Rābā's story as a subset of the distinction:

> And these words [the perfume exception] apply to establish a traveling [salesman] but not to establish a fixed salesman.
> But if the salesman is a rabbinic scholar, even to establish a fixed salesman, like the case in which:
> Rābā permitted Rab Josiah and Rab Obadiah to be established [in the local marketplace] not according to Halakhah.
> What is the reason? Since they were rabbis, they would come to be bothered[24] from their study.[25]

Taken on its own, the story indicates that Rābā violated the rules of market protection in allowing Rab Josiah and Rab Obadiah to sell in the market. But by creating a dichotomy within the exemption of Rab Naḥmān, the *stam* turns Rābā's violation of the law into an expansion of a restriction on the exemption. Where the exemption entitles perfume salesmen to sell as travelers in the city, Rābā permitted Rab Josiah and Rab Obadiah to become permanently fixed as salesmen in the city. This permanent settling is justified by the *stam*'s comment after the story that the men's rabbinic pursuit of Torah study demanded that they be fixed within the city.

The story as a whole describes Rābā as preferring rabbis in the commercial marketplace because of their status as rabbis. In this way, wealth in one field translates into another through a slippage that Bourdieu argues is common in parallel fields. One of the advantages of Bourdieu's framework is the way it allows us to see that cultural capital can often be exchanged for financial gain. The *stam*'s concluding line, meant to help establish that Rābā's actions only violated a subrestriction of an exemption, nicely exemplifies the core principle of slippage that allows the valuation of the competitive energy of the Torah field to trump the values of the commercial marketplace. Precisely because one market operates on the basis of communal good and the other on individual rights, the overlap between the two creates a moment in which a choice must be made and the values of the knowledge field (communal good) trump those of the commercial market (individual rights). At the same time, though, it is difficult not to judge this moment of overlap by the rules of the field in which it transpires and note the way Rābā's action tramples the rights of the local nonrabbinic merchants who suffer from this foreign competition.

The narrator's explicit declaration that Rābā acted "not according to Halakhah" is difficult for the *stam*. In truth, the explicit statement is only shocking for its explicitness. Implicit in all legal narrative, I have argued, is a sense in which the action described is antinomian; otherwise, there is little purpose to the narration. A narrator tells a story because it is interesting, and legal narratives are almost always more interesting for describing protagonists whose actions trump the expectations established by the rules of law. This antinomian character of talmudic legal narratives as sources makes them a challenge for the *stam*. While the *stam* often deals with differing theoretical opinions and customary distinctions, these still testify to the importance of the legal discourse and demand adherence to its rules. The challenge of legal narratives is that they present themselves as antinomian in the sense that they describe an antirules reality that is more difficult to treat as a mere opposing view.

The mildly antinomian character of legal narrative emerges implicitly in the two subsequent legal narratives in this story cycle. The second story narrates a scenario in which Rabînā is asked as the local judge to enforce the restrictions on foreign salespersons and creatively declines to do so:

A group of basket salesmen brought their baskets to Bābel.[26]
 The local residents sought to prevent them.
 They came before Rabînā[27] and he said to them, "they brought from outside the city, let them sell to the world."

Faced with a real instance of competition restriction, Rabînā creates a clever loophole—permitting outsiders to sell to other outsiders—that allows foreigners to sell in the local market. The story does not explain Rabînā's motivation, but one can speculate about the root cause of Rabînā's refusal to enforce the law. Such a refusal might stem from a fundamental dislike of the rule itself or from the empathy Rabînā feels for the foreign merchants. Either way, the story critiques the earlier discussion of competition restriction by noting the law's essential unfairness. Since the city marketplace is a gathering point for visiting sellers and buyers, the limitation on selling to city residents, while sensible from a tax perspective, is unfair in that it permits outsiders to buy but not to sell. Faced with a request by locals to enforce this restriction, Rabîna creates an exception that defangs the law: the foreigners are allowed to sell to foreigners. This exception puts the locals on the defensive by highlighting their unfair advantage relative to the foreigners whom the locals expect to arrive as buyers but not as sellers.

As in the case of the prior legal narrative, the *stam* does not like the general tenor of this story inasmuch as it reduces the importance of the law crafted in the theoretical laboratory. Again the *stam* tries to control the damage by framing the story:

> And this is the case on the market days, but not on nonmarket days.
> And even on market days, they are only allowed to sell in the market,
>   but not to circulate [in the city].[28]

These two restrictions attempt to limit Rabîna's ruling so that it does not completely undermine the general rule restricting competition, but that undermining is precisely the reason such a narrative is reported or narrated.

The third legal narrative continues the theme by again describing a ruling that goes against the rules of law; this time the factor motivating the ruling is empathy for the foreign merchants:

> A group of wool merchants[29] brought wool to Pûm Naharā. The local residents came to prevent [the foreigners].
>   They came before Rab Kahanā [30] [ca. 330–ca. 390 C.E.] [and] he said to [the foreigners], "By law they may prevent you."
>   [The foreigners] said to him, "We have [extended] credit."
>   He said to them, "go and sell an amount equivalent to your minimal subsistence until your debts have been repaid and [then] you should leave."

While in the second story Rabîna challenged the theoretical underpinnings of the local residents who attempted to eliminate the foreigners as competition, in this story Rab Kahanā recognizes that the law favors the locals against the foreigners. Nevertheless, in the face of considerable economic loss Rab Kahanā allows the foreigners to survive in the local market until they can recoup their debts before leaving town. The *stam* does not modify this story. One could argue that no modification is necessary since the story recognizes the power of precedent, only allowing for exigent circumstance to create an exception. The message of the story is that rabbinic arbiters of the market sometimes recognize that the proprietary rules of competition restriction must be ignored for pragmatic purposes.

Taken as a group, the three terse legal narratives evidence the gap between hypothetical study and real-world application, at least in the context of monopoly laws. In all three cases, the normative expectation of legal mandate is bucked in light of competing cultural realities. By incorporating these stories into the discursive legal conversation, the passage expands the theoretical discourse to incorporate the cultural realities of rabbinic privilege and judicial empathy.

The Nonnormative Narratives

The three terse legal narratives are connected to a set of three nonnormative narratives through a long narrative that bridges their contents. I am deferring treatment of that bridge narrative and will focus now on the final three nonnormative narratives.

The three nonnormative narratives depict rabbinic competitiveness and describe internal rabbinic hierarchy. I believe that these three stories are associated with the discussions of restricted competition because they thematize scholarly envy. These narratives are unified within this text by an introductory formula in which a protagonist claims credit for the death of Rab 'Addā bar 'Ahabâ (ca. 320–ca. 380 C.E.): "I killed him, because . . ." In general, such introductory formulas are either original to the story cycle and explain how these stories became linked or represent a later reader's attempt to thematically unify disparate subject matter. Because of the variation within the textual witnesses, Richard Kalmin argues that in the case of these three nonnormative narratives the introductory formula is the product of later readers.[31] In other words, even in its final form, the redacted Talmud did not unify these stories on the basis of such a formula. What unifies these stories, I would argue, is their treatment of scholarly envy. The three stories are built around the themes of jealousy, the tension between individual desires and group needs and the slippage of markets already apparent in the first legal narrative.

The first of the three stories narrates a rivalry between the study halls of 'Abayê and Rābā:

> 'Abayê [ca. 290–ca. 350 C.E.] said, "I punished [Rab 'Addā bar 'Ahabâ] for he used to say to the students, 'instead of gnawing bones[32] at the house of 'Abayê go eat meat at the house of Rābā.'"

Traditional rabbinic historiography reads this story as evidence of the rivalry between 'Abayê's yeshiva at Pûmbědîtā and Rābā's yeshiva at Měḥôzā. The imagined image of these yeshivas is of large highly bureaucratized institutions with clear hierarchy and political authority. But in light of Goodblatt's work on the yeshiva and my assumption that this story is an amoraic source, one should understand the two respective educational contexts as disciple circles and the "house of 'Abayê" and "house of Rābā" to refer literally to the homes in which these scholars conducted their pedagogy.[33] The text confirms the work of the previous chapter by demonstrating the extent to which scholars needed their students. One can also think of the students as a form of capital.

Rab 'Addā is accused by 'Abayê in this story of advertising for Rābā's study hall through an analogy to the consumption of meat. This commodification of Torah study is yet another example of the way in which Torah knowledge is turned into its mirror opposite—the market of goods—by this passage.

Meat moves from metaphor to context in the second narrative:

> Rābā said, "I punished [Rab 'Addā bar 'Ahabâ] for[34] he used to tell the butcher, 'I [deserve to] take meat before the messenger of Rābā [because I am more important.]' "[35]

Where 'Abayê had used meat consumption as Rab 'Addā's metaphor for qualitative difference in Torah study, Rābā refers to the meat market as an instantiation of Rab 'Addā's envious assertion of priority. Rābā is no stranger to priority in the marketplace. I referred in the legal narratives above to the preferential treatment Rābā offers to Rab Obadiah and Rab Josiah in his own marketplace and to Rābā's explicit claim (at Nědārîm 62a) that scholars may ask for priority in the marketplace because of their status as scholars. This story contributes additionally the notion that the marketplace is the arena in which the relative and internal hierarchies of rabbinic Judaism are played out. Not only can rabbinic Jews expect the butcher to serve them meat before serving nonrabbinic Jews, but the butcher is also expected to make relative evaluations of the clientele and serve them in order of their Torah capital.[36]

Rab 'Addā is described by this story as a hypercompetitive rabbinic athlete who insists on his own status and the priority that his Torah capital deserves. From this story alone it is not clear whether Rab 'Addā bar 'Ahabâ is a student of Rābā's or a rival. The statement demanding priority is ambiguous about Rab 'Addā's claim: he may demand priority over Rābā's agent or, alternatively, over Rābā himself. Given the previous story's testimony about Rab 'Addā's loyalty to Rābā's study hall, there is here the picture of a social-climbing student who is both laudatory of his teacher and eager to catapult himself from his middle-class status into the upper echelon.

Both 'Abayê's and Rābā's stories about Rab 'Addā describe an individual who is highly competitive and interested in creating intrarabbinic hierarchy. But the speakers themselves are no less implicated in the same charges. 'Abayê and Rābā both object to Rab 'Addā because of the way his own social aspirations in the Torah field threaten their own positions within that field. Both scholars externalize their own subjective criticisms of Rab 'Addā: 'Abayê in his study hall and Rābā in the character of his butcher store agent. Yet both are ultimately afraid of the competition Rab 'Addā represents.

The third narrative in this cycle is the longest of the three. The length of this story suggests a later provenance than the preceding two stories. Additionally, this story blatantly invokes the context of institutional yeshivas, a phenomenon that seems to have begun in the period of the *stammaim*:[37]

> Rab Naḥmān bar Isaac [ca. 320–ca. 380 C.E.] said, "I punished [Rab 'Addā bar 'Ahabâ]."
>   Because Rab Naḥmān was the head of a row.[38]
>   Every day before entering the row, Rab 'Addā bar 'Ahabâ would review the teaching with [Rab Naḥmān] and then enter the row.
>   That day Rab Pāppā and Rab Hûnā the son of Rab Joshua [ca. 320–ca. 380 C.E.] held up Rab 'Addā bar 'Ahabâ because they weren't there for the conclusion [of Rābā's lecture].
>   They said to him, "Tell us the teaching of the tithing of the animal, how did Rābā teach it?"
>   [Rab 'Addā bar 'Ahabâ] said to them, "this is what Rābā said."
>   Meanwhile, it became late and Rab 'Addā bar 'Ahabâ didn't come.
>   And the rabbis said to Rab Naḥmān bar Isaac, "Arise because it is late for us, why is [our] master sitting?"
>   [Rab Naḥmān] said to them, "I am sitting and guarding the bier of Rab 'Addā bar 'Ahabâ."
>   Meanwhile, a voice went out that Rab 'Addā bar 'Ahabâ died.

Above I referenced Richard Kalmin's claim that the introductory formula about the death of Rab 'Addā was appended to these respective stories by a subsequent redactor. One of Kalmin's strongest arguments for the lateness of the introductory formula is the ill fit of the formula with what transpires in the respective stories. This final story works most poorly with the introductory formula because the formula implies that Rab 'Addā's cursed death was a punishment for his own iniquity. According to this story, though, the iniquity lies not with Rab 'Addā but with Rab Naḥmān bar Isaac.

The structures that operate within this story's description of the amoraic yeshiva suggest that this story reflects the stammaitic institutional yeshiva. Within this institution, there are hierarchical marking points: a lecturer is highest on the totem pole, but students sit within the study hall according to the status accorded them by their Torah knowledge. Rab Naḥmān bar Isaac is described as the head of a row, a position at the head of his social stratum that also, as appears from the story, accords him the right to teach his inferiors. The institutional context allows the storyteller access to a rich visible semiotics of hierarchy.[39]

Though Rab Naḥmān is the head of the row and Rab 'Addā seated within it, the former scholar relies on the latter to prepare the lecture. In this way Rab 'Addā is Cyrano-like in his support of an inferior scholar in a hierarchically superior position.[40] Rab 'Addā's strong command of the teaching—his Torah capital—is known to other members of Rāba's audience. Though the story does not describe the hierarchical status of Rab Pāppā and Rab Hûnā son of Rab Joshua, these two names are, along with Rab Naḥmān bar Isaac, the best known of all of Rāba's students in the Talmud. That such students would turn to Rab 'Addā evidences the story's sense of the latter's greatness.

At every level the story alerts the reader to the tensions surrounding capital within the Torah field as students jockey for position within the internal hierarchy. Rab Naḥmān bar Isaac's position as head of a row may have been originally earned through Torah capital, but it now functions as power in the service of power as Rab Naḥmān relies on an underling to sustain his reputation. The students who request that Rab Naḥmān get on with his lecture pose a threat to their teacher, who refuses to lecture for fear that a poor performance will undermine his hierarchical standing. Various textual witnesses contain an alternative version of this story. In that version Rab Naḥmān actually stands to deliver the lecture and is unable to execute. This final story does not highlight Rab 'Addā's competitive ego; if anything, Rab 'Addā is the one actor in the story who acts on behalf of the larger field, teaching his poorer colleagues without receiving the hierarchical advantages; his own assistance of Rab Naḥmān is self-detrimental.

The Bridge Narrative: An Encounter

Having reviewed six of the seven narratives that close out the Bābā Batrā 20b–22a passage, I return now to the narrative, bracketed above, that bridges the three legal narratives with the three nonnormative narratives. Like the final narrative of Rab Naḥmān bar Isaac, this is a lengthy narrative. Though it does not have blatant institutional markings, the story has later provenance because, like other late narratives, it borrows both from other Bavli passages and from its own context.[41] The adjacent collage-like *sugya* and the two story cycles provide helpful context for a strong literary analysis of this story because their materials are incorporated within the narrative.[42]

> Rab[43] Dîmmî of Nĕhardĕʿaʿ brought figs by boat (to Mĕḫôzā).[44]
>
> The exilarch said to Rābā, "Go out and see! If [Rab Dîmmî] is a scholar, grab[45] the market for him."
>
> Rābā said to Rab ʾAddā bar ʾAhabâ,[46] "Go sniff his flasks."
>
> [Rab ʾAddā] went out[47] and asked [Rab Dîmmî], "An elephant who swallows a reed basket and expels it via its anus, what is it[s status]?"[48]
>
> [Rab Dîmmî] did not have it in his hands.
>
> [Rab Dîmmî] said to [Rab ʾAddā], "The master is Rābā?"[49]
>
> [Rab ʾAddā] struck [Rab Dîmmî] with his sandal[50] [and] said to him, "between me and Rābā there is a lot,[51] but undeniably I am your master, and your master's master."[52]
>
> They did not grab for him a market, [and] he lost his figs.
>
> [Rab Dîmmî] came before Rab Joseph [and] said to him, "See, master, what they have done to me."
>
> [Rab Joseph] responded, "The one who did not delay the debt of retribution on the king of Edom will not delay your debt," as it is written (Amos 2:1): "On three sins of Moab and on the fourth I will not take them back for they burned the bones of the king of Edom into lime."
>
> Rab ʾAddā bar ʾAhabâ died.
>
> Rab Joseph said, "I punished him because I cursed him."
>
> Rab Dîmmî [of Nĕhardĕʾāʿ][53] said, "I punished him (for he caused the loss of my figs)."[54]

Rab Dîmmî travels by boat to Mĕḫôzā[55] to sell figs. The exilarch, excited by the arrival of a scholar in his town, asks Rābā to personally greet the visitor and extend to Rab Dîmmî special market privileges. Rābā dispatches Rab 'Addā bar 'Ahabā, who asks Rab Dîmmî a question that Rab Dîmmî is unable to answer. Because of the difficulty of the question, Rab Dîmmî assumes his questioner is Rābā. Rab 'Addā, in response, smacks Rab Dîmmî with a sandal and informs him that the chasm between Rab Dîmmî and Rābā is unbridgeable. Rab Dîmmî is denied special market privileges, and his figs spoil. Upon his return to Pûmbĕdîtā, Rab Joseph curses Rab 'Addā who dies. Both Rab Joseph and Rab Dîmmî take credit for Rab 'Addā's death.

Rab Dîmmî of Nĕhardĕ'āʿ, the fig merchant who is also a scholar, arrives in Mĕḥôzā rich in two forms of capital—figs and knowledge. Though the market for each of these commodities is distinct, it is clear that the town of Mĕḥôzā institutionalizes a slippage between the two because the renowned scholar Rābā is the arbiter of the commodities market (as was the case in the first legal narrative above) and can grant the visiting fig merchant special privileges. The exilarch instructs Rābā to certify that Rab Dîmmî is a member of the rabbinic class and to "grab for him" the market for figs. Medieval commentators and Jewish legal codes have understood this line to mean that Rab Dîmmî would have the right of first sale in the marketplace.[56] While the exilarch's instruction might simply emerge from the respect owed to a member of the rabbinic class, it could also be understood as stemming from the exilarch's desire for increased knowledge capital in the city. If Rab Dîmmî is granted special standing in the market, he is more likely to linger in town and dispense his knowledge to the locals.

While the exilarch's motivation is ambiguous, Rābā's response to the imperative is underwhelming. Though the exilarch commands Rābā with an imperative to "see" Rab Dîmmî, Rābā does not deem Rab Dîmmî worthy of such a greeting and dispatches his student instead. The Yemenite textual tradents of this passage highlight Rābā's refusal by inserting an additional scene in which Rab Dîmmî "came before the exilarch and was *seen*, before Rābā and was *not seen*."[57] Though this line is not original to the talmudic text, it picks up on the subtler ways in which Rābā begins the process of mistreating Rab Dîmmî.

Rābā uses the language "sniff his flasks" to instruct Rab 'Addā to inspect Rab Dîmmî's wares. The expression "sniff his flasks" appears only one other time in the Talmud—in a story at Šabbāt 108a that describes the arrival of the important early amora Rab in Babylonia. In that context, the term is used by Samuel to instruct his student Qarnā to interview/intimidate Samuel's rival Rab.

The analogous language of sniffing flasks here highlights the extent to which the story's Rābā fears the competition represented by Rab Dîmmî. If one reads Rābā's selection of Rab ʾAddā in light of the stories in which Rābā and ʾAbayê testify that Rab ʾAddā was a hypercompetitive rabbinic athlete, the choice of Rab ʾAddā has greater resonance. Rābā chooses Rab ʾAddā to test Rab Dîmmî because Rab ʾAddā can be relied upon to insist on his own position in the hierarchy. The analogy of the bridge story to Šabbāt 108a suggests that the actions of the students in both cases—Qarnā in Šabbāt and Rab ʾAddā bar ʾAhabâ here—are intended by their teachers.

The question posed to Rab Dîmmî is itself both scatological and picayune. Richard Kalmin has noted the inappropriate nature of the scatological question as a greeting for a rabbinic colleague.[58] And yet, within the rabbinic world a question about the purity of animal feces is a serious question. The exact question posed to Rab Dîmmî is posed within a discussion at Měnāḥôt 69b, and the Talmud analyzes it but leaves it unresolved.[59] The Talmud's failure to decide this matter of law at Měnāḥôt 69b does not mean that the question is undecidable, only that the redactor of Měnāḥôt 69b chooses to leave the question unresolved. Nevertheless, the lack of resolution at Měnāḥôt 69b suggests that this is not a question testing basic competence, but a legal dilemma or paradox. The redactor's choice of such a question as a test of knowledge suggests that the content of the question participates in the rude welcome of Rab Dîmmî. Simply put, the test is designed to produce failure rather than success. As R. ʾElʿāzār says at Bābā Batrā 81b: "do you ask me a question that earlier scholars could not resolve in order to shame me?"[60]

This bridge narrative employs capitalist rhetoric to describe Rab Dîmmî's inability to answer: it was not "in his hands." The notion of knowledge that can be contained and carried in one's hands turns this capital into the parallel of Rab Dîmmî's figs in order to establish that the absence of one form of capital (Torah knowledge) prevents access to the market for the other (figs).

In failure, Rab Dîmmî is not extended the rabbinic benefit of (exclusive) access to the market. Though the letter of the law precludes such a benefit, the earlier legal narratives established the expectation of such a benefit for visiting rabbis. Rabînā's critique of the exclusionary law that permits foreigners to sell to other foreigners, Rab Kahanā's empathic permission to the foreign sellers to eliminate their credit, and Rābā's blanket permission for other rabbinic visitors create a real-world precedent that transcends the exclusionary letter of the law. The legal narratives create the expectation that rabbis act empathically for visitors and never allow such merchants, and especially rabbis, to suffer the loss of their goods because of exclusionary rules. The story of Rab Dîmmî is narrated as if his failure to receive market access is a miscarriage of justice, which it is only if one ignores the rules of law in favor of the legal narratives that contextualize Rab Dîmmî's treatment as particularly cruel. In other words, the narrator of the bridge encounter constructs an image of law around the cultural realities established by the legal narratives, not the precedents of the legal statutes.

Rab Dîmmî's inability to answer the entrance-exam question and his expectation regarding his greeter lead him to suspect that the man confronting him at the city gate is the renowned Rābā. When Rab Dîmmî suggests this to Rab 'Addā, the latter smacks him with a sandal and rebukes him.[61] Both the action and its accompanying verbal content demean Rab Dîmmî and continue the pattern of abusive welcome. Rab 'Addā informs Rab Dîmmî that several classes of rabbinic hierarchy separate Rab Dîmmî from Rābā. Rābā does not deign to greet Rab Dîmmî personally because Rab 'Addā, who is himself lower on the hierarchical totem pole than Rābā, is greater than Rab Dîmmî's teachers: "I am your master's master." Some of the variants explicate an implicit pun here on the name "Rābā," which means "the master" in Aramaic. Though lower criticism argues against these as the original text of the Talmud, they do highlight an implicit pun that is part of the original text: Rab Dîmmî is told that he cannot see "the master" because that master is several classes removed.

The picture of the hierarchy of rabbinic culture that emerges from this retort to Rab Dîmmî is reminiscent of the nonnormative narratives that follow the bridge narrative in the lengthy talmudic passage that is the subject of this chapter. Rābā's story of relative priority in the meat market, 'Abayê's story of preference for one institution over another, and Rab Naḥmān bar Isaac's story of the institutional middle classes' negotiating their own positions are echoed in Rab 'Addā's response; that backdrop forces the reader to confront Rab 'Addā's own envy within his treatment of Rab Dîmmî. As a competitor for Rābā's accolades and his own standing in the competitive *beit midrash*, Rab 'Addā could hardly afford a new competitor.

Rab Dîmmî returns to Rab Joseph and asks him to see what they have done with him. The use of the imperative "see" recalls the exilarch's identical instruction to Rābā, who ignored the instruction and began the whole cycle of abuse. Rab Joseph responds to Rab Dîmmî's abuse by invoking God to repay Rab Dîmmî's debt. The language of debt and repayment continues within the curse. The notion of a divine system of justice that works as a merchant's ledger is a legacy of Jewish life in a majority Zoroastrian culture.[62] Within this divine economy, adherence to the commandments and Torah study generate metaphysical, capital while the violation of prohibitive norms or the devaluation of Torah study results in their reduction. For most of this passage, the accumulation of Torah capital is reward in and of itself. At this juncture, the notion of heavenly reward allows the storyteller to invoke a heavenly arbiter within the human Torah field. Seeking redress from rabbinic competitors who have behaved badly, Rab Joseph turns to heaven. This human manipulation of divine justice is not uncharacteristic as a last resort for rabbinic storytellers and legists. In cases where their own power cannot enforce the ethically correct ruling, the rabbis are forced to assume that God's justice will rectify all wrongs. It is noteworthy that God's law sides with Rab Dîmmî and against enforcement of legal precedent. The rules of the rabbinic class in the real, Rab Joseph would argue, trump the theoretical exclusionary rules of restricted competition.

The Bridge Narrative as Cultural Capsule

An important feature of the bridge narrative is its dramatis personae. The historical Rab Dîmmî of Nĕhardĕ'ā' is a well-attested amora, but the evidence of his citation throughout the Talmud indicates that he lived and was active considerably later than either Rābā or Rab Joseph and would not have encountered either. The recurrence of these names (Rab Dîmmî, Rābā, Rab Joseph) with their historical incongruence immediately after a discursive legal conversation in which these names are featured is remarkable.[63] I outlined above the problem of the Talmud's attributing an aphorism to Rab Dîmmî and not to Rab Joseph though the passage later attributes the statement to Rab Joseph.[64] The storyteller responsible for the bridge narrative attempts to resolve this problem via the story's plot. The story creates a historical framework in which such interactions are possible. The story's movement follows the trajectory of the earlier discursive conversation as it begins with an encounter between Rab Dîmmî and Rābā's proxy before following Rab Dîmmî back to Rab Joseph. The story suggests that Rab Dîmmî is a young student (lower class) during Rābā's initial years and Rab Joseph's final years of teaching. This suggestion is taken up by various talmudic prosopographers who treat the story as reliable historiography and conclude from this story that Rābā was an active teacher even during Rab Joseph's period of activity and that Rab Dîmmî lived an inordinately long time.[65]

It is not simply the dramatis personae that recur within the story, but the content of the earlier legal discussion. Rābā and Rab Dîmmî have two debates within the legal discussion about the qualities of schoolteachers and the criteria by which their relative quality should be judged. As I discussed in Chapter 4, within the Greco-Roman *paideia* there was also a hierarchy of teachers in which the lower class of teachers were grammar-school teachers while the higher class of teachers were rhetors. Despite the separation of tasks, there was fluidity within these categories through the usurpation of the other's job. Among the higher class, it was common to protest this fluidity by insisting on hierarchy.[66] That insistence, I noted above, fuels the umbrage Rābā takes when his students categorize him as a schoolteacher.[67] Thus when Rab Dîmmî comes to town as a potential rival to Rābā, one can understand this arrival as akin to the arrival of a new schoolteacher even though the teaching in question is within a different class.

In one of the debates between Rābā and Rab Dîmmî treated above, the two scholars debate whether the metric for determining teacher quality should be gross knowledge or pedagogical skill, with Rābā opting for knowledge and Rab Dîmmî for pedagogy. Within that debate, the two scholars register their justifications entirely within the realm of pedagogy, debating the question of the lasting quality of errors; neither scholar discusses the benefits of greater knowledge. Rab Dîmmî's arrival in town is taken as a competitive threat to Rābā, presumably to Rābā's standing as the premier amoraic teacher in town. The questioning of Rab Dîmmî highlights his lack of knowledge—serving to replicate Rābā's criterion for judging teachers as replaceable.

The second debate between Rābā and Rab Dîmmî centers around the impact of scholarly envy on the rabbinic psyche and learning productivity. Recall that Rab Dîmmî forces the debate to center around the net benefit of envy on the individual scholar who will be inspired by competition to acquire greater knowledge. Rābā's initial position, by contrast, focuses not on the market and capital but on a teacher's psyche. Rab Dîmmî's failure in Rābā's town results in his own crushed psyche and not in his renewed commitment to study. The story stages the interaction between Rab Dîmmî and Rābā in order to perform the idealized issues of the previous discussion on the realistic stage and to allow Rab Dîmmî to feel the brunt of competition's force.

Beyond the issue of their debates, the stories can be seen as a specific response to the capitalistic aphorism "Scholarly envy will increase wisdom" and the larger difference between the Torah field and the commercial market that the discursive legal conversation so carefully constructs. Where the legal conversation punctuates its general discussion of competition restriction with Rab Joseph's reminder that the Torah field is different, the benefits that a rabbi may assume within the commercial market point to the impossibility of separating the Torah field from the commercial market or of allowing competition to be restricted in one field but not another. The bridge narrative echoes the general feeling of the passage's final three nonnormative stories by suggesting that the productive valuation of rabbinic competition is more idealized than real.

One can make a strong case for understanding the bridge narrative as the final piece of the talmudic passage, composed out of its adjacent parts.[68] Three of its character names (Rābā, Rab Dîmmî, and Rab Joseph) are taken from the preceding discursive conversation, while the name Rab 'Addā bar 'Ahabâ comes from the historical narratives that follow it. The legal content is a response to the earlier theoretical conversation and deconstructs the divide between the economic and knowledge fields as separate fields, reifying their distinction but recognizing the slippage that occurs between the two fields.[69]

Both the microcosm of the narrative and the macrocosm of the larger three-page passage alert us to Torah's position as cultural capital in amoraic and stammaitic Babylonia. As capital, Torah motivated competitions of accumulation that established reputations and led to a jockeying for hierarchical position. While the passage testifies to these social dynamics within rabbinic Babylonia, it also grapples with the value of such dynamics. The most explicit grappling is the discursive conversation that tries to separate education as its own market or, in Bourdieu's language, field. Within that dialectical conversation, scholars disagree within the confines of clear normative recommendations about hiring and firing. The nonnormative narratives do not speak to the realities of hiring and firing, but they thematize competition and stage it, withholding normative judgment.[70]

The bridge narrative connects these two units within the *sugya*, combining thematization with an explicit treatment of the normative. The combination of these (which others would term Halakhah and Aggadah) creates a narrative of multiple characters that reflects a different pluralism than is possible within dialectical debate. The host rabbis who are anxious about their authority manipulate the law in one direction while the guest rabbi and his supporters rail against the miscarriage of justice. In the bridge narrative neither is right nor the other wrong. Rather, the narrative form allows for a picture of the issues of monopoly, competition, and privilege not as abstract theories but as performances within a complex culture.

The framework of fields and capital allows for a recognition of the core similarities between the Torah *paideia* of the rabbis and the economic marketplace in which they also participated. It establishes a framework in which to understand both the larger social forces and the role of the individual within society. One of the advantages of Bourdieu's theoretical framework is the way it enables a detached look at issues of rabbinic power and authority.

While some have argued for the rabbis as a special class of moral actors, the material examined in this chapter demonstrates the timeless humanity of these rabbis.[71] Various characters in the stories act out of self-interest and manipulate the flexibility of law for their own gain. These rabbis sometimes translate Torah capital into financial capital in ways that other, theoretical, passages of rabbinic literature explicitly decry. Bourdieu's work suggests that these are not signs of political corruption, per se, but of natural human behaviors within a cultural field. The bridge narrative encapsulates the *sugya*'s central issues, staging them, but leaving them both unresolved and without normative recommendation. Chapter 6 will explore this tendency within late Bavli narrative.

Chapter 6

Lengthy Bavli Narratives: A New Theory of Reading

Much of this book has treated the brief legal episode and the tension between such stories and the nonnarrative legal sources among which they are ordinarily juxtaposed. A central feature of this dynamic is the relationship between the episode and its respective amoraic interpretation. I have posited thus far that the *stam* is animated by a centripetal (tending to unify) dynamic that struggles to resolve the seemingly deviant case story with less complex nonnarrative legal texts.[1] The Talmud contains another narrative type worth introducing to the conversation—the lengthy narrative. This narrative type contains more scenes and relatively elaborate characterizations and plots.[2] These narratives have been treated as Aggadah by traditional and critical scholar alike and are often included in compendiums of talmudic narrative. But since I have argued that Halakhah/Aggadah is not an essential division in the literature, I would like to consider lengthy talmudic narrative its own genre. This process will enable those who insist on the ability to differentiate along these lines to properly name the different literary features of halakhic *sugyot* and lengthy narratives, respectively. To be more precise, the reconstruction of Halakhah/Aggadah as a division between *sugya* genres will end up pitting dialectical talmudic *sugyot* (whether legal or theological) against lengthy narratives.

Legal episodes are perceived as deviant because their very marks of "tellability" deviate from the cultural expectations represented in statutes and codes. Such texts often appear within collage-like talmudic legal discussions that incorporate tannaitic and amoraic statements, midrashim, rationales, questions, answers, and stories. The *stam* generally plays an active role in such *sugyot*, visibly working to introduce, interpret, frame, and anonymously contribute to the materials inherited from rabbinic predecessors. The work of the source critic is aided in such passages by the text's practice of attributing inherited materials—statutes, midrashim, rationales, and even stories—to named rabbis; it is also helped by the general tendency of later redactors to switch from the Hebrew of attributed sources to Babylonian Aramaic.[3] The significant contribution of the *stammaim* is evident from the frequency and volume of their textual contributions to such conversations.

A contrasting situation obtains with respect to the Talmud's lengthy narratives. Such narratives are not interrupted by citations to named authorities. There is generally no attribution of authorship or narration of the story in toto to a named tanna or amora. Shifts in language (Hebrew/Aramaic) are less common in such stories. The Talmud's longer stories are only infrequently interrupted and commented upon by the *stammaim*. There is, however, another ubiquitous redactional phenomenon that pertains to lengthy talmudic narratives—the propensity to borrow materials from elsewhere in rabbinic literature and even other Bavli contexts.[4] Scholars presume that this extensive borrowing marks lengthy Bavli narrative as a relatively late redactional phenomenon.[5]

The picture I have painted thus far separates Bavli stories into two categories: small attributed narratives incorporated in conversational *sugyot* and anonymously credited lengthy narratives that stand on their own or in a cycle of similar stories.[6] This categorization is, of necessity, a not unproblematic heuristic device as there are some stories in the Talmud that are hard to categorize as belonging to one or the other.[7] This is one reason scholars have resisted such categorizations. Scholars of talmudic composition have considered stories a coherent category and treated stammaitic framing and interpretation in conversational *sugyot* along lines identical to the treatment of stammaitic redactional manipulations of lengthy narratives; both are instances of editorial modification.[8]

In two monographs and various articles Jeffrey Rubenstein has begun to treat lengthy talmudic narratives as the project of the late editors responsible for giving them finished form.[9] Rubenstein argues that these editors are identical to the *stammaim* responsible for the loud activity in the Talmud's conversational *sugyot* and, on the basis of this equation, uses cultural insights culled from comparative readings of lengthy talmudic narratives (mostly with Palestinian parallels) to construct a *Sitz im Leben* for the *stammaim* responsible for the majority of the Talmud—its conversational *sugyot*.

Richard Kalmin, whose work mines much of the same comparative Babylonian-Palestinian narrative terrain, has critiqued Rubenstein.[10] Most of

Kalmin's critique centers around Rubenstein's treatment of the *stammaim* as the "authors" of lengthy talmudic narrative. Part of Kalmin's critique reflects incredulity over the equation of the anonymous storyteller and the *stam* of conversational *sugyot*. As a paradigmatic counterexample Kalmin points to the unethical portrayal of amoraim: while the *stammaim* in conversational *sugyot* work to suppress such portrayals, lengthy talmudic narratives often consist significantly of such portrayals. Kalmin asks: "if the anonymous editors authored the Talmud's greatest stories, why do the overwhelmingly prosaic, legal preoccupations of these commentators throughout the Talmud reveal them to be the very antithesis of deft storytellers and imaginative artists?"[11] The remainder of this chapter stands as an answer to this question.[12]

This chapter focuses on a narrative longer than those that have been treated thus far in the book. This story, found at Qîddûšîn 70a–b, is marked as a late-redacted text by its habit of borrowing from passages found elsewhere in the Talmud.[13] The passage is particularly intriguing because its borrowings include materials taken from two passages treated in earlier chapters above; the overlap allows for comparative analysis of the same motifs in two different genre contexts of the Talmud. In analyzing this lengthy narrative, this chapter demonstrates the ways in which the cultural complexity that is suppressed by the monological energy of talmudic dialectical *sugyot* is embraced, magnified, and even augmented within lengthy talmudic narratives. The very example of ethical conflict that forms the basis for stammaitic interpretive suppression in the context of a legal *sugya* is central to a lengthy narrative's characterization and plot.

This paradigmatic lengthy narrative is difficult to read as a didactic instructional text.[14] As such, it directly challenges the approach to rabbinic narrative that seeks to discover the didactic moral of such texts.[15] In reading this narrative I will argue that narratives be considered not as attempts to communicate fixed cultural values or ideas but as vehicles for storytellers to process their cultural worlds. The end result is that much of what has been argued about the narrativity of legal episodes is also true of longer narratives though such texts are rarely filtered through the strong monological lens of the *stam*'s conversational *sugya* voice or the post-talmudic legal discourse.

Qîddûšîn 70

The fourth chapter of Mishnah Qîddûšîn outlines several caste-based marriage prohibitions. The caste categories divide the Jewish community on the basis of privilege and scandal, both of which are transmitted from parents to children. Within the talmudic discussion of the opening mishnah, there is a lengthy narrative in which a rabbi declares an otherwise ordinary Israelite to be of servant status because of his behavior. See the appendix to the present chapter for a full translation; due to the narrative's prohibitive length, I present here only a schematic paraphrase:

Scene 1: A man shopping for meat in Pûmbĕdîtā is told to wait and give queue priority to the agent of Rab Judah son of Ezekiel, an amora active in the mid-third century.

Incensed by this treatment, the man challenges the status quo, asking, "who is Judah Šĕwisqîêl [a linguistically difficult term related to the physicality of meat production] that he takes before me."

Scene 2: Upon hearing of the incident, Rab Judah excommunicates the man.

When Rab Judah further learns that the man routinely defames others as "servants," Rab Judah judicially declares that this man has servant status.

Scene 3: The excommunicated man petitions Rab Naḥmān, who summons Rab Judah to his court.

Rab Hûnā advises Rab Judah that though Rab Judah is not obliged to respond to the summons, Rab Judah should appear before Rab Naḥmān out of respect for the prestige of the exilarchate.

Scene 4: Rab Judah engages Rab Naḥmān at his home in an intellectual duel.

The initial exchange involves a series of linguistic "corrections" designed to demonstrate Rab Judah's preeminence.

When Rab Naḥmān tries to change course by playing the proper host, Rab Naḥmān implicates the female members of his house in a service role as a means of drawing common ground with his guest.

Rab Judah resists the entreaty, insisting upon his own stricter gender separation that further communicates a loftier social position.

Rab Naḥmān's wife Yaltā concludes the scene by pleading with her husband[16] to dispose of the visitor's business before the visitor completely destroys Rab Naḥmān's reputation.

Scene 5: Rab Naḥmān begins to discuss the case with Rab Judah before the excommunicated man arrives.

Rab Naḥmān challenges Rab Judah to justify his behavior.

When asked why he excommunicated the man, Rab Judah explains: "because [the man] pained the rabbinic emissary."

When asked why he declared him a servant, Rab Judah cites Samuel's statement that "one who defames uses his own calumny for the purpose." Rab Naḥmān challenges Rab Judah over the actionable intent of Samuel's claim though this challenge is left unresolved.

The excommunicated man arrives and accuses Rab Judah of labeling him a servant because of the man's descent from the Hasmonean dynasty. When Rab Judah cites another precedent of Samuel's that one who claims descent from the Hasmoneans is a servant, the excommunicated man questions the provenance of the precedent.

Rab Judah defends the provenance of the story by invoking Rab Matneh as a witness to Samuel's original utterance.

Rab Matneh appears and recites Samuel's original statement with an additional coda: "whoever claims descent from the house of the Hasmonean dynasty is a servant. *Broadcast of him that he is a servant.*"

Scene 6: Various *kĕtûbôt* are ripped up (marriages are called off) because of Rab Judah's court case.

The locals follow Rab Judah out of the city to stone him, but he prevents them by threatening to reveal another tradition of Samuel that might prove damaging to their lineage.

This lengthy narrative coheres as a unit; despite its length, it is not interrupted by a stammaitic commentarial voice. Even so, it is juxtaposed within the Mishnaic *sugya*, framed on either side by texts that encourage a certain focalization. The text that precedes the lengthy narrative is a statutory discussion that recurs in the story. The passage includes a tannaitic *baraita* and the amora Samuel's commentary on this *baraita*:

"One who defames[17] [another] is [himself] defamed
and does not ever speak in praise."
    Samuel [ca. 230–ca. 290 C.E.] said, "And with his own calumny he defames."

The tannaitic *baraita* has two clauses.[18] The initial clause is an active sentence describing a hypothetical scenario with a specifically claimed outcome: "one who defames is defamed." This clause is ambiguous as to the nature of the outcome: is the sentence a descriptive psychological characterization or an actionable legal prescription?[19]

An investigation of the sentence's original intent must focus on the second clause of the sentence: "and does not ever speak in praise." Since this clause would seem to be psychological commentary (that is, this type of person has a character defect that proscribes praise), it is likely that the opening clause is intended similarly as psychological description (that is, one who slanders others is masking a personal flaw). The *baraita* is a moralistic psychological sentence with normative implications for individual moral evaluation but without function as a precedential statute.

Another level of ambiguity enters the picture with Samuel's comment on the *baraita*: "And with his own calumny he defames." It is possible to read Samuel's statement as further psychological description: one who scandalizes others usually does so to mask deeply personal flaws.[20] But the talionic nature of Samuel's statement lends itself to a reading that focuses on the initial clause's potential for interpretation as a normative prescription. Such a reading presumes the *baraita* to call for a judicial scandalizing of the rumormonger, with Samuel's comment providing the specifics for that call. In this way, the *baraita*'s opening clause instructs a court to formally announce the lowered status of one who scandalizes others; Samuel's comment instructs that the court's announcement should reflect the attempted scandalizing.

The ambiguity within Samuel and the *baraita* forms the spine of the lengthy narrative. Several moments in the story testify to the centrality of this ambiguity. Most explicitly, Rab Naḥmān (or the narrator) challenges Rab Judah on this very ambiguity ("When Samuel made his comment, it was to suspect someone, but did he mean to *announce* about someone?"). But the ambiguity also appears in one of the story's stranger turns. When the excommunicated man arrives and offers an alternate legal explanation of Rab Judah's actions (because of the man's Hasmonean descent), the story never returns to answer the story's explicit questioning of Rab Judah's practical interpretation of the seemingly psychological principle. In the course of the discussion that ensues over his opponent's theory (that Rab Judah declared him a servant because of his family's dynastic claim to originate from the Hasmoneans), Rab Judah eventually cites another statement of Samuel's ("whoever is of Hasmonean descent is a servant") that shares the same ambiguity of psychological evaluation/legal mandate. The excommunicated man then challenges the provenance of that statement (all but accusing Rab Judah of making it up to suit his purposes).[21] Like a deus ex machina, Rab Matneh miraculously appears and corroborates the citation. But Rab Matneh's corroboration is more than a repetition of the attribution to Samuel. When Rab Matneh quotes his memory of Samuel, he adds a line. Rab Judah had quoted Samuel ambiguously: "whoever claims descent from the house of the Hasmonean dynasty is a servant." Rab Matneh recites the same opening sentence with a coda: "*broadcast of him* that he is a servant." This additional line has the narrative purpose of justifying Rab Judah's initial jump from the *baraita* and Samuel to a judicial announcement even as the story's circuitous path from the original statement to this final justification draws energy from the ambiguity.[22]

Within the historical evolution of talmudic law, statements of opprobrium are often interpreted as normative precedents by later interpreters because of the increasingly normative interests of later interpreters and the monological program of redactors and other late readers.[23] This transition from moralizing sentiment to actionable statute is captured within Rab Judah's announcement, suggesting that this process is related to rabbinic self-interest; Rab Judah's desire to put this man in his place is the immediate cause of the leap from moralizing to precedent.

Borrowing

As a late-redacted lengthy narrative, the narrative of Qîddûšîn 70 borrows from a number of other Talmudic passages.[24] The notion that anyone claiming Hasmonean lineage is a servant is found at Bābā Batrā 3b.[25] Though in this story this is attributed to Samuel, it is the only statement of Samuel's in this passage voiced in Aramaic. The evident lateness of the Qîddûšîn 70a–b story and its construction of the story in conversation with various statements attributed to Samuel make it likely that this statement was originally composed in the late narrative of Bābā Batrā 3b and attributed to Samuel here pseudepigraphically.

The story (treated above in Chapter 5) that Rābā tells at Bābā Batrā 22a about Rab 'Addā bar 'Ahabā's objecting to the priority of Rābā's agent at the butcher's line is the direct source for the Qîddûšîn narrative's opening scene in the butcher's line. There is a telling difference between the stories, though. The point of the Bābā Batrā 22a story is rabbinic competitiveness. As such, Rab 'Addā bar 'Ahabā plays within the system of rabbinic cultural capital; he is a social climber who believes he has surpassed his superiors. The adapted scene of Qîddûšîn 70, by contrast, narrates the anonymous man's mocking the notion of rabbinic priority. Punning Rab Judah's father's name with a word associated with butchering, the man questions the very slippage of social capital by asking whether he need defer to butcher's nepotism.

The larger Bābā Batrā passage discussed in Chapter 5 contains many contexts of capital slippage wherein rabbis use their Torah knowledge for commercial gain. In the Qîddûšîn passage, though, the slippage is between the markets of Torah capital and social capital. Among the dominant myths of rabbinic historiography is the idea that the destruction of the Temple transformed the separatist milieu of the sectarians into the unified world of the rabbis. Concomitant with the loss of the temple was a loss of the importance of certain Temple-associated social capital and its replacement with the ideational. The intellectual world of the rabbis, according to this, created a meritocracy surrounding Torah knowledge that replaced the oligarchy of the priesthood.[26] Increasingly scholars are showing the ways in which this myth is historically inaccurate. Geoffrey Herman's recent work on the importance of priestly status within Babylonian rabbinic culture demonstrates the continued significance of caste within rabbinic culture.[27] The durability of caste status as socially significant explains why the rabbis would seek to control its articulation and suggests the strong implications of such control for rabbinic power.

The talmudic passage with the most significant influence on the Qîddûšîn story is the Šĕbûʿôt 30 passage treated in Chapter 3. That passage is ideationally proximate as it shines light on the construction of rabbinic identity through the other. A story in that passage describes Rab Joseph's sending a letter to Rab Naḥmān to look out for an upcoming litigant named ʿÛllā. The *stam* there mitigates the story's ethical damage by claiming that the purpose of the letter was not to encourage rank favoritism, but to move ʿÛllā's matter up the docket. Both the supposition of favoritism and the notion of moving up the docket appear in Qîddûšîn 70 with the identical (rare) language.

Another instance of borrowing from Šĕbûʿôt 30 is Yaltā's argument to move Rab Judah's case up the docket so that Rab Judah not ruin Rab Naḥmān's reputation and equate him with everyone else. In Chapter 3 I highlighted the extent to which Šĕbûʿôt 30 is animated by the rabbinic need to constitute rabbinic standing within the larger Jewish society. The obsession with courtroom postures is a function of that need. I also argued that the fluid noninstitutionalized nature of rabbinic cultural life created a crisis in rabbinic self-perception that found its crux in the need to distinguish both the rabbinic program from regular society and individual rabbis from among the regular population. It is this second sense of distinguishing rabbis from one another that is the basis of Yaltā's suggestion to Rab Naḥmān that he move Rab Judah's case up the docket to avoid losing face.

The most significant interface between the Šĕbûʿôt passage and the Qîddûšîn passage is not a moment of explicit borrowing, but of deliberate ignorance. Šĕbûʿôt 30 includes a series of statutory statements attributed to Rabbâ bar Rab Hûnā. Among these statements is the following statement that encodes an ethic of judicial equity:

> Rabbâ bar Rab Hûnā said [when] a *ṣûrbā mērabbānān* and an am haarez oppose [each other] at trial, the *ṣûrbā mērabbānān* should not sit down [before the judge] before [the am haarez does] because it looks like [the judge] is arranging [the *ṣûrbā mērabbānān*'s] judgment.

In the Qîddûšîn story Rab Naḥmān contradicts Rabbâ bar Rab Hûnā's statute by opening his discussion of the case before Rab Judah's opponent arrives. Were the *stam* in full monological mode, an anonymous voice would note this violation of ethics and statute in the narrative. In this lengthy narrative *sugya*, though, no such interruption takes place. Furthermore, it is evident that the storyteller deliberately narrates this violation of ethics and statute, for the story could have easily introduced the opponent to the scene before the discussion began. While there are good aesthetic reasons for deferring the man's arrival, an author exercised by the contradiction of ethics and legal precedent would have certainly narrated the story in such a manner.

When Rab Naḥmān begins to discuss the case prior to the arrival of the opponent, he justifies this move by saying, "so that they not say that rabbis favor one another." The term for favoritism utilizes a verbal root (rare in the Talmud) that appears in Šĕbûʿôt 30 within the story of Rab Joseph's letter to Rab Naḥmān. The root is employed by the *stam* in Šĕbûʿôt 30 within a rhetorical question that rejects as an absurdity the possibility of rabbinic favoritism. In this verbal wink, the Qîddûšîn storyteller admits to familiarity with the Šĕbûʿôt 30 passage. But here the context is different. Rabbinic favoritism is not an absurdity. The presumption of the statement is that rabbinic favoritism exists, but it should not be named. The issue is not rabbinic favoritism but public awareness of such favoritism. The contrast is even greater when one takes into account the rhetoric of Rabbâ bar Rab Hûnā's statute (cited above) which avoids equitable situations that have the appearance of impropriety: "because it *looks like* arranging judgment." Simply put, the lengthy narrative of Qîddûšîn embraces the cultural realities of rabbinic favoritism, while the legal *sugya* of Šĕbûʿôt 30 works hard to legislatively control not only the manifestation of such but its appearance.

The lengthy Qîddûšîn 70 narrative is concluded by a set of short episodes.

These are amoraic stories of the type treated in earlier chapters that are included within the Talmud's dialectical *sugyot*.

> Rab Judah announced in Pûmbědîtā, "'Adā and Jonathan are servants, Judah son of Pāppā is a bastard."

> Rab Naḥmān announced in Šekněṣîb, "'Adā, 'Adā and Jonathan are servants, Isaac son of Pāpā is a bastard. Baṭî son of Tôbîyâ in haughtiness did not receive a freedom *geṭ* [from servitude]."

> Rābā announced in Měḥôzā, "Balaites, Danaites, Talaites, and Zagaites are all defamed."

> Rab Judah said, "Gobaites are Gibeonites, and Dorninites are generations of the *Něṯînîm*."

> Rab Joseph said, "The house of Kobê in Pûmbědîtā are all servants."

> Rab Judah said in the name of Samuel, "Pašḥur son of 'Êmar had four hundred servants and some say four thousand, and all of them became mixed with the priests. Any priest who is angry is one of them."

These six pronouncements compose a story cycle unified by their common theme of lineage announcements. Five of the stories (all but the last) reflect a putative contemporaneous historical occurrence and testify to rabbinic attempts to function as social authorities vis-à-vis caste. The third story is troubling as historiography because Rab Judah pronounces caste status on the basis of midrashic reasoning; similarities between place names in Babylonia and caste designations become equations for purposes of caste.[28] The final text is not a story but a midrashic pronouncement attributed to Samuel.

As in Chapter 5, the lengthy narrative seems to draw some of its pieces from local inherited materials. The protagonist of the lengthy Qîddûšîn narrative who jumps to judicial declarations of caste is Rab Judah, the same rabbi who problematically uses midrash to scandalize whole communities. Samuel's midrashic statement dismissing priests on the basis of psychology ("Any priest who is angry") again partakes of a descriptive/prescriptive ambiguity and contributes the notion of a man claiming priestly (Hasmonean) descent who is declared a servant.

The focalization permitted by this set of texts that follows the lengthy narrative at Qîddûšîn 70 suggests that the storyteller uses this narrative to struggle with a central component of rabbinic power—rabbinic authority over caste and its related marriage and divorce issues.

The basic caste laws outlined in Mishnah Qîddûšîn are derived from the Bible. These are preexisting categories that were, in some cases, important during second temple times. The caste laws seem as natural as biology—one's status depends on the lineage and sexual propriety of one's forebears. But any society in which serious rewards exist for those of higher caste needs bureaucratic means of memorializing calumnies and prestige of various kinds. If no such means exist, the entire system is only as good as collective memory and the situation is ripe for abuses by those eager to shed their untouchable designation or those who would use the power of rumor to intimidate social foes. In a caste system with no official bureaucracy, social capital is an arena of significant potential violence.

In his critique of violence, Walter Benjamin speaks of the way in which modern democracies choose not to outlaw violence completely but to monopolize it.[29] Through its police, military, and penal system, contemporary democracies maintain the capacity to do violence to citizens and foreigners alike. Such violence is theoretically justified by the violence it curtails, but it creates opportunities for corruption, abuse, and personal use and it often loses sight of its own violent nature. This leads Benjamin to reevaluate the basic morality of state violence.

The Qîddûšîn passage articulates a rabbinic attempt to monopolize rather than eliminate caste scandal.[30] The introductory *baraita* and Samuel's comments testify to the rabbinic suspicion of one who scandalizes someone else. And yet, the concluding four stories evidence the degree to which amoraim arrogated to themselves the power to declare about the caste status of members of their community.[31] The problem with such a move is that rabbinic scandalizing is also potentially violent and possibly immoral.[32] A midrashic scandalizing ("Gobaites are Gibeonites") testifies to rabbinic utilization of caste in the service of their own power. The late storyteller uses the lengthy narrative to thematize the potential problem of rabbis employing their caste authority as a reflexive weapon because it might have been the sharpest arrow in the quiver.[33]

The preceding chapters have largely critiqued the notion of the rabbis as a social leadership group with institutional authority and stature. The caste situation is the rare instance in which extant power within the community was there for the rabbinic taking. Several scholars have noted the importance of lineage to rabbinic Babylonia; these legal narratives describing amoraic declarations testify to some rabbinic control as the reality of genealogy in amoraic Babylonia.[34] The danger of such power, though, is that the rabbis could use it to buttress their own authority in other matters or simply to increase the value of Torah capital and its market.[35] Rab Judah first excommunicates the man who challenges his standing. But that move is unsatisfying to Rab Judah, who also declares about the man's caste. The storyteller plays out the fear (that emerges from Rab Judah's midrash) that rabbis use their power over marriage and divorce more for their own stature than as a reflection of historical and biological realities.[36]

The story nicely imagines an appeals court associated with the exilarch to which the man can turn. Even so, the story reduces the authority of that court, insisting on the reader's awareness that Rab Judah need not report; there is, ultimately, no check on charismatic rabbinic power. The conversation between Rab Judah and Rab Naḥmān strikes the foundation of the appellate court by showing the extent to which even such an institution derives its power from the competition for Torah capital.

Within the lengthy narrative format, the storyteller is able to challenge the moral standing of rabbinic power. The court case begins with a moment of rabbinic nepotism, but the substance of the case challenges Rab Judah's use of caste. When the opponent arrives and changes the legal basis for Rab Judah's behavior, the man explicitly attacks the provenance of Rab Judah's citation, suspecting that Rab Judah here produces a convenient theoretical teaching much as he conveniently altered Samuel's citation to declare the man a servant.[37] The storyteller ultimately identifies with Rab Judah, but the narrative format permits the inclusion of a character who challenges the integrity and the ethics of rabbinic manipulation of caste, casting aspersions on Rab Judah by accusing him of playing fast and loose with source citations.[38]

The final scene uses several images to describe the sheer power of rabbinic caste control. Several hundred *kĕtûbôt* are ripped up as a result of the proceeding; a river is dammed up with the stones generated by Rab Judah's investigation of Pûmbĕdîtā caste. Rab Judah is the story's central character, but it is hard to characterize him as its hero since his behavior is morally problematic and there is no growth in his character from the beginning of the story to its end. The problematic nature of Rab Judah and the behavior he models make this story difficult to explain according to the regnant theory of rabbinic narrative introduced by Yonah Fraenkel.

Implications for Rabbinic Narrative

Yonah Fraenkel is largely responsible for the narrative turn in the study of rabbinics. Part of Fraenkel's methodology is an assumption that rabbinic narratives are didactic texts and that a proper interpretation of such a text appreciates its message or moral.[39] There are certainly rabbinic narratives that work well as didactic texts and Fraenkel's methodology yields creative insights beyond the limits of its methodology. I would argue, though, that narratives are not simply vehicles for communicating messages that are easily formulated as simple declarative statements. Narrative has the advantage of transpired time, the possibility for multiple characters, voices, scenes, and registers. Following psychoanalysis, one may recognize narrative as a medium through which individuals process the social world that they inhabit. In this sense, narratives are process rather than product. Instead of trying to reduce narratives to the simple single-sentence moral, one can appreciate the way storytellers use narrative to struggle with themselves in evaluating their community, political arena, and normative responsibilities.[40]

This approach to narrative explains why scholars sense a palpable difference between the dialectical *sugyot* redacted by the *stammaim* and late lengthy narratives. The inherent difference is that the storyteller processes issues through narrative, allowing and even encouraging the full cultural complexity of lived life to shine through in order to make sense of the cultural world. Since the storyteller of Qîddûšîn 70 struggles with the potential problems of rabbinic power and authority with respect to caste, the storyteller deliberately narrates scenes with more problematic ethics and deliberately antistatutory behavior. Rabbinic favoritism is embraced as a feature of life rather than suppressed as a negative paradigm.[41]

The *stam* in conversational *sugyot* functions in a monological mode animated by a dynamic energy to unify received precedents as much as possible. As part of this mode, the *stam* regularly suppresses the exceptional because it is hard to make such behavior function as a usable paradigm. In lengthy narrative mode, by contrast, the centripetal energy is absent, replaced by a centrifugal (tending away from unity) energy that is willing to follow the contours of life to more dialogical places. This allows such narratives to reach for the kind of aesthetic achievement Bakhtin lionized in the novel's refusal to suppress the dialogical.[42]

I have encountered some resistance to the deconstruction of Halakhah/Aggadah among those who claim the ability to sort along the lines of this dichotomy. I would suggest that we more specifically differentiate between *sugyot* with a monological dialectic framework (that sometimes uncomfortably contain narratives) and *sugyot* composed of lengthy narratives that embrace dialogical realities by refusing to filter the rabbinic cultural experience.

Appendix: Translation of Qîddûšîn 70

"One who defames [another] is [himself] defamed, and does not ever speak in praise." Samuel said, "And with his own calumny he defames."

A certain man[43] entered the butcher shop in Pûmbĕdîtâ. He said to them, "bring me meat."

They said to him, "Watch[44] until the agent of Rab Judah son of Ezekiel takes, and we will seat[45] you."

He said [to them],[46] "Who is Judah Šĕwisqîēl that he takes before me."

They went and told [this] to Rab Judah [son of Ezekiel];

[Rab Judah] excommunicated[47] him."

[The people] reported to [Rab Judah] that [the man] was wont to call people "servants;"

[Rab Judah] broadcast of him that he was a servant.

[The man] went and brought a letter of summons from the house of Rab Naḥmān.

Rab Judah went before Rab Hûnā and [asked] him, "Should I go or not go?"

[Rab Hûnā] said to [Rab Judah] "you do not need to go,[48] but [go][49] out of respect for the house of the Nāsî.[50]

[Rab Judah went][51] and found [Rab Naḥmān] as he was building a fence.[52]

[Rab Judah] said to [Rab Naḥmān], "Does the master not agree with that which Rab Nĕhîlā'î[53] said in the name of Rab,[54] 'once a man is appointed a *pārnas* on the community, he is prohibited from performing labor before three.'"

[Rab Naḥmān] said to [Rab Judah], "I was making a bit of a balustrade."

[Rab Judah] said to [Rab Naḥmān], "Do you despise[55] the term *Maʿakeh* as is written in the Torah or *Mĕḥîṣâ* of the rabbis?"

[Rab Naḥmān] said to [Rab Judah], "Let my master sit on a couch?"[56]

[Rab Judah] said to [Rab Naḥmān], "Do you despise the term *sapsāl* of the rabbis or *'Îṣṭĕbā*[57] of the populace?"

[Rab Naḥmān] said to [Rab Judah], "Let my master eat a citron [pronounced *'itrûngā*]?"

[Rab Judah] said to [Rab Naḥmān], "This is what Samuel said, 'Whoever pronounces *'itrûngā* has three level of haughtiness.' Either say *'etrôg* of the rabbis or *'etrôgā* of the populace."

[Rab Naḥmān] said to [Rab Judah], "Let my master drink wine [pronounced *'anbag*]?[58]

[Rab Judah] said to [Rab Naḥmān], "Do you despise the term *'ispargûs* of the rabbis or *'anpeq* of the populace?"

[Rab Naḥmān] said to [Rab Judah], "Let Dûnāg come and let her serve us drinks."

[Rab Judah] said to [Rab Naḥmān], "This is what Samuel said, 'One may not take service of a woman.'"

[Rab Naḥmān said] but she is a minor?

[Rab Judah] said, "Samuel said explicitly regardless of whether she is an adult or a minor"

[Rab Naḥmān] said to [Rab Judah], "Let my master send greetings to Yalta?"

[Rab Judah] said to [Rab Naḥmān], "This is what Samuel said, 'a woman's voice is taboo.'"

[Rab Naḥmān said], "Through an emissary?"

[Rab Judah] said to [Rab Naḥmān], "This is what Samuel said,[59] 'One may not greet a woman.'"

Through her husband?

This is what Samuel said: "One may not greet a woman at all."

Yaltā[60] sent to him, "Prioritize his business in order that he not equate you to the regular people."[61]

[Rab Naḥmān] said to [Rab Judah], "What is the reason for your traveling here?"

[Rab Judah] said to [Rab Naḥmān], "My master sent after me a letter of summons."[62]

[Rab Naḥmān] said to [Rab Judah], "My master's speech[63] I have not learned, but I sent the master a letter of summons?"[64]

[Rab Judah] brought out the letter of summons[65] and showed it to [Rab Naḥmān].[66]

[Rab Naḥmān] said to [Rab Judah], "Since the master came, let us discuss things so they should not say that rabbis privilege one another."

[Rab Naḥmān asked Rab Judah] "Why did the master excommunicate that man?"

"Because he pained the rabbinic emissary."[67]

"Why did you announce about him that he is a servant?"

"Because he routinely called people servants, and it is taught, 'whoever disqualifies is disqualified and one does not ever speak in his praise.'"[68]

And Samuel said, "And he disqualifies with his own blemish."

When Samuel made his comment, it was to suspect someone, but did he mean to announce about someone?

Meanwhile, [Rab Judah's] opponent arrived.[69]

[The opponent] said, "You called me a servant because I descend from the house of the Hasmonean dynasty."

[Rab Judah responded] Thus said Samuel, "Whoever claims descent from the house of the Hasmonean dynasty is a servant."

[The opponent] said to Rab Judah], "But does the master not agree with that which Rab 'Abā said in the name of Rab,[70] 'Any rabbinical scholar who teaches a law, if it comes before its scenario transpires, we listen to it, but if not, we do not listen to it.'"

[Rab Judah] said to him, "Rab Matneh was with him [meaning "me"]."

Rab Matneh had not seen Něhardĕ'ā for thirteen years. That day he came.

[Rab Judah] said to [Rab Matneh], "Does the master remember what Samuel said when he was with one knee on the shore and one knee on the bridge?"

[Rab Matneh] said to him, "This is what Samuel said, 'Whoever claims descent from the house of the Hasmonean dynasty is a servant. Broadcast[71] of him that he is a servant.'"[72]

[On that day][73] several *kětûbôt* were ripped up in Něhardĕ'ā.

When [Rab Judah] went out, they went out after him to stone him.

[Rab Judah] said to them, "If you will be silent, you will be silent, but if not, I will reveal that Samuel said, 'Two lineages exist in Něhardĕ'ā: one is called "sons of the dove" and one is called "sons of the raven," and your mnemonic is *ṭāmē ṭāmē ṭāhôr ṭāhôr*.'"

They cast their stones from their hands, and the river Malka was dammed up.

Rab Judah[74] announced in Pûmbědîtā,[75] "'Adā and Jonathan are servants, Judah bar Pāppā is a bastard."[76]

Baṭî bar Tôbîyâ in haughtiness did not receive a freedom *geṭ* [from servitude].

Rābā announced in Měḥôzā, "Balaites, Danaites, Talaites, and Zagaites are all defamed."

Rab Judah said, "Gobaites are Gibeonites, and Dorninites are generations of the *Nětînîm*."

Rab Joseph said, "The house of Kobê in Pûmběḏîtā are all servants."

Rab Judah said in the name of Samuel, "Pašḥur bar ʾÊmar[77] had four hundred servants and some say four thousand, and all of them became mixed with the priests. Any priest who is angry is one of them."[78]

Conclusion

This book aims to develop an appropriate hermeneutics for the study of Bavli legal narratives. It begins by recognizing the ways in which the dominant hermeneutics for reading these narratives is limited. The discourse of Jewish legal interpretation has often operated (and continues to operate in many contexts) with a default understanding of law as a set of rules. This picture of Jewish law encourages readers to transform legal texts that are not penned within the genre of rules into legal rules. In the case of the genre of legal narrative, this occasions a flattening of the story into a singular moral or didactic legal message.

The minimization of a legal story's meaning is often, though not always, performed by readers located within the Bavli (amoraim or the *stam*). Since the Bavli includes varying layers of interpretation within its pages, its treatment of legal narrative sources frequently includes such a minimization. Though some legal narratives are minimized within the Bavli by named amoraim, a greater number of such narratives are transformed into legal rules by the *stam*, the anonymous voice that dominates the Bavli and structures the dialogues of the Bavli's smallest unit, the *sugya*.

Critical scholarship has focused significant energy on the extent to which the *stam* is responsible for structuring Bavli *sugyot* and for determining the meaning of the final redacted text we call the Bavli. In some ways, one can conceive of the *stam* as having created the *sugya* through the process of digesting the earlier sources it employs in the fabrication of a *sugya*: each earlier source is not only cited within the *sugya* but juxtaposed with other sources from which it is distinguished and commented on by the *stam*. Because the process of the *stam*'s digestion of a *sugya* often centers on the production of seemingly contradictory materials, there is a dialectical energy to many legal *sugyot* characterized by a presentation of contradiction and resolution. Despite the *sugya*'s celebrated pluralistic diversity of legal positions or midrashic justifications, the poetic energy of the genre is in the direction of minimized controversy and resolution. The mechanics of Bavli questions and answers drives toward a unifying coherence.

As a source being digested by the *stam* in the creation of a *sugya*, the legal narrative represents a genre problem. The hermeneutic drive toward a rule-based understanding of law with energy toward minimized controversy creates the perception that legal narratives are problematic; stories are often interesting because they describe unexpected behavior (behavior that breaches canonicity) and because stories are narrated within a world broader than the narrow discourse of law in which actors' behavior is motivated by many factors.

The perceived problematic nature of legal narrative within the hermeneutics of Jewish law encourages the creation of a different hermeneutics to properly address these sources. This reading methodology moves in the direction of the perceived problems, acting to celebrate the breadth of legal narratives rather than to suppress that breadth. Rather than reading legal narratives within a rules-based discourse of law, the new hermeneutics of talmudic legal narratives imagines an interdisciplinary cultural space within which such texts can be understood to operate.

Robert Cover introduced the term *nomos* to describe a complex legal space whose contours are not completely defined by the rules of law or legal institutions. This complex legal space is one that myths and other narratives help construct and maintain. If one reads Bavli legal narratives within the Bavli *nomos*, one is not reading such narratives as if they are exceptions to a law established by the rules among which the narratives are juxtaposed. Rather, one recognizes the narratives as texts with an equally strong claim to define legal meaning. Such a reading resists the energy of the dominant Jewish legal hermeneutics by importing into its definition of the legal other discourses such as economics, politics, psychology, and sociology. Moreover, it imports such other fields as equal partners to the legal rules in defining legal meaning. In doing so, legal narratives become the basis for a reading of the legal *sugya* in toto that often runs counter to the grain of its internal dynamics.

If, for example, a legal narrative is highly affected through the emotional behavior of its characters, the dominant hermeneutics of Jewish law (even in the Bavli itself) generally suppresses the emotional material in favor of the rules-based discourse to which the narrative can contribute. But within the complex legal space of the *nomos*, the emotional content is not only not suppressed, but moved from the margins to the center, raising awareness of the extent to which the actions of the characters within the Bavli's *nomos* are highly cathected.

The transformation of Jewish discursive legal space into a *nomos* that reflects a broader multilingual cultural territory has ramifications not only for the poetics of Bavli legal narrative but also for the poetics of Bavli legal *sugyot* in general. In altering the dominant hermeneutics of Jewish law to appropriately contend with the complex meaning of legal narrative, this book aims to establish a framework for aesthetic and social literary analysis that neither privileges the legal as a uniquely normative world of rules nor ignores legal statutes or statements of legal rationale within the pursuit of literary meaning. The result is the possibility of literary readings of Bavli legal *sugyot* that highlight the often unrecognized thematic coherence of these *sugyot* while exploring the way these legal discussions, often treated entirely through the lens of legal rules, reflect the multidiscursive cultural realities of amoraic Babylonia.

This book further argues for literary analysis of Bavli texts for their social dynamics. This approach runs counter to more typical static treatments of Babylonian rabbinic historiography. Instead of struggling to make talmudic texts reveal the institutional frameworks and clear political relationships that moderns look to for sociological clarity, turning to talmudic legal narratives for indications of rabbinic social life allows scholars to be more responsive to the texts, permitting the texts a greater ability to speak for themselves. The assorted readings of the earlier chapters work to articulate a picture of mundane rabbinic power in its locally negotiated sense. The rabbis as a group utilize existing mechanisms of power (marriage/divorce; civil jurisprudence) to cement their own prestige and authority. When outside the confines of definitive areas of rabbinic authority, the rabbis act in ways that testify to feelings of powerlessness and cultural instability both collectively and individually.

The stories treated herein shine a spotlight on the Babylonian rabbis of the third to seventh centuries C.E. This includes the final five generations of amoraim and the era of the *stammaim*. In evaluating this historical period I distinguish between the amoraic and stammaitic periods only inasmuch as the latter is a more bureaucratically institutionalized society. This difference comes across both in instances of stammaitic interpretation of earlier amoraic narratives and in narratives that are more purely stammaitic.

In the course of analyzing talmudic legal narratives I have deconstructed the Halakhah/Aggadah binary distinction. But good deconstruction involves both destruction and construction. Though I claim the dichotomy as fundamentally foreign to the Bavli and the product of geonic utilization of the Talmud rather than the text itself, I have also reinscribed some of the dichotomy as a difference between types of Bavli passages. The typical Bavli *sugya*, which most associate with the legal conversations it often (but not always) conducts, has a centripetal energy that drives toward neatly defined arguments with basic consensus. The late lengthy Bavli narrative *sugya*, by contrast, embraces narrative's potential for exploring extreme scenarios, characters, or plots in the interests of processing and constructing one's cultural world. Such passages are difficult to reduce to normative arguments and post-talmudic readers have generally declined to make the attempt by claiming such passages as Aggadah. In clarifying the way these different genre types work, I am both outlining the ways in which the texts encourage readers to read these genres and paving the way for readings that resist that encouragement. Much as I have resisted the monological interpreters within and outside the Talmud to read the Talmud's legal narratives as descriptors of a culturally complex law, one could resist the genre expectation of late Bavli narratives to read these as encouraging normative responses and similarly implicating a complex legal precedent. Similarly, as I have demonstrated here, one can read even nonnarrative legal materials in thicker ways, bringing disparate fields of knowledge and methodologies as equal partners to statutory law in the reading of such materials.

Though this book focuses on a narrow subgenre of talmudic text—the talmudic legal narrative—it has implications for the Talmud as a whole. This work intervenes within the millennium-long discourse of talmudic interpretation to question some of the assumptions basic to traditional and critical reader alike. In addition to its deconstruction of Halakhah/Aggadah, this book ushers in a source criticism that draws upon compositional history in an exploration of textual poetics. The implication of such a source criticism is the separation of talmudic layers as an initial step in literary analysis rather than as a tool for charting ideational evolution. My hope is that this book empowers readers to critique the reading strategies that have come to dominate both traditional and critical understandings of the Talmud.

Notes

Introduction

1. It is common for people to define Aggadah in positive terms as narrative. As explained below, though, this definition is imprecise. The negative definition "non-legal" better captures the full range of texts treated as Aggadah and allows the two sides of the binary to together encompass all rabbinic texts.

2. Though the tosafists of medieval Germany and France are not as statute-oriented as Maimonides and other codifiers, the dynamic energy of their project presumes the inherently statutory nature of the talmudic statements they routinely juxtapose and distinguish.

3. A good comparative example is Robert A. Ferguson, "Untold Stories in the Law," in *Law's Stories: Narrative and Rhetoric in the Law*, ed. Peter Brooks and Paul D. Gewirtz (New Haven, Conn.: Yale University Press, 1996).

4. This now universally accepted fact was established in David M. Goodblatt, *Rabbinic Instruction in Sasanian Babylonia*, Studies in Judaism in Late Antiquity, vol. 9 (Leiden: Brill, 1975).

5. David Weiss Halivni, *Měqôrôt Û-Měsôrôt: Šabbāt* (Jerusalem: Jewish Theological Seminary of America, 1975); Shamma Friedman, "Mābô Kĕlālî ʿAl Derek Ḥēqer Ha-Sûgyâ," in *Meḥqārîm Û-Měqôrôt*, ed. H. Z. Dmitrovsky (New York: Jewish Theological Seminary of America, 1978), 283–321.

6. Exceptions include David Charles Kraemer, *Reading the Rabbis: The Talmud as Literature* (New York: Oxford University Press, 1996); Aryeh Cohen, *Rereading Talmud: Gender, Law, and the Poetics of Sugyot*, Brown Judaic Studies (Atlanta, Ga.: Scholars Press, 1998); and Louis Jacobs, *Structure and Form in the Babylonian Talmud* (Cambridge and New York: Cambridge University Press, 1991).

7. The appearance of randomness creates a climate in which the discovery of organizational schema is indeed a discovery. Such discoveries animate Louis Jacobs's work on the Talmud. See his *Studies in Talmudic Logic and Methodology* (London: Vallentine, 1961), *Structure and Form in the Babylonian Talmud*, and *Rabbinic Thought in the Talmud* (Edgware, Middlesex, and Portland, Ore.: Vallentine Mitchell, 2005).

8. Friedman, "Mābô Kĕlālî ʿAl Derek Ḥēqer Ha-Sûgyâ"; Halivni, *Měqôrôt Û-Měsôrôt: Šabbāt*.

9. Daniel Boyarin, *Carnal Israel: Reading Sex in Talmudic Culture* (Berkeley: University of California Press, 1993).

10. Shoshana Felman, *Jacques Lacan and the Adventure of Insight: Psychoanalysis in Contemporary Culture* (Cambridge, Mass.: Harvard University Press, 1987), 92.

Chapter 1

1. This tension is treated in Steven D. Fraade, "Nomos and Narrative Before *Nomos and Narrative*," *Yale Journal of Law and the Humanities* 17, no. 1 (2005); Menachem Elon, *Jewish Law: History, Sources, Principles*, trans. Bernard Auerbach and Melvin Sykes (Philadelphia: Jewish Publication Society, 1994), 3:1367–1422; Moshe Halbertal, *People of the Book: Canon, Meaning, and Authority* (Cambridge, Mass.: Harvard University Press, 1997), 72–81; and Chaim Tchernowitz, *Tôldôt Ha-Pôsqîm* (New York: Jubilee Committee, 1947), 3:73–137.

2. Elon, *Jewish Law*, 3:1144–45, describes as axiomatic the notion that Jewish law could never be fully reduced to a code since even Maimonides would have to reckon with the reliance of his code on prior traditional materials that could never be abrogated. But the intention of the author and the functional performance of the literature are separable, and one can make the claim, pace Maimonides' rejections, that *Mishneh Torah* does reduce Jewish law to a code. This is the direction of Halbertal, *People of the Book*, 73: "Maimonides apparently viewed his code as a comprehensive and self-sufficient summary of all Halakhah, so that it can serve as an authoritative text in and of itself."

3. Though this mixing of genres was deplored by scientific scholarship, it has recently come to be celebrated; see David Damrosch, *The Narrative Covenant: Transformations of Genre in the Growth of Biblical Literature* (San Francisco: Harper & Row, 1987), 35: "The mixing of law and narrative was not a crude blunder by incompetent editors whom even the young Goethe could only deplore; rather, it was the most important generic innovation of its age."

4. Eliezer Segal, *Case Citation in the Babylonian Talmud: The Evidence of Tractate Neziqin*, Brown Judaic Studies, no. 210 (Atlanta, Ga.: Scholars Press, 1990), 216. Others who note the same phenomenon without naming it as such include Hanina Ben-Menahem, *Judicial Deviation in Talmudic Law: Governed by Men, Not by Rules*, Jewish Law in Context, vol. 1 (Chur, Switzerland, and New York: Harwood Academic Publishers, 1991), 32; and Richard Lee Kalmin, *Sages, Stories, Authors, and Editors in Rabbinic Babylonia*, Brown Judaic Studies, no. 300 (Atlanta, Ga.: Scholars Press, 1994).

5. Hanokh Albeck, *Mābô La-Mišnâ* (Jerusalem: Môsad Bialik, 1966).

6. For a related connection between midrash and Talmud as genres, see David Halivni, *Midrash, Mishnah, and Gemara: The Jewish Predilection for Justified Law* (Cambridge, Mass.: Harvard University Press, 1986).

7. Halbertal, *People of the Book*, 72: "While the Mishnah is a flexible code, the Talmud seems to be even farther away from being a code of any sort. . . . In many talmudic

discussions the *sugiya* does not proceed by way of selection aimed at approaching or approximating the right answer. Astonishingly, many of the discussions manifest the opposite tendency as they progress dialectically."

8. This notion of literary dynamics is informed by Peter Brooks, *Reading for the Plot: Design and Intention in Narrative* (New York: A. A. Knopf, 1984); see, for example, p. 47: "But I think we do well to recognize the existence of textual force, and that we can use such a concept to move beyond the static models of much formalism, toward a dynamics of reading and writing."

9. The notion of the Bavli's celebration of argumentation for its own sake (anticode) is developed in David Charles Kraemer, *The Mind of the Talmud: An Intellectual History of the Bavli* (New York: Oxford University Press, 1990). I do not say here "legal discussions," because this is equally true of the Talmud's theological passages constructed in the discursive question-and-answer format that typifies the *stam*'s monological presentation. This is beautifully illustrated in Daniel Boyarin, *Socrates and the Fat Rabbis* (Chicago and London: University of Chicago Press, 2009), 146–48.

10. Elon, *Jewish Law*, 3:1144ff.

11. This central tension over the impulse toward codification plays itself out on the surface of the talmudic text. Consider BT ʿÊrûbîn 46b in which Rab Měšaršîya rejects out of hand the use of decision-making rules to reach final rulings.

12. Tchernowitz, *Tolĕdôt Ha-Pôsqîm*, 73–137.

13. Shamma Friedman has alerted me to an excellent example of this phenomenon at BT Bābā Měṣîʿā 86a. The story of Rabbâ bar Naḥmēnî's death narrates a heavenly debate between God and the other members of the heavenly academy about the legal issue of doubtful leprosy. When the heavenly debate needs resolution, they decide to appeal to Rabbâ bar Naḥmēnî. Elsewhere in the Talmud, Rabbâ is credited with a position on this issue, and the debate on a matter of purities law allows the story to narrate Rabbâ's dying with the word "pure" on his lips, a literary motif that is explicitly identified by the text.

14. Tchernowitz, *Tolĕdôt Ha-Pôsqîm*, 93–100.

15. Ibid., 97.

16. Halbertal, *People of the Book*, 80.

17. See, for example, Joseph Dov Soloveitchik, *Halakhic Man*, 1st English ed. (Philadelphia: Jewish Publication Society of America, 1983); Joel Roth, *The Halakhic Process: A Systemic Analysis*, Moreshet Series (New York: Jewish Theological Seminary of America, 1986); and Elliot N. Dorff, Arthur I. Rosett, and Jewish Theological Seminary of America, *A Living Tree: The Roots and Growth of Jewish Law* (Albany: State University of New York Press, 1988).

18. Wai-chee Dimock, "Deploying Law and Legal Ideas in Culture and Society: Rules of Law, Laws of Science," *Yale Journal of Law and the Humanities* 13 (2001).

19. Rachel Adler, *Engendering Judaism: An Inclusive Theology and Ethics* (Philadelphia: Jewish Publication Society, 1998); Tamar Ross, *Expanding the Palace of Torah: Orthodoxy and Feminism*, Brandeis Series on Jewish Women (Hanover: Brandeis University Press, published by University Press of New England, 2004).

20. Gary Saul Morson and Caryl Emerson, *Mikhail Bakhtin: Creation of a Prosaics* (Stanford, Calif.: Stanford University Press, 1990), 15–32.

21. Ibid., 23–27.

22. M. M. Bakhtin, *The Dialogic Imagination: Four Essays*, ed. Michael Holquist, trans. Caryl Emerson and Michael Holquist, University of Texas Press Slavic Series, no. 1 (Austin: University of Texas Press, 1981), xxvi–xxx.

23. Bakhtin (ibid., 299) writes: "The prose writer as a novelist does not strip away the intentions of others from the heteroglot language of his works, he does not violate those socio-ideological cultural horizons (big and little worlds) that open up behind heteroglot languages—rather, he welcomes them into his work." See Morson and Emerson, *Mikhail Bakhtin*, 21–27.

24. Bakhtin (*Dialogic Imagination*, 296) writes: "The poet is a poet insofar as he accepts the idea of a unitary and singular language and a unitary, monologically sealed-off utterance."

25. See note 4 above.

26. Morson and Emerson, *Mikhail Bakhtin*, 27–32.

27. Morson and Emerson (ibid., 25) note that "In Bakhtin's view, all approaches to ethics in terms of rules not only ignore essential particulars that fail to fit a rule, but also function in a fundamentally mechanical way."

28. Ibid., 26.

29. Robert M. Cover, *Narrative, Violence, and the Law: The Essays of Robert Cover*, ed. Martha Minow, Michael Ryan, and Austin Sarat, Law, Meaning, and Violence (Ann Arbor: University of Michigan Press, 1992), 175.

30. Austin Sarat and Thomas Kearns, "Making Peace with Violence: Robert Cover on Law and Legal Theory," in *Law's Violence*, ed. Austin Sarat and Thomas Kearns (Ann Arbor: University of Michigan Press, 1995).

31. For a critique of this state, see Paul W. Kahn, *The Cultural Study of Law: Reconstructing Legal Scholarship* (Chicago: University of Chicago Press, 1999). Pierre Schlag, in *The Enchantment of Reason* (Durham, N.C.: Duke University Press, 1998), 117, writes: "Hence it is that even in scholarly journals, American legal academics spend most of their prose imitating the poses, the idioms, the concerns, and sometimes the imperious tones of presiding judges . . . Legal academics, as they see things, are on the side of the law (and 'law' is, presumptively, a good thing). The dominant supposition among legal academics is that law review scholarship ought to provide solutions (read: *legal* solutions); it ought to be constructive (read: prescribe *more law*); and it ought to deal with concrete legal problems (read: address the world in the terms and categories constructed by the official legal apparatus)."

32. Schlag (*Enchantment of Reason*, 97) writes: "Thus, while American legal thinkers will inquire, often in a sustained, sophisticated, and quite critical manner, into the consequences, meanings, value, and formal definitions of artifacts like 'rights,' 'principles,' or 'rules,' they virtually never question the *ontological identity or status* of such legal artifacts. They will presume (when talking about such legal

artifacts) that there is an identifiable referent there and that the only question is what to say about 'it.'"

33. A taxonomy of "law and literature" scholarship is found in Jane Baron, "Law, Literature and the Problems of Interdisciplinarity," *Yale Law Journal* 108 (1999). An extensive bibliography of the field is offered in Shoshana Felman, *The Juridical Unconscious: Trials and Traumas in the Twentieth Century* (Cambridge, Mass.: Harvard University Press, 2002), 192–94.

34. Felman (*Juridical Unconscious*, 55) notes:

> The dialogue between the disciplines of law and literature has so far been primarily thematic (that is, essentially conservative of the integrity and of the stable epistemological boundaries of the two fields): when not borrowing the tools of literature to analyze (rhetorically) legal opinions, scholars in the field of law and literature most often deal with the explicit thematized reflection (or "representation") of the institutions of the law in works of the imagination, focusing on the analysis of fictional trials in a literary plot and on the psychology or the sociology of literary characters whose fate or whose profession ties them to the law (lawyers, judges, or accused).

35. Robert M. Cover, "The Supreme Court, 1982 Term—Foreword: *Nomos* and Narrative," *Harvard Law Review* 97, no. 4 (1983); and Cover, *Narrative, Violence, and the Law,* pp. 95–172. Cornel West, *Keeping Faith: Philosophy and Race in America* (New York: Routledge, 1993), 306, argues that Cover's work "was not [simply] interdisciplinary but de-disciplinizing."

36. Jewish Publication Society, *Tanakh: A New Translation of the Holy Scriptures According to the Traditional Hebrew Text* (Philadelphia: Jewish Publication Society, 1985), 307. Subsequent biblical quotations rely on the JPS translation unless otherwise specified.

37. Cover, "*Nomos* and Narrative," 19 n. 50. Cover realizes that the statute's discussion of love complicates the usage to which he is putting the Genesis deviation from the norm; because of this, Cover imagines a parallel legal world where the rule is followed without protest. But the imagination of such a legal world for heuristic purposes is not unproblematic.

38. Cover circumvents the problems of biblical source criticism by asserting that his argument does not rely on the canonical union of the later Deuteronomy statute with the earlier Genesis narratives, but on the shared heritage of the two: "The Deuteronomic material has been included in a biblical canon together with a rich set of accompanying narratives. Long before the final redaction of the canon, many of the texts and stories existed as parts of a common sacred heritage of the people who produced Deuteronomy" (ibid., 20).

39. Cain and Abel (Genesis 4), Ishmael and Isaac (Genesis 16–22), Esau and Jacob (Genesis 23–26), Reuben and Judah (Genesis 43–45), Judah and Joseph (Genesis 37, 40–50), Manasseh and Ephraim (Genesis 48).

40. Cover, "*Nomos* and Narrative," 21. I would add that one could establish the norm from the description of its subversion in the Genesis stories themselves.

41. Ibid., 19.

42. Clifford Geertz, *The Interpretation of Cultures: Selected Essays* (New York: Basic Books, 1973), 3–30.

43. Cover, "*Nomos* and Narrative," 5 n. 7. Geertz himself draws the term from Gilbert Ryle, *Collected Papers*, 2 vols. (London: Hutchinson, 1971).

44. Geertz, *Interpretation of Cultures*, 5.

45. Ibid., emphasis mine.

46. Kahn, *Cultural Study of Law*, 18–30.

47. This is one of the things critiqued in Suzanne Last Stone, "In Pursuit of the Countertext: The Turn to the Jewish Legal Model in Contemporary American Legal Theory," *Harvard Law Review* 106, no. 4 (1993).

48. I highlight here one sense of the term *nomos*. Steven Fraade ("Nomos and Narrative Before *Nomos and Narrative*") has noted the linguistic connection between *nomos* and Torah, and Joseph Lukinsky ("Law in Education: A Reminiscence with Some Footnotes to Robert Cover's *Nomos and Narrative*," *Yale Law Journal* 96, no. 8 [1987]) has observed the connection between *nomos* and the literary space of the Talmud.

49. It is in this sense that "*Nomos* and Narrative" can be considered a founding text for the critical legal studies movement. West, *Keeping Faith*, 195–206.

50. See *Sĕpôrnô* Deuteronomy 19:16.

51. Cover, "*Nomos* and Narrative," 22.

52. "This does not mean that the formal precept was not obeyed. Indeed, the narratives in question would lose most if not all of their force were it not for the fact that the rule *was* followed routinely in ordinary life." Ibid., 21.

53. Compare Cover's reference to Irving Howe and the Yiddishists who routinely held their annual balls on Kol Nidre night. Ibid., 8 n. 18.

54. Cover (ibid., 7) writes: "I must stress that what I am describing is not the distinction between the 'law in action' and the 'law in the books.' Surely a law may be successfully enforced but actively resented." Geertz (*Interpretation of Cultures*, 11) criticizes the rules-oriented approach of cognitive anthropologists: "If, leaving our winks and sheep behind for the moment, we take, say, a Beethoven quartet as an, admittedly rather special but, for these purposes, nicely illustrative, sample of culture, no one would, I think, identify it with its score, with the skills and knowledge needed to play it, with the understanding of it possessed by its performers or auditors, nor, to take care, *en passant*, of the reductionists and reifiers, with a particular performance of it or with some mysterious entity transcending material existence."

55. See above note 4.

56. Jerome Bruner, "The Narrative Construction of Reality," *Critical Inquiry* 18, no. 1 (1991): 11ff. I thank Joshua Levinson for suggesting these categories.

57. Catherine Kohler Riessman, *Narrative Analysis*, Qualitative Research Methods (Newbury Park, Calif.: Sage Publications, 1993), 85–113; David Herman, *Story Logic:*

Problems and Possibilities of Narrative, Frontiers of Narrative (Lincoln: University of Nebraska Press, 2002).

58. Bruner, "Narrative Construction of Reality."

59. William Labov and Joshua Waletzky, "Narrative Analysis: Oral Versions of Personal Experience," in *Essays on the Verbal and Visual Arts*, ed. June Helm (Seattle: University of Washington Press, 1967).

60. Bruner, "Narrative Construction of Reality," 11. Hayden V. White, "The Value of Narrativity in the Representation of Reality," *Critical Inquiry* 7, no. 1 (1980): 16–17, says: "The reality which lends itself to narrative representation is the conflict between desire, on the one side, and the law, on the other. Where there is no rule of law, there can be neither a subject nor the kind of event which lends itself to narrative representation." White continues:

> [W]e cannot but be struck by the frequency with which narrativity, whether of the fictional or the factual sort, presupposes the existence of a legal system against or on behalf of which the typical agents of a narrative account militate. And this raises the suspicion that narrative in general, from the folktale to the novel, from the annals to the fully realized "history," has to do with the topics of law, legality, legitimacy, or, more generally, authority. . . . Interest in the social system, which is nothing other than a system of human relationships governed by law, creates the possibility of conceiving the kinds of tensions, conflicts, struggles, and their various kinds of resolutions that we are accustomed to find in any representation of reality presenting itself to us as a history.

61. See Richard Delgado, "Storytelling for Oppositionists and Others," *Michigan Law Review* 87 (1989); Patricia J. Williams, *The Alchemy of Race and Rights* (Cambridge, Mass.: Harvard University Press, 1991).

62. See literature cited in Baron, "Law, Literature and the Problems of Interdisciplinarity."

63. Peter Brooks, "The Law as Narrative and Rhetoric," in *Law's Stories: Narrative and Rhetoric in the Law*, ed. Peter Brooks and Paul D. Gewirtz (New Haven, Conn.: Yale University Press, 1996), 16, notes: "Narrative has a unique ability to embody the concrete experience of individuals and communities, to make other voices heard, to contest the very assumptions of legal judgment. Narrative is thus a form of countermajoritarian argument, a genre for oppositionists intent on showing up the exclusions that occur in legal business-as-usual—a way of saying, you cannot understand until you have listened to our story."

64. Martha Minow, "Stories in Law," in *Law's Stories*, ed. Peter Brooks and Paul D. Gewirtz (New Haven, Conn.: Yale University Press, 1996), 36.

65. See Morson and Emerson, *Mikhail Bakhtin*, 25.

66. Gerald L. Bruns, *Hermeneutics, Ancient and Modern* (New Haven, Conn.: Yale

University Press, 1992), 104–23. Daniel Boyarin once wrote: "Speaking in Bakhtinian terms, the texts are not monological but dialogical, presenting different views on most issues dialectically at nearly every turn" (*Carnal Israel*, 27). For a reversal, see Boyarin, *Socrates and the Fat Rabbis*, 142 n. 30.

67. Bakhtin (*Dialogic Imagination*, 88) writes: "The idea begins to live, that is, to take shape, to develop, to find and renew its verbal expression, to give birth to new ideas, only when it enters into genuine dialogic relationships with other ideas, with the ideas of others. Human thought becomes genuine thought, that is, an idea, only under conditions of living contact with another and alien thought, a thought embodied in someone else's voice, that is, in someone else's consciousness expressed in discourse. At that point of contact between voice-consciousnesses the idea is born and lives."

68. Morson and Emerson, *Mikhail Bakhtin*, 28.

69. Michael Holquist, "Introduction," in Bakhtin, *Dialogic Imagination*, xxvi–xxvii.

70. Bakhtin (*Dialogic Imagination*, 299) writes: "The prose writer as a novelist does not strip away the intentions of others from the heteroglot language of his works, he does not violate those socio-ideological cultural horizons (big and little worlds) that open up behind heteroglot languages—rather, he welcomes them into his work."

71. Bakhtin (ibid., 296) says: "The poet is a poet insofar as he accepts the idea of a unitary and singular language and a unitary, monologically sealed-off utterance."

72. This dialogical gap helps explain the ethical problematics of talmudic narratives. See Chapter 6.

73. Bakhtin, *Dialogic Imagination*, 283–84.

74. Peter Brooks, "Narrativity of the Law," *Law and Literature* 14, no. 1 (2002), discusses hermeticism as a feature of American law. For a critique of monological dialogue in Plato, see Boyarin, *Socrates and the Fat Rabbis*, 33–132.

75. Minow, "Stories in Law," 35–36.

76. Cover, "*Nomos* and Narrative," 21.

77. Boyarin, *Socrates and the Fat Rabbis*.

78. Rashi Bābā Mĕṣī'ā 33a defines "Talmud" as a verb: "I have already explained above that it means to pay attention in order to understand what the unexplicated reasons for Mishnaic law are, *or when two sources contradict he will understand to distinguish so that both of them can endure* or to comprehend the words of two disagreeing tannaim and let us say, 'this is according to whom—to such and such a scholar'" (translation and emphasis mine).

79. Eryl W. Davies, "The Inheritance of the First-Born in Israel and the Ancient Near East," *Journal of Semitic Studies* 38, no. 2 (1993). I thank Jonathan Milgram for drawing this to my attention.

80. For the assumption that Deuteronomy legislates against accepted prior practice, see Nahum M. Sarna, *Understanding Genesis*, Heritage of Biblical Israel (New York: Jewish Theological Seminary of America, 1966), 185–88.

81. According to the *itpe'el* form found in the British Library Harley 5508 (400) and Columbia X 893 T 141 manuscripts.

82. The problem of differentiating between Rabbâ and Râbâ is outlined in Shamma Friedman, "Kĕtîb Ha-Šēmôt 'Rabbâ' Wĕ-'Râbâ' Bĕ-Talmûd Ha-Bablî," *Sinai* 110 (1992). Any combination of the two names is possible in these two citations. For my purposes it is more powerful to assume that the name to which the dictum is attributed is the same as the name of the story's problematic protagonist. Since Rabbâ is R. Zêrâ's contemporary, it is likely that the story is about Rabbâ; I likewise chose to attribute the statute to Rabbâ.

83. This implicit bracketed statement is explicated in Gottingen 3, Vatican 134, Munich 140, British Library Harley 5508 (400), and Columbia X 893 T 141 manuscripts as well as in the Pesaro *editio princeps*.

84. Vatican 134, Munich 95, Munich 140, British Library Harley 5508 (400), and Pesaro claim this happened in the morning. British Library Harley 5508 (400)and marginal notes in both Vatican 134 and Munich 140 add "when his wine was better." The absence of explicit drinking in the original text of this narrative (as per this note and the preceding) makes that implicit aspect of the narrative explicit only through its juxtaposition with the preceding precept. It is clear, then, that on this basic level the narration of the story in this context is done with the intention of drawing it into conversation with the preceding precept.

85. This implicit bracketed term is explicated in Columbia X 893 T 141 and Pesaro.

86. Vatican 134, Munich 95, Munich 140, British Library Harley 5508 (400), and Pesaro emphasize the effect of the conclusion by adding a term: "each and every time."

87. *Hamā'ôr Haqātān*, Mĕgîllâ 3b (Rîf) (emphasis mine).

88. See for example *Bêt Yōsêp 'Ōraḥ Ḥayyîm* 695b.

89. *Yad 'Eprayim* at *Shulḥan Arukh 'Ōraḥ Ḥayyîm* 695:2 (emphasis mine).

90. See Henry A. Fischel, "Story and History: Observations on Greco-Roman Rhetoric and Pharisaism," in *Essays in Greco-Roman and Related Talmudic Literature*, ed. Henry A. Fischel (New York: Ktav, 1977); Yonah Fraenkel, *Sippûr Ha-'Aggādâ: 'Aḥdût Šel Tōken Wĕ-Ṣûrâ* (Tel Aviv: Ben Ḥayyîm, 2001); Galit Hasan-Rokem, *Riqmat Ḥayyîm* (Tel Aviv: 'Am 'Ôbēd, 1996); and Eli Yassif, *The Hebrew Folktale: History, Genre, Meaning*, trans. Jacqueline S. Teitelbaum, Folklore Studies in Translation (Bloomington: Indiana University Press, 1999).

91. Boyarin, *Socrates and the Fat Rabbis*. Boyarin rightly notes that in this passage, the juxtaposed contradictory statements are not challenged within the Talmud and one could therefore characterize the Talmud in this passage as willing to tolerate the combination of serious statute and satirical narrative. My own interest lies primarily with talmudic legal narrative and the way it is often framed and transformed into statutory form whether this happens in the Talmud or in subsequent talmudic commentarial discourse.

92. M. M. Bakhtin, *Rabelais and His World*, trans. Hélène Iswolsky (Bloomington: Indiana University Press, 1984).

93. Carey A. Moore, *Esther: Introduction, Translation, and Notes*, Anchor Bible, vol. 7B (Garden City, N.Y.: Doubleday, 1971), xlvi–xlix. Adele Berlin, *Esther: The Traditional Hebrew Text with the New JPS Translation*, JPS Bible Commentary (Philadelphia: Jewish Publication Society, 2001), xx.

94. The explicit normative instructions about the holiday of Purim toward the end of the biblical book are particularly parsed for their legal meaning. See, for example, the discussion at BT Mĕgîllâ 2a about the word *bizmanēhem*.

95. Last year my son's Jewish community center day care enclosed a note with its *mišlōaḥ mānōt* (holiday gift packages) letting all parents know that they would not be performing the ritual correctly if they gifted friends through the agency of a minor.

96. I am indebted to Naftali Cohn for noting this parallelism between the rabbinic story and the biblical story.

97. Cover, "*Nomos* and Narrative," 21: "Indeed, the narratives in question would lose most if not all of their force were it not for the fact that the rule *was* followed routinely in ordinary life."

Chapter 2

1. Quoted from Gideon Libson, "Halakhah and Law in the Period of the Geonim," in *An Introduction to the History and Sources of Jewish Law*, ed. Neil S. Hecht et al. (Oxford: Oxford University Press, 1996), 217.

2. For a recent attempt to grapple with the definitional dilemmas of the dichotomy, see Berachyahu Lifshitz, "'Aggādâ Bĕ-Tôlĕdôt Tôrâ Šebĕ-'al Peh," *Shenaton Hamishpat Haivri* 22 (2004).

3. Though Fraenkel (*Sippûr Ha-'Aggādâ*, 222–23) claims that there are works of later Aggadah (*Vayiqra Rabbah* and *Pesiqta De-Rab Kahana*) that are self-consciously confined to Aggadah alone.

4. See Yair Lorberbaum, *Ṣelem 'Elôhîm: Halākâ Wĕ-'Aggādâ* (Jerusalem: Schocken Press, 2004); Yair Lorberbaum, "Reflections on the Halakhic Status of Aggadah," *Dînê Yiśra'el* 24 (2007).

5. Lifshitz, "'Aggādâ Bĕ-Tôlĕdôt Tôrâ Šebĕ-'al Peh."

6. The famous exception to this is at Bābā Qamā 60b, but this text does not use the term "Halakhah" at all.

7. Lorberbaum, "Reflections on the Halakhic Status of Aggadah," 30. "The terms '*Halakhah*' and '*Aggadah*' actually appear as distinct categories in the tannaitic sources, but they are neither mutually exclusive nor antithetical."

8. Robert Brody, *The Geonim of Babylonia and the Shaping of Medieval Jewish Culture* (New Haven, Conn.: Yale University Press, 1998), xix–xxi.

9. Jane S. Gerber, "My Heart Is in the East," in *The Illustrated History of the Jewish People*, ed. Nicholas De Lange (New York: Harcourt Brace, 1997), 159.

10. Brody, *Geonim of Babylonia*, 100–122, 147–54.

11. Ibid., 43–48.

12. Ibid., 45.

13. Ibid., 43–48.

14. Lawrence H. Schiffman, *From Text to Tradition: A History of Second Temple and Rabbinic Judaism* (Hoboken, N.J.: Ktav, 1991), 266–69.

15. Lorberbaum ("Reflections on the Halakhic Status of Aggadah," 34) writes: "For

the Geonim, *Halakhah* and *Aggadah* . . . do not belong to the same literary corpus, nor do they even belong to the same ideational world." See also Lorberbaum, *Ṣelem 'Elôhîm*, 109–13.

16. Benjamin Manasseh Lewin, ed. and pub., '*Ôṣar Ha-Gĕônîm* (Haifa, 1928), Berakhot, Commentaries 271, p. 91. See Saul Lieberman, *Šĕqî'în* (1970), 83.

17. Though it has been suggested that the geonic strong division was cemented in Spain and North Africa but resisted in France and Germany. See Lorberbaum, *Ṣelem 'Elôhîm*, 111 nn. 18–19.

18. Compare this with Schlag, *The Enchantment of Reason*, 26–27: "Reason as transcendence is established through what might be called an 'exclusionary gesture.' This gesture distinguishes reason sharply from other sources or kinds of belief. The exclusionary gesture serves at once to protect the integrity of reason from contaminants and to enable the exclusion of undesirable views from law's empire. The exclusionary gesture enables legal thinkers and actors to retain a faith that the manifold legal materials and operations are organized in a coherent whole by a transcendent source: reason as *central command*." To borrow Schlag's hypothesis, then, Halakhah excludes Aggadah as part of a monopolizing strategy central to its claim to authority.

19. In my own work on this monograph I discovered that TS FII(2).14, a fragment of Hilkôt Gĕdōlōt, had been misidentified as a Bavli text witness.

20. Provençal commentators of the twelfth and thirteenth centuries comment on *Halakôt Rabātî* rather than the Talmud.

21. H. N. Bialik, *Kol Kitbê H. N. Bialik* (Tel Aviv: Dvir, 1947), 207ff.

22. For a comparable view, see Elon, *Jewish Law*, 1: 94–104.

23. Boyarin, *Carnal Israel*, 15: "I assume that both the halakha and the aggada represent attempts to work out the same cultural, political, social, ideological, and religious problems."

24. Felman, *The Juridical Unconscious*, 5.

25. Yehudah Brandes, '*Aggadâ Lĕ-Ma'aśeh: 'Iyûnîm Bĕ-Sûgyôt Mišpāḥâ, Ḥebrâ, Wĕ-'abôdat Ha-Šem* (Jerusalem: Eliner Library, Jewish Agency for Israel, Beit Morasha of Jerusalem, 2005).

26. Lorberbaum, *Ṣelem 'Elôhîm*, 130–45.

27. "Our rabbis teach," a typical tannaitic introductory formula, appears in Yalqûṭ Šim'ônî Mišlê preceding this story; see Raphael Nathan Nata Rabbinovicz, *Seper Diqdûqê Sôprîm* (Jerusalem: 'Ôr ha-Ḥokmâ, 2002), Sanhedrin, 210. These words also appear in the version found in Moses Gaster, *The Exempla of the Rabbis* (New York: Ktav, 1968), 159, but since they appear as an introductory formula before every story in Gaster, they cannot be used as evidence of tannaitic provenance.

28. "In the name of Rab" is absent from the body of MS Karlsruhe-Reuchlin 2 and added in the margins. A number of words, including some essential ones, are similarly added in the margins of Karlsruhe-Reuchlin 2.

29. MS Karlsruhe-Reuchlin 2 has the deleted term "in fire" before "black bile." For "black bile," see below, at notes 64ff.

30. The implicit bracketed verb is absent in MS Herzog.

31. BT Sanhedrîn 75a.

32. Hilkōt ʿAbōdâ Zārâ.

33. See Jean Baumgarten and Jerold C. Frakes, *Introduction to Old Yiddish Literature* (Oxford and New York: Oxford University Press, 2005). Some early Yiddish literature specifies its purpose for women and less-educated men. Daniel Boyarin, *Unheroic Conduct: The Rise of Heterosexuality and the Invention of the Jewish Man*, Contraversions: Critical Studies in Jewish Literature, Culture, and Society, 8 (Berkeley: University of California Press, 1997), explores the uniquely Jewish description of masculinity.

34. Though this was not the initial aim of the work's author, the popularity of this work is related to its adoption as a woman's study Bible. See description in Vanessa L. Ochs, *Words on Fire: One Woman's Journey into the Sacred* (San Diego: Harcourt Brace Jovanovich, 1990), 36.

35. See Jay Michael Harris, *Nachman Krochmal: Guiding the Perplexed of the Modern Age*, Modern Jewish Masters Series (New York: New York University Press, 1991), 274–99.

36. I thank Eliyahu Stern for noting that the Vilna Gaon refers to midrashim indivisibly as *midrěšê ha-Tôrâ*.

37. See, for example, Leopold Zunz, *Die gottesdienstlichen Vorträge der Juden, historisch entwickelt: Ein Beitrag zur Alterthumskunde und biblischen Kritik, zur Literatur- und Religionsgeschichte* (Berlin: A. Asher, 1832).

38. Yonah Fraenkel, *Darkê Ha-ʾAggādâ Wěha-Midraš* (Masada, Israel: Yad la-Talmûd, 1991); and Fraenkel, *Sîppûr Ha-ʾAggādâ*.

39. Fraenkel, *Darkê Ha-ʾAggādâ Wěha-Midraš*, 236–39; Fraenkel, *Sîppûr Ha-ʾAggādâ*, 23–32; Yonah Fraenkel, *Midraš Wě-ʾAggadah* (Tel Aviv: Open University, 1996), 346–61; and Yonah Fraenkel, *ʿIyûnîm Bě-ʿOlāmô Ha-Rûhānî Šel Sippûr Ha-ʾAggādâ* (Tel Aviv: Ha-Kîbbûṣ Ha-Měʾûḥād, 1981), 66–69.

40. Fraenkel, *Darkê Ha-ʾAggādâ Wěha-Midraš*, 282; Fraenkel, *Sipûr Ha-ʾAggādâ*, 240–52; Fraenkel, *ʿIyûnîm*, 13–18.

41. Jeffrey L. Rubenstein, *Talmudic Stories: Narrative Art, Composition, and Culture* (Baltimore: Johns Hopkins University Press, 1999), 12–15; Boyarin, *Carnal Israel*, 12–16.

42. Fraenkel, *Sippûr Ha-ʾAggādâ*.

43. Ibid.

44. Ibid., 220–35.

45. Ibid., 223. Fraenkel argues that some later redacted works are exclusively aggadic. This supports his general notion that there is a classical period of rabbinic literary composition and a postclassical period. Fraenkel argues later in this piece that it is no accident that the classical period overlaps with the period in which rabbinic works did not care to differentiate themselves as exclusively Halakhah or Aggadah.

46. That the Bavli is often more elaborate in its telling is demonstrated extensively in Rubenstein, *Talmudic Stories*.

47. Michael Sokoloff, *A Dictionary of Jewish Babylonian Aramaic of the Talmudic*

and Geonic Periods (Ramat Gan, Israel: Bar Ilan University Press; and Baltimore: Johns Hopkins University Press, 2002), 394.

48. Moshe Simon-Shoshan's distinction between the relative narrativity of parallel texts is helpful here. See his "Halachah Lemaʿaseh: Narrative and Legal Discourse in the Mishnah" (Ph.D. diss., University of Pennsylvania, 2005).

49. Rashi Sanhedrîn 31b in the name of *Sēper Hā-ʾAggadah*. The Nātān Ṣûṣîtā story requires its own study, an endeavor I hope to undertake in the near future. There are two fundamental problems in dealing with the story—the nature of the story itself and the name Nātān Ṣûṣîtā.

The story itself is found at Rashi Sanhedrîn 31b where it shares much with the central narrative of this chapter and is written in a precise middle Hebrew. The language alone suggests that Rashi's version is an authentic rabbinic narrative, which Rashi attributes to a *Sēper Ha-ʾAggadah* that is not extant. Another version of the story is found in Rabênû Nisîm Gāôn's *Ḥibbûr Yāpeh Min Ha-Yĕšûʿâ*. Because Rabênû Nisîm expanded his stories in general, and this one in particular, and because Rabênû Nisîm's work was originally in Arabic, it is difficult to extract from this work a pre-geonic version. As one of his expansions, Rabênû Nisîm borrows the interaction of doctors and rabbis in the narrative at Sanhedrin 75a for dramatic effect. Rashi and Rabênû Nisîm share both the overall plot and the name of the male protagonist. Šĕʿîltôt Vāʾērā contains a halakhic discussion of martyrdom in which the story of Sanhedrîn 75a has a prominent place. In introducing that story, Šĕʿîltôt adds details familiar from both Rashi and Rabbênû Nisîm as associated with the other narrative. Šĕʿîltôt names the male protagonist Nātān Ṣûṣîtā and the female protagonist Ḥannâ, and claims that Ḥannâ is a married woman, a feature that appears in all accounts. The troubling aspect of this final feature is that Ḥannâ's being married conflicts with the early amoraic debate about her marital status that Šĕʿîltôt quotes after citing the body of the narrative of Sanhedrîn 75a. Because of this contradiction, I posit that Šĕʿîltôt's version of the narrative must have been, like Rashi's, remarkably similar to Sanhedrîn 75a in both content and language. Such similarity led to the borrowing of details even when these did not work in their new contexts.

The name *Nātān Ṣûṣîtā* has been the subject of considerable discussion. Daniel Boyarin, "Lĕ-Leqsîqôn Ha-Talmûdî," *Tarbiz* 50 (1981), is the seminal piece on the lexicography of this term. I would like to suggest an explanation for the term that is based on Boyarin's research but unsuggested in that piece. Boyarin writes that the word is related to a part of the wheat stalk that the rabbis referred to as "the manhood of the wheat." It is very possible, then, that the word *ṣûṣîtā* is associated with this narrative not because of the heavenly halo, but because the protagonist attempts to give (*nātan*) his manhood (*ṣûṣîtā*) to the woman with whom he is obsessed.

50. See Šĕʿîltôt Vāʾērā and preceding note.

51. MS Yad Harav Herzog 1 has R' Ishmael bar Naḥmēnî. We can posit a possible transition then from Yerushalmi's text to that of the printed editions. "R"Y bar Naḥmēnî" for Rab Isaac bar Naḥmān became the more prevalent Rab Ishmael bar Naḥmēnî,

which is easily mistaken for Rab Samuel bar Naḥmēnî. But MS Karlsruhe-Reuchlin 2 has the variant R. Samuel alone, so the transition may work in the opposite direction.

52. Haym Soloveitchik, "Halakhah, Hermeneutics, and Martyrdom in Medieval Ashkenaz (Part I of II)," *Jewish Quarterly Review* 94, no. 1 (2004); Avraham Grossman, "The Sources of Kiddush Hashem in Early Ashkenaz" (Hebrew), in *Sanctity of Life and Martyrdom: Studies in Memory of Amir Yekutiel*, ed. Isaiah Gafni and Aviezer Ravitzky (Jerusalem: Hebrew University, 1991); Ephraim Kanarfogel, "Halakha and *Metziut* (Realia) in Medieval Ashkenaz: Surveying the Parameters and Defining the Limits," *Jewish Law Annual* 14 (2003); and Israel Ta-Shma, "Suicide and Murder for the Sake of Kiddush Hashem" (Hebrew), in *Facing the Cross: The Persecutions of 1096 in History and Historiography*, ed. Y. T. Assis et al. (Jerusalem: Hebrew University, 2000). The *rishonim* postdate the geonim and certainly have a strong notion of the Halakhah/Aggadah dichotomy. But even the best definition of such a dichotomy is bound to have liminal cases. Furthermore, both the Crusade Chronicles and the aggadic narratives employed by the tosafists to support their position are narratives and rise to that level owing to their breach of canonicity, to use the categories developed above in the Introduction. That is, the chronicler deliberately describes extralegal behavior to make a point (as Soloveitchik notes) much as the rabbinic storyteller describes the mass suicide in ways that deliberately surpass the canonical expectations established by legal precedent.

53. This is similar to the phenomenon of scholars being named because of their attributions. Shamma Friedman, "*Nomen est Omen*—Dicta of the Talmudic Sages Which Echo the Author's Name" (Hebrew), in *These Are the Names: Studies in Jewish Onomastics*, vol. 2, ed. Aaron Demsky (Ramat Gan: Bar Ilan University Press, 1999).

54. According to Rabbinovicz, *Seper Diqdûqê Sôprîm*, 10:211, "son of Rab 'Îqqā" is missing in Yalqûṭ Šimʿônî Mišlê.

55. This reading marks the passage as potentially progressive in supporting a woman's right of refusal. As such, it is the best possible answer. My only critique is that it fails by the standards of talmudic legal reasoning since it does not neatly tie up all the loose ends.

56. Bakhtin (*Dialogic Imagination*, 187) writes:

> Nevertheless, heteroglossia (other socio-ideological languages) can be introduced into purely poetic genres, primarily in the speeches of characters. But in such a context it is objective. It appears, in essence, as a *thing*, it does not lie on the *same* plane with the real language of the work: it is the depicted gesture of one of the characters and does not appear as an aspect of the word doing the depicting. *Elements of heteroglossia enter here not in the capacity of another language carrying its own particular points of view, about which one can say things not expressible in one's own language, but rather in the capacity of a depicted thing. Even when speaking of alien things, the poet speaks in his own language* [emphasis mine]. To shed light on an alien world, he never resorts to an alien language, even though it might in fact be more adequate to that world.

57. The language of "bring me" is odd and is likely based on the parallel discussion of idolatry wherein the point is made that even if the patient doesn't say "bring me idolatrous herbs [the action can rise to the level of a cardinal sin.]" Alternatively, the text is trying to maintain the patient's agency.

58. Shamma Friedman, " Mābô Klālî ʿal Derek Ḥeqer Ha-Sûgyâ " and *Talmûd ʿārûk: Pereq Ha-Śôḥēr Et Ha-'ûmanîn*, 2 vols. (Jerusalem: Jewish Theological Seminary of America, 1990); and David Weiss Halivni, *Měqôrôt Û-Měsôrôt: Nāšîm* (Tel Aviv: Dvir, 1968), *Mê-Yômā ʿad Ḥăgîgâ* (Jerusalem: Jewish Theological Seminary of America, 1975), *Šabbāt* (1975), *ʿĒrûbîn Û-Pěsaḥîm* (Jerusalem: Jewish Theological Seminary of America, 1982), *Bābā Qammā* (Jerusalem: Magnes, 1993), and *Bābā Měṣîʿā* (Jerusalem: Magnes, 2003).

59. Adiel Schremer, "Stammaitic Historiography," in *Creation and Composition: The Contribution of the Bavli Redactors (Stammaim) to the Aggada*, ed. Jeffrey L. Rubenstein (Tübingen: Mohr Siebeck, 2005); Richard Kalmin, "The Formation and Character of the Babylonian Talmud," in *Cambridge History of Judaism*, vol. 4, *The Late Roman-Rabbinic Period*, ed. Steven T. Katz (Cambridge: Cambridge University Press, 2006); Richard Kalmin, *Jewish Babylonia Between Persia and Roman Palestine* (New York: Oxford University Press, 2006).

60. This is not the first work to treat the *stam* from a literary perspective. It is preceded by Cohen, *Rereading Talmud*; and Kraemer, *Mind of the Talmud* and *Reading the Rabbis*.

61. Though see Boyarin, *Socrates and the Fat Rabbis*, which embraces authorial anonymity as a defining feature of the Talmud.

62. Friedman, "Mābô Klālî ʿal Derek Ḥeqer Ha-Sûgyâ," 314 n. 12.

63. Yaakov Zussman, "Wě-Šûb Lě-Yěrûšalmî Něziqîn," *Mehqārê Talmûd* 1 (1990): 55–133. See also Alyssa M. Gray, *A Talmud in Exile: The Influence of Yerushalmi Avodah Zarah on the Formation of Bavli Avodah Zarah* (Providence, R.I.: Brown Judaic Studies, 2005).

64. Marcus Jastrow, *A Dictionary of the Targumim, the Talmud Babli and Yerushalmi, and the Midrashic Literature* (Brooklyn: Traditional Press, 1975), 1:532; Michael Sokoloff, *A Dictionary of Jewish Palestinian Aramaic of the Byzantine Period*, 2nd ed. (Ramat Gan, Israel: Bar Ilan University Press; and Baltimore: Johns Hopkins University Press, 2002), 224.

65. See also Šabbāt 67a where *ṭīnā* and *ṭīṭ* are grouped together in a curse.

66. Sokoloff, *Dictionary of Jewish Palestinian Aramaic*, 7.

67. Peter Toohey, "Love, Lovesickness and Melancholy," *Illinois Classical Studies* 17 (1992).

68. Ibid.

69. Ibid., 269–74. For a treatment of lovesickness in the Jewish context, see Joshua Levinson, "An-Other Woman: Joseph and Potiphar's Wife—Staging the Body Politic," *Jewish Quarterly Review* 87, nos. 3–4 (1997).

70. Toohey, "Love, Lovesickness and Melancholy," 269–74.

71. Fischel, "Story and History," 450–66, suggests that the sage story genre is derived from the Greco-Roman *chreia*. David Stern, "The Captive Woman: Hellenization, Greco-Roman Erotic Narrative, and Rabbinic Literature," *Poetics Today* 19, no. 1 (1998), discusses two ways in which the Greco-Roman genre of erotic narrative affects rabbinic literature.

72. Yassif, *Hebrew Folktale*, 140, connects these two tales as two iterations of one folk motif.

73. Both Tessa Rajak, "Dying for the Law: The Martyr's Portrait in Jewish-Greek Literature," in *The Jewish Dialogue with Greece and Rome*, ed. Tessa Rajak (Leiden: Brill, 2001), and Daniel Boyarin, *Dying for God: Martyrdom and the Making of Christianity and Judaism* (Stanford, Calif.: Stanford University Press, 1999), are apposite here.

74. This name is a late insertion in MS Leiden Or. 4720.

75. Palestinian Talmud ʿAbôdâ Zārâ 2:2 (40d–41a); Šabbāt 14:4 (14d).

76. Boyarin (*Dying for God*, 34–35) reads Tosefta's version of this story as an instantiation of the porous boundary between Judaism and Christianity in the tannaitic period.

77. For a contextualization of the Babylonian Talmud in the Greco-Roman context, see Daniel Boyarin, "Hellenism in Jewish Babylonia," in *The Cambridge Companion to the Talmud and Rabbinic Literature*, ed. Charlotte Elisheva Fonrobert and Martin S. Jaffee (Cambridge: Cambridge University Press, 2007).

78. Mary Frances Wack, *Lovesickness in the Middle Ages: The Viaticum and Its Commentaries* (Philadelphia: University of Pennsylvania Press, 1990), 7; Jackie Pigeaud, *La maladie de l'âme: Étude sur la relation de l'âme et du corps dans la tradition médico-philosophique antique*, Collection d'études anciennes (Paris: Société d'édition "Les Belles lettres," 1981).

79. The latter half of R. Isaac's claim is a midrashic reading of Proverbs 9:17 whose meaning varies dramatically depending on how much of the biblical text is incorporated. Proverbs 9 constructs two opposing female paradigms: the lady of wisdom and the lady of folly. Verse 17 is uttered by the lady of folly, who sits as a prostitute outside her door, enticing men inside by telling them that "stolen waters are sweet and bread eaten furtively is tasty." But verse 18 announces that these men do not realize that death and hell await them on the other side of the door. If R. Isaac's statement means to include verse 18 as well as verse 17, then the message of his statement is hopeful: even though sinners appear to be deriving pleasure now, they will eventually pay the price. But if, as it seems from the citation, the statement only adduces verse 17, then R. Isaac's message is depressingly pessimistic for rabbinic Jews; not only are they unable to experience sexual pleasure because of the Temple's loss, but such pleasure is transferred to sinners.

80. R. Joshua ben Ḥananyâ was a second-generation tanna and student of R. Yôḥānān ben Zakka'y who lived during the time of the destruction.

81. Tosefta Sôṭâ considerably expands the aggadic content of Mishnah Sôṭâ 9 and tells the following story of the same R. Joshua:

When the Temple was destroyed there were many separatists in Israel who would not eat meat nor drink wine. R. Joshua took an interest in them and said to them, "My children, why are you not eating meat?" They replied, "Shall we eat meat when every day the daily sacrifice [of meat] was brought on the altar and now is no longer?" He asked them, "Why are you not drinking wine?" They replied, "Shall we drink wine when every day wine was poured on the altar and now is no longer?" He said to them, "then figs and grapes we should not eat for from them were the first fruits brought at Pentecost, bread we should not eat because from it they would bring the two loaves and the showbread, water we should not drink because from it they would pour on Tabernacles." They were silent. He said to them, "to mourn too much is impossible and not to mourn at all is impossible. So the rabbis said, 'let a man lime his house with limestone and leave a small piece in memory of Jerusalem, let a man prepare all of his feast needs and leave something over in memory of Jerusalem, let a woman make jewelry and leave a little bit in memory of Jerusalem' as it says, 'If I forget you, O Jerusalem, let my right hand wither; let my tongue stick to my palate if I cease to think of you, if I do not keep Jerusalem in memory even at my happiest hour'" (Psalm 137:5-6). (Tosefta Sôṭâ 15:10-15)

82. R. Yôsî's argument can be understood to reflect the insufficiency of language in the service of the mourned loss/lack.

83. The fact that the formula generally expresses rabbinic powerlessness adds another layer of understanding to the strong assertion of power latent in arguably the most famous iteration of this formula found at Bĕrākôt 8a: "Rab Ḥîyyā bar 'Ammî said in the name of 'Ûllā, 'From the day the Temple was destroyed, the Holy One, blessed be He, only has in his world the four cubits of Halakhah.'" The statement is arguably the quintessential description of Judaism's transition from a Temple-based religion to one predicated on rabbinic law. One reason the formulation is compelling is its simultaneous replication in form (through the use of the property notion of four cubits of personal space as in Mishnah 'Erûbîn 1:4) of what it claims in content—namely that God's space has shifted from physical construction to theoretical construct. But this famous terse formulation is not so innocent; the purpose of this text is an assertion of authority over God. By cloaking such a text in a formulaic expression of powerlessness, the author masks its aspirations.

84. One could also imagine the attempt to lose oneself in legal statutes as deriving similarly from rabbinic anxiety about their own power.

85. Brooks ("Narrativity of the Law") considers such hermeticism an inherently problematic part of American law as well.

Chapter 3

1. I have in mind traditional histories that begin with and continue the traditions of *'Iggeret Rab Šĕrîrā Gaôn* and *Sēper Haqabbālâ*. Works of this kind continue to proliferate in contemporary traditional circles.

2. For a more rigorous and somewhat overlapping treatment of rabbinic historiography, see Seth Schwartz, "Historiography on the Jews in the Talmudic Period," in *The Oxford Handbook of Jewish Studies*, ed. Martin Goodman, Jeremy Cohen, and David Sorkin (Oxford: Oxford University Press, 2002); and Seth Schwartz, "The Political Geography of Rabbinic Texts," in *The Cambridge Companion to the Talmud and Rabbinic Literature*, ed. Charlotte Elisheva Fonrobert and Martin S. Jaffee (Cambridge: Cambridge University Press, 2007).

3. I. M. Jost, *Allgemeine Geschichte des israelitischen Volkes, sowohl seines zweimaligen Staatslebens als auch der zerstreuten Gemeinden und Sekten bis in die neueste Zeit . . . aus den Quellen* (Berlin: C. F. Amelang, 1832); Heinrich Graetz, *History of the Jews*, 6 vols., ed. Bella Löwy (Philadelphia: Jewish Publication Society of America, 1891–98); Isaak Halevy, *Dôrôt Ha-Rîšonîm* (Frankfurt am Main: Slobotzky, 1901); Isaac Hirsch Weiss, *Dôr Dôr Wĕ-Dôrshāyw* 5 vols. (Vilna: Romm, 1904); Gedalia Alon, *Jews, Judaism, and the Classical World: Studies in Jewish History in the Times of the Second Temple and Talmud* (Jerusalem: Magnes Press, 1977); and Gedalia Alon, *The Jews in Their Land in the Talmudic Age, 70–640 C.E.* (Jerusalem: Magnes Press, Hebrew University, 1980).

4. See, for example, Louis Finkelstein, *Akiba: Scholar, Saint and Martyr* (New York: Covici, 1936).

5. Jacob Neusner, *A Life of Yohanan ben Zakkai, ca. 1–80 C.E*, 2nd ed., Studia Post-Biblica, vol. 6 (Leiden: Brill, 1970).

6. For a comprehensive overview of rabbinic historiography, see Schwartz, "Historiography on the Jews in the Talmudic Period."

7. See, for example, Seth Schwartz, *Imperialism and Jewish Society, 200 B.C.E. to 640 C.E.*, Jews, Christians, and Muslims from the Ancient to the Modern World (Princeton, N.J.: Princeton University Press, 2001).

8. See the description of the Babylonian context in Schwartz, "Historiography on the Jews in the Talmudic Period"; Schwartz, "Political Geography of Rabbinic Texts."

9. Jacob Neusner, *A History of the Jews in Babylonia*, Studia Post-Biblica (Leiden: E. J. Brill, 1965), 2:204. Ben-Menahem (*Judicial Deviation in Talmudic Law*, 33) credits Y. Weissberg, "'Ôdôt Batê Dîn Bi-Zĕman Ha-Talmûd," *Festschrift zu M. A. Bloch* (Budapest: Singer és Wolfner, 1905), with the observation that such stories are more historically reliable.

10. See Gafni's *Yahadût Bābel Û-Môsdôtehā Bi-Tĕqûpat Ha-Talmûd* (Jerusalem: Zalman Shazar Center, 1975); "Yĕšîbâ Û-Mĕṭibtā," *Zion* 43 (1978); "Maʿaśĕh Bêt Dîn Bĕ-Talmûd Ha-Bablî," *Proceedings of the American Academy of Jewish Research* 49 (1982); and *Yĕhûdê Babel Bi-Tĕqûpat Ha-Talmûd* (Jerusalem: Zalman Shazar Center, 1990); and Goodblatt's "History of the Babylonian Academies," in *The Cambridge History of*

Judaism, vol. 4, *The Late Roman Rabbinic Period*, ed. Steven T. Katz (Cambridge: Cambridge University Press, 2006) and *Rabbinic Instruction in Sasanian Babylonia*.

11. Hayden V. White, *Tropics of Discourse: Essays in Cultural Criticism* (Baltimore: Johns Hopkins University Press, 1978), 84.

12. Schwartz, "Political Geography of Rabbinic Texts."

13. Jacob Neusner, *A History of the Jews in Babylonia*, Studia Post-Biblica (Leiden: E. J. Brill, 1965), 3:265–71.

14. For the role of Zionism, see Schwartz, "Historiography on the Jews in the Talmudic Period."

15. There is a tendency within talmudic historiography to focus heavily on divisions (between amoraic and stammaitic, between Babylonia and Israel). In a recent work, Richard Kalmin (*Jewish Babylonia Between Persia and Roman Palestine*) revives the work of Zvi Dor that considers the fourth generation of amoraim a more significant watershed.

16. This is evident both from Tosefta and from Mishnaic citations to earlier works of Mishnah.

17. For a fuller treatment of this material, see Segal, *Case Citation in the Babylonian Talmud*; Gafni, "Maʿăśēh Bêt Dîn Bĕ-Talmûd Ha-Bablî," 226–32; and Gafni, *Yĕhûdê Babel Bi-Tĕqûpat Ha-Talmûd*.

18. Louis Finkelstein and H. S. Horovitz, *Sifre Deuteronomy* (Berlin: Ha-Aggûdâ ha-Tarbûtît ha-Yĕhûdîm bĕ-Germāniyâ, 1940), 230, puts the commandment on the litigants. Menahem Kahana, ed., *Sifre Zuta on Deuteronomy: Citations from a New Tannaitic Midrash* (in Hebrew), including text of Jeshua ben Judah's commentary on Deuteronomy (Jerusalem: Magnes, 2002), 284 n. 6, corrects this on the basis of a lower critical reconstruction and argues that the commandment is on the judges to force the litigants to stand. There is no evidence for that reading in the present text.

19. Based on Vatican 156. Other witnesses have "the two of them."

20. This implied "but" is explicated in Vatican 140 and 156, Munich 95, and Florence II-I-9. I have translated on the basis of Vatican 140, but Vatican 156, Munich 95, Florence II-I-9, and the print editions all add "What is a prohibition?" This line is found in parallel texts at Tosefta Sanhedrîn 6:2, Siprā Qĕdôšîm 2:4, ʾĀbôt Dĕrabbî Nātān A 10, Palestinian Talmud Yômā 5:7 (43b), and modified slightly at Palestinian Talmud Šĕbûʿôt 4:7 (35b). It is absent from Palestinian Talmud Sanhedrîn 3:8 (21c). The Palestinian Talmud evidence points to an addition from Tosefta; the same might be happening here. I discuss the ramifications of this additional line below.

21. The abbreviated verb is completed as a singular form in Pesaro and subsequent print editions, but context calls for a plural—the court would be telling the litigant to shorten his words.

22. Vatican 140 and Florence II-I-9 read "Rābā."

23. Vatican 140, Munich 95, and Florence II-I-9 nest Rab Hûnā's limitation within ʿŪllā's limitation by saying that the *baraita*'s argument refers to litigants during deliberations, as opposed to litigants during the verdict or witnesses during deliberations. Pesaro's

text, however, leaves open the possibility that Rab Hûnā's statement is completely independent of 'Ûllā's, with both attempting to limit the scope of the argument. 'Ûllā maintains that everyone agrees that *the witnesses* are required to stand based on the verse. Rab Hûnā maintains that *all present* must stand during the verdict. Rab Hûnā might believe, though, that witnesses need not stand during their testimony or other deliberations and certainly that such a posture would not be governed by a biblical mandate.

24. Florence II-I-9 adds a line that equates witnesses with the time of the verdict. This statement once again attempts to say that Rab Hûnā agrees with 'Ûllā's hypothesis that witnesses must stand; only this time, the witnesses are standing because their testimony is akin to the time of the verdict. Though the very point of this appendage seems to be to justify 'Ûllā's position through the derivative use of Exodus 18:13, *Halākôt Gĕdôlôt* and *Midraš Haggādôl* on Deuteronomy 19:17 add a reference to Deuteronomy 19:17. The Pesaro *editio princeps* completes the reference to Deuteronomy 19:17. Because this position is really a second scriptural derivation, it becomes a full-blown independent version in *Yalqûṭ Šimʿônî Yitrô* 270. The Vilna edition attempts to clarify the nature of this second position by stating it as an alternative text and beginning again at the beginning of the sentence. Rabbinovicz (*Seper Diqdûqê Sôprîm*, Šĕbûʿôt, p. 58) observes that one cannot require judges to sit from Deuteronomy 19:17. Such a position is only mandated by Vilna's attempt to turn a simple addition into a complete alternate position.

25. James Kugel, "Two Introductions to Midrash," *Prooftexts* 3, no. 2 (1983); Yosef Hayim Yerushalmi, *Zakhor, Jewish History and Jewish Memory*, Samuel and Althea Stroum Lectures in Jewish Studies (Seattle: University of Washington Press, 1982).

26. The implicit bracketed word is explicated in Yad Harav Herzog 1.

27. The implicit bracketed word is explicated in Florence II-I-9, Karlsruhe-Reuchlin 2, and the Barko edition princeps.

28. The first half of the verse evokes the language of Qôraḥ's rebellion at Numbers 16:3, while the second half evokes the Golden Calf of Exodus 32:4, 8.

29. The idea that only davidic kings may sit in the Temple appears as the basis of redactive questions at BT Yômā 25a and 69b, and PT Pĕsāḥîm 5:10 (34d), and Sôṭā 7:7 (21a). The existence of tannaitic statements in these passages that contradict suggests that the principle was not well known or uniformly held within the tannaitic period, but becomes uniformly held in the amoraic period. In all of these instances, the Talmuds adopt compromise answers. The Babylonian Talmud suggests that the event took place in the women's gallery, while the Palestinian Talmud asserts that the individuals are leaning against the wall—a physical compromise reminiscent of what we will see below with R. Naḥmān.

30. Adam Lehto, "Divine Law, Asceticism and Gender in Aphrahat's *Demonstrations*, with a Complete Annotated Translation of the Text and Comprehensive Syriac Glossary" (Ph.D. diss., University of Toronto, 2003), 310.

31. Jastrow, *Dictionary of the Targumim*, 939.

32. J. N. Epstein and E. Z. Melamed, *Mĕkîltā Dĕ-Rabbî Šimʿôn Ben Yôḥa'y* (Jerusalem: Mĕqîṣê Nirdāmîm, 1955), 131–32. The second half of the story appears in the

critical edition in the small letters associated with reconstruction from Midraš Haggādôl rather than the large letters of the midrash as found in the Cairo Genizah.

33. The rhetoric is an especially powerful critique of the *sugya*'s claim that rabbinic honor is really God's honor.

34. See Shamma Friedman, "A Good Story Deserves Retelling: The Unfolding of the Akiva Legend," in *Creation and Composition*, ed. Jeffrey L. Rubenstein (Tübingen: Mohr Siebeck, 2005). For the slippage between Rābā and Rab Pāppā, see Tosafot Bābā Qammā 67b, "Rābā 'Āmar."

35. There are two earlier amoraim with this name that are more prominent, but this individual must be a contemporary of Rab Pāppā.

36. Note the statement attributed to R. 'El'āzār toward the end of the *sugya*: "Any rabbi who does not stand for his teacher is called wicked, will not live long and will forget his learning, as it says (Ecclesiastes 8:13) 'and it will not be well with the scoundrel, and he will not live long, because he does not revere God.'"

37. In fact, the statement of Rab Joseph in a series of midrashim seems a random product of free association unless you read the entire *sugya* and recognize its importance to the later discussion.

38. Vatican 140 attributes this midrash to the tanna R. Yose. Either this is the original and Joseph is the expansion of an abbreviation or vice versa.

39. *'Aggadōt Hatalmûd* makes this another alternative reading of the same *baraita*.

40. An additional *yāpeh* is added in Vatican 140 and 156, Munich 95, and Florence II-I-9.

41. While the translation "kinsman" cited above (from Jewish Publication Society, *Tanakh*, 185) has the same connotation as Rab Joseph's midrash, it hardly implies a normative instruction to act inequitably to nonkinsmen.

42. Mar bar Rab 'Aši's argument bears a strong resemblance to the reasons provided in the Talmud why a man cannot testify against his spouse. See BT Běkôrôt 35b.

43. Vatican 140 and Florence II-I-9 add the honorific "Rab" for this individual while Munich 95 and the Pesaro *editio princeps* provide the full name Rab 'Ûllā son of Rab 'Illā'i. I speculate that this addition is made so that the reader will not assume that the 'Ûllā in question is the Palestinian second-generation amora who is generally referenced, simply, as 'Ûllā and who appears later in this *sugya*. Instead, 'Ûllā bar Rab 'Illā'î, a third-generation Babylonian amora, is identified. Because the point of the story is that this individual is being honored because of R. Joseph's introduction, the addition is unnecessary as the story could refer to any 'Ûllā. The story of Rab 'Ānān sending an unknown individual to Rab Naḥmān at Kětûbôt 105b also argues for an unknown 'Ûllā.

44. I have translated based on Munich 95. All other witnesses have some description of 'Ûllā as a friend.

45. I have translated based on Florence II-I-9. All other witnesses attribute an internal monologue to Rab Naḥmān. This omniscient narration is in keeping with the story at Kětûbôt 105b and the goose story found later in this passage.

46. Jastrow, *Dictionary of the Targumim*, 485. The root may be related to pollution as in Numbers 35:33 and other biblical sources.

47. The implicit bracketed word is explicated in Vatican 140, Munich 95, Florence II-I-9, and Pesaro.

48. The implicit bracketed word is explicated in Pesaro.

49. Abraham Weiss, *Lĕ-Ḥēqer Ha-Talmûd* (New York: Feldheim, 1954); Abraham Weiss, ʿ*Al Ha-Yĕṣîrâ Ha-Siprûtît Šel Ha-ʾamôraʾîm* (New York, 1961).

50. The implicit bracketed word is explicated in Vatican 140 and Florence II-I-9. Pesaro and *ʾAgadōt Hatalmûd* enumerate the ṣûrbā mērabbānān and am haarez by name here by saying "We seat the ṣûrbā mērabbānān and to the am haarez we also say 'sit' but if he stands, it is not our concern."

51. Rashi claims the root *btš* (pester) for this word and suggests a meaning of bothering, but the word is not attested elsewhere.

52. Pesaro and *ʾAggadōt Hatalmûd* simplify the language by saying that "we seat the ṣûrbā mērabbānān and tell the am haarez to sit, but if [the am haarez] stands, it is not our business."

53. Lee I. Levine (*The Rabbinic Class of Roman Palestine in Late Antiquity* [Jerusalem: Yad Izhak Ben-Zvi; New York: Jewish Theological Seminary of America, 1989], 68 n. 121) writes: "The Babylonian Talmud uses such terms as *Rabānān* or *Ṣûrbā Mērabbānān* to designate the lesser members of the academy."

54. The implicit bracketed words are explicated in Vatican 140, Florence II-I-9, and Pesaro. This parallels the below passage in which all text witnesses have these words.

55. The implicit bracketed words are explicated in Vatican 140 and Florence II-I-9.

56. The "house of judges" as a courtroom term is unattested elsewhere and some have taken it to refer to the judge's residence. Munich 95 and Florence II-I-9 attempt to clarify by turning "to the house" into "in front of" but this ultimately doesn't work with the singular enclitic of "before it."

57. At Šabbāt 23b Rābā says, "one who loves the rabbis will have children who are rabbis, if one values rabbis, one will have in-laws who are rabbis, one who is in awe of the rabbis will become himself a ṣûrbā mērabbānān and if he is incapable, his words will be heard as if he were a ṣûrbā mērabbānān." Here the term means both a rabbi in training and a rabbi for purposes of respect. Benjamin Mermelstein, "Ṣûrbā Mērabbānān," in *Abhandlungen zur Erinnerung an Hirsch Perez Chajes*, ed. V. Aptowitzer and A. Z. Schwartz (Vienna: Alexander Kohut Memorial Foundation, 1933), suggests that the word ṣûrbā originally meant "deer" and referred to the young student in the academy. Over time the word evolved to include even the old and distinguished.

58. Aharon Oppenheimer, *The Am Ha-Aretz: A Study in the Social History of the Jewish People in the Hellenistic-Roman Period*, trans. I. H. Levine, Arbeiten zur Literatur und Geschichte des Hellenistischen Judentums 8 (Leiden: E. J. Brill, 1977); Solomon Zeitlin, "The Am Haarez: A Study in the Social and Economic Life of the Jews Before and After the Destruction of the Second Temple," *Jewish Quarterly Review* 23, no. 1 (1932).

59. Stephen G. Wald, "Am Ha-Areẓ," in *Encyclopaedia Judaica*, ed. Fred Skolnick and Michael Berenbaum (Detroit: Macmillan Reference, 2007); Jeffrey L. Rubenstein, *The Culture of the Babylonian Talmud* (Baltimore: Johns Hopkins University Press, 2003).

60. Rubenstein, *Culture of the Babylonian Talmud*; Stephen G. Wald, *Pereq 'ēlû 'ôbrîn: Bablî Pĕsāḥîm, Pereq Šĕlîšî* (New York: Jewish Theological Seminary of America, 2000); and Wald, "Am Haarez."

61. Wald ("Am Ha-Areẓ," 67) writes: "As a result, the varying rabbinic descriptions and testimonies which either describe or characterize the *am ha-areẓ* should be understood as reflecting variations in the self-perception and self-definition of the rabbinic elite."

62. Rubenstein, *Culture of the Babylonian Talmud*; Wald, "Am Ha-Areẓ."

63. Pesaro adds that "[the opponent] will certainly say that [the *ṣûrbā mērabbānān*] is busy with his regular learning [and not discussing or deciding the pressing case]."

64. Isaiah Gafni, "The Political, Social, and Economic History of Babylonian Jewry, 224–638 CE," in *The Cambridge History of Judaism*, vol. 4, *The Late Roman-Rabbinic Period*, ed. Steven T. Katz (Cambridge: Cambridge University Press, 2006); Jeffrey L. Rubenstein, "The Rise of the Babylonian Rabbinic Academy: A Reexamination of the Talmudic Evidence," *Jewish Studies, an Internet Journal* 1 (2002).

65. Michael L. Satlow, *Creating Judaism: History, Tradition, Practice* (New York: Columbia University Press, 2006), 196.

66. Goodblatt, *Rabbinic Instruction in Sasanian Babylonia*, 108–53.

67. Shalom Albeck, *Batê Ha-Dîn Bî-Yĕmê Ha-Talmûd* (Ramat Gan: Bar Ilan University, 1980).

68. Gafni, *Yĕhûdê Babel Bi-Tĕqûpat Ha-Talmûd*; Geoffrey Herman, "Rāšût Ha-Gôlâ Bĕ-Babel Bi-Tĕqûpat Ha-Talmûd" (Ph.D. diss., Hebrew University, 2005); Neusner, *History of the Jews in Babylonia*; and Schwartz, "Political Geography of Rabbinic Texts."

69. Albeck, *Batê Ha-Dîn Bî-Yĕmê Ha-Talmûd*; and Shalom Albeck, *Mābo La-Mišpat Hā-'ibri Bi-Yĕmê Ha-Talmûd* (Ramat Gan: Bar Ilan University, 1999).

70. Gafni, "Ma'aśêh Bêt Dîn Bĕ-Talmûd Ha-Bablî"; Gafni, *Yĕhûdê Babel Bi-Tĕqûpat Ha-Talmûd*; and Goodblatt, *Rabbinic Instruction in Sasanian Babylonia*.

71. Ryle, *Collected Papers*, 2:480–96.

72. Geertz, *Interpretation of Cultures*.

73. Stephen Greenblatt, "The Touch of the Real," *Representations* 59 (Summer 1997).

74. Geertz, *Interpretation of Cultures*, 7.

75. Ibid., 7–9.

76. Greenblatt, "Touch of the Real," 15.

77. Ibid.

78. Ibid.

79. Ibid., 17–18.

80. Geertz, *Interpretation of Cultures*, 19.

81. Florence II-I-9 has Mĕrêmar.

82. Pesaro uses a plural form to indicate that 'Amêmar "seated all of them." While

there is no need for equality here since R. Yêmar is a witness rather than a litigant, it stands to reason that Mar Zûtrā would also have merited being seated because of his own stature.

83. BT Zĕbāḥîm 16a.

84. Pesaro claims that this question is posed by R. 'Ašî to 'Amêmar. The subsequent verb "say" is a reply by 'Amêmar to R. 'Ašî. Pesaro is trying to fend off the search for the identity of the final speaker.

85. Who is the final speaker here? Pesaro tries to make 'Amêmar the final speaker, but it seems that this last statement is a quotation. It is possible that the text here explicitly marks a transfer from BT Kĕtûbôt 105b. Tanḥûmā makes 'Amêmar the final speaker. This could be the source for Pesaro.

86. Pesaro makes the father's name Šerbîā, while Florence II-I-9 turns the son into Rabbâ.

87. Vatican 140, Munich 95, and Florence II-I-9 add that Rab had an opponent in this litigation.

88. The implicit bracketed term is explicated in Pesaro.

89. Pesaro and the margins of Vatican 140 continue "And Rab Pāppā absolutely did not tell him to sit."

90. The implicit bracketed name is explicated in Vatican 140, Munich 95, and Florence II-I-9.

91. The implicit bracketed word is added in Vatican 140, Munich 95, and Florence II-I-9.

92. Sokoloff, *Dictionary of Jewish Babylonian Aramaic*, 900, defines this as "the messenger of the court who has not been bribed by me." I do not think this is necessary; once the litigant distinguishes between bailiff and judge, he can still consider the judge impartial.

93. The limiting function of the *stam* is sometimes performed by later amoraim. See Šĕbûʿôt 41a in which Rab 'Ašî suggests that a *ṣûrbā mērabbānān* has credibility without an oath, and Rab Yêmar asks, "Because he is a *ṣûrbā mērabbānān*, he can take other people's shirts?"

94. Richard Kalmin (*Sages, Stories, Authors, and Editors*, 82–83) discusses the fact that Hûnā is generally considered greater than Naḥmān in the academic context but not in the judicial. Compare Herman, "Rāšût Ha-Gôlâ Bĕ-Babel Bi-Tĕqûpat Ha-Talmûd," 108.

95. Pesaro has Rab Naḥmān speaking to himself using the first person plural.

96. Vatican 140, Munich 95, and Florence II-I-9 explicate that he will look like "one who gets up before a goose."

97. Rab Naḥmān's attention to the ritualized rules of procedure and the ways in which rituals of respect, treated formalistically, undermine their purpose is echoed in the following story told about Marie-Antoinette's levee in David I. Kertzer, *Ritual, Politics, and Power* (New Haven, Conn.: Yale University Press, 1988), 106.

This extravagant ritualization could take on a life of its own, just because to change precedent meant to change rank. The results were occasionally ludicrous. The *levée* (rising from bed) of the French king and queen formed part of this system of ritually denoting rank. When the seventeenth-century king, Louis XIV, got out of bed it was no simple matter: dozens of aristocrats and others were involved in a complex choreography of power. Still in the eighteenth century, Marie-Antoinette underwent such a rite each morning. The queen's maid of honor had the right to give her her chemise, while the lady-in-waiting then helped her get into her petticoat and dress. If, however, a royal princess happened to be present, she had the honor of putting the chemise on the queen. One day, after Marie-Antoinette had been entirely undressed by her attendants, the maid of honor was about to give her her chemise when in walked the Duchess of Orléans. Attentive to the duchess's higher rank, the maid of honor handed the chemise back to the chambermaid, so that she could then pass it to the duchess. No sooner had the duchess acquired the chemise than the higher-ranking Countess of Provence made her entry. Though the queen still stood entirely naked before the noble crowd, the duchess had no choice but to pass the chemise back to the chambermaid, so that it could then be given to the countess. Fortunately for the queen, the countess was able to get the chemise to her before any higher-ranking noblewoman arrived.

98. Pesaro adds the first half of Rab Hûnā's statement.
99. Geertz, *Interpretation of Cultures*, 5.
100. Simha Assaf, *Těšûbôt Ha-Gě'ônîm* (Jerusalem, 1928), 100.
101. Gideon Libson, *Jewish and Islamic Law: A Comparative Study of Custom During the Geonic Period*, Harvard Series in Islamic Law 1 (Cambridge, Mass.: Islamic Legal Studies Program, Harvard Law School, 2003), 105–7.
102. Berachyahu Lifshitz, "Minhāg Měbaṭēl Halākâ," *Sinai* 86, nos. 1–2 (1980); Israel M. Ta-Shma, *Minhag 'Ašqěnaz Ha-Qadmôn: Ḥēqer Wě-'Îyûn* (Jerusalem: Magnes, Hebrew University, 1992), 61–85.
103. For a related analysis of the relationship between law and custom, see Ta-Shma, *Minhag 'Ašqěnaz Ha-Qadmôn*, 61–85.

Chapter 4

1. For a thorough collection of texts related to rabbinic education and an appendix describing secondary sources about rabbinic education, see Marc G. Hirshman, *The Stabilization of Rabbinic Culture, 100 C.E.–350 C.E.: Texts on Education and Their Late Antique Context* (New York: Oxford University Press, 2009).
2. Goodblatt, *Rabbinic Instruction in Sasanian Babylonia*.
3. Schwartz, *Imperialism and Jewish Society*.

4. See studies cited in ibid., 111 no. 20.

5. Schwartz, "Political Geography of Rabbinic Texts," 90–93; Herman, "Rāšût Ha-Gôlâ Bĕ-Babel Bi-Tĕqûpat Ha-Talmûd."

6. Schwartz, *Imperialism and Jewish Society*, 121.

7. See *Rašbam* Exodus 22:6.

8. See Epstein and Melamed, *Mĕkîltā Dĕ-Rabbî Šim'ôn Ben Yôḥa'y*, 206–7; Tosefta Bābā Mĕṣî'ā 8:20–21; BT Bābā Mĕṣî'ā 95a; and PT Bābā Mĕṣî'ā 8:1, 11c–d.

9. The contextual *pĕšaṭ* reading of *Rašbam* Exodus 22:6 that distinguishes between objects watched does not presume such an understanding. Rather, it connects liability to the presumed level of commitment to watch implied by the arrangement. By agreeing to watch an animal rather than an object, the bailee accepts a greater level of responsibility.

10. For a rich discussion of these issues, see David Henshke, *Mišnâ Rišônâ Bĕ-Talmûdam Šel Tannā'îm 'aḥărônîm: Sugyôt Bĕ-Dînê Šômrîm* (Ramat Gan: Bar Ilan University, 1997).

11. The debate over the meaning of *wĕnišbar 'ûmēt* (and it is crippled or it dies) is relevant for determining the verse's rationale. A prior verse (Exodus 22:9) contains the triad *ûmēt 'ô nišbar 'ô nišbâ* (and it dies or is crippled or taken captive). The absence of the third term for captivity in our verse and the change in order present the initial problems of understanding this verse. The Septuagint reverses the order and contains the third term (though it changes the form of the verb for death from τελετάω in verse 9 to ἀποθνήσκω). It is possible that this reversal and addition represent an original text, or (after *lectio difficilior*) the work of an early tradent bothered by the problems in the Masoretic text. Abraham Geiger, *Ha-Miqrā Wĕ-Targûmāyw*, trans. Y. L. Barukh (Jerusalem: Môsad Bialik 1949), 302–3, assumes that the difficulty of the missing term prompted some Samaritan versions to omit the middle word *'ô* (or) and replace it with a *waw* (and), which creates a hendiadys: "it was crippled and died." This variant confirms the order of the Masoretic text and explains why this text is different from verse 9—in this case the verse describes a two-step process. Though this beautifully explains the verse, it is again possible that the Masoretic text's confusion caused the change in the Samaritan texts. Shalom M. Paul, *Studies in the Book of the Covenant in the Light of Cuneiform and Biblical Law*, Supplements to Vetus Testamentum (Leiden: E. J. Brill, 1970), 94, explains that the new JPS translation "it dies of injuries" is based on the Akkadian parallel in Nuzi documents wherein the hendiadys seen in the Samaritan texts is clear. Naphtali Herz Tur-Sinai, *Pĕšûṭô Šel Miqrā* (Jerusalem: Qiryat Sēper, 1962), 1:118–20, speculates that the original text had different terms in both verse 13 and the end of verse 14. Verse 13 had *wĕnišbâ 'ô mēt* (it was taken captive or died) and 14 had *'im šābûr hû' bā bišbārô* (if it were broken, it comes in its brokenness). This allows us to understand full payment for a missing or dead animal, and partial payment for a broken one. While this reading fits well with the context in Exodus 22, Henshke (*Mišnâ Rišônâ*, 202, no. 4) correctly criticizes this hypothesis as highly speculative. A possible support for the hendiadys might be found in the midrashic text found in both Mĕkiltôt and the later cited Tosefta. In this text we read "it fell and died" in place of *wĕnišbar 'ô mēt* (it was crippled or died).

Perhaps this hendiadys reflects an initial biblical text of *wĕnišbar 'ûmēt* (it was crippled and died).

12. It is possible that the biblical text meant to include renting within borrowing unlike later rabbinic readers. That would make even more sense with the exception.

13. Tosefta Bābā Mĕṣîʿā 8:20–21 and Mishnah Bābā Mĕṣîʿā 8:1.

14. Tosefta Bābā Mĕṣîʿā 8:20. The Mishnah, here the later text (Henshke, *Mišnâ Rišônâ*, 56, no. 204), omits the phrase that indicates this position, an omission that arguably opens the door to Rab Hamĕnûnâ's statement on Bābā Mĕṣîʿā 95a requiring physical as well as contractual presence.

15. *Pisqē Hāroš* Bābā Mĕṣîʿā 8:6 reads "Rab 'Ašî" here. This is likely an orthographic shift from "Rābā" to "Rab 'A." Halivni, *Mĕqôrôt Û-Mĕsôrôt: Bābā Qammā*, 449, no. 7, cites other examples of this phenomenon.

16. This statement in parentheses, missing from the Florence II-I-8, Hamburg 165, and Cremona T. IV 10 manuscripts, is probably an explanatory addition.

17. This scenario strains the formal definition of owner presence, since the finite act of pouring is independent of the borrowing and is terminated before the borrowing commences. *Šiṭâ*, cited in *Šiṭâ Mĕqûbeṣet*, explains that the borrower performs the act of acquiring the animal while in the process of pouring. An analogous position is found in the Hebrew/Judaeo-Arabic commentary in S. Schechter, Louis Ginzberg, and Israel Davidson, *Ginzê Shekter*, 3 vols., Texts and Studies of the Jewish Theological Seminary of America (Jerusalem: Hôṣa'at Maqôr, 1969), 2:392. *'Ôr Zārûʿa* (Bābā Mĕṣîʿā 8:311) explains that the borrowing transpires between the verbal commitment to pour and the act of pouring. *Talmîd Hārašba* (Moshe Yehuda Blau, *Šiṭat Ha-Qadmônîm: ʿal Maseket Baba Mĕṣîʿâ* [New York: n.p., 1966], 251) suggests that the borrowing transpires after the act of pouring, but that the verbal commitment connects the discrete actions and creates owner presence. Furthermore, this scholar is so taken by the simple reading of this passage that he interprets the Mishnah's requirement of owner priority to describe such a case.

These solutions recall similar ones regarding a passage on Bābā Mĕṣîʿā 81a–b. In that passage, the *stam* responds to two tannaitic sources that describe exchanges in watch duty by saying that these constitute owner presence. Shamma Friedman (*Talmûd 'ārûk*, II: 268–73, 88–89) notes that the notion of an owner's being present not through physical work in the hirer's domain is unparalleled in the essential texts that describe owner presence. In light of the difficulty, Friedman suggests a reading of Rab Pāppā that is independent of the *stam* and unrelated to the notion of owner presence. In the present passage, there is no possibility of separating amoraic statement from post-amoraic commentary. Rather, our passage unequivocally states that two discrete actions that place both the lender and the object in the borrower's employ can constitute owner presence though the owner's employment is terminated before the object's acquisition. Though the contract for the pitcher is never mentioned, we must assume that an oral agreement binds these actions together and that the contract can create priority/simultanaeity and owner presence. If this is the case, then Rab Pāppā (or the usage of Rab Pāppā by the author of the questions that precede his *mêmrā*) can be understood as limiting the power of contract by saying that if one contracts for actions to take place at different times, this does not constitute owner presence. This reading is explicit in Isaiah ben Mali, *Pisqê Ha-Rîd* (Jerusalem: Mākôn ha-Talmûd ha-Yiśra'elî ha-Šalem, 1964), 176.

18. All extant manuscripts have "Rābā," while the print editions based on Soncino *editio princeps* read "Rabbâ." See Friedman, "Kĕtîb Ha-Šēmôt 'Rabbâ' Wĕ-'Rābā' Bĕ-Talmûd Ha-Bablî." The intertext is significant here regardless of whether the figure in the intertext is Rabbâ the teacher or Rābā the student.

19. Meir Ayali, *'Ôṣar Kînûy 'ôbdîm Bĕ-Siprût Ha-Talmûd Wĕha-Midrāš* (Tel Aviv: Ha-Qibûṣ ha-Mĕ'uḥād, 1984), 77, notes that the term *maqrî dardĕqî* (teacher of children) is exclusive to the Babylonian Talmud.

20. This is also a Bavli exclusive term (ibid., 25). Among medieval commentators, the array of definitions for this term includes: planter (Rabbênû Ḥanan'el, *'Arûk*); public planter (Rambam, *Ginzê Shekter, Bêt Habĕḥîrâ*); sharecropper (Rashi, *Nimmûqê Yôsēp*, Rab Yĕš'ayâ 'Aḥarôn, *'Ôr Zārû'a*).

21. According to the medievals: bloodletter (Rabbênû Ḥanan'el, Rambam, *Ginzê Shekter*, Rashi 97a, *Bêt Habĕḥîrâ, Nimmûqê Yôsēp*, Rab Yĕš'ayâ 'Aḥarôn, *'Ôr Zārû'a*); circumciser (Rabbênû Ḥanan'el, *Ginzê Shekter* in name of Yēš Mĕpārśîm, Rashi Bābā Batrā 109a); barber/bloodletter (*Talmîd Hārašba*).

22. *Magîd Mishnah Sĕkirût* 10:7 suggests that the term *matā*, or town, might be distributed to every term in the list. In light of my contention in "Legal Narratives in the Babylonian Talmud" (Ph.D. diss., Columbia University, 2005), 412–24 that the term *sôpēr matā* is drawn into the *mêmrā* in Bābā Batrā 21b from the context of Bābā Batrā 21a, this cannot be sustained.

23. According to the medievals: barber (Rashi 97a, one position found in *Nimmûqê Yôsēp, 'Ôr Zārû'a*); scribe (variant cited in Rabbênû Ḥanan'el, *'Arûk*, Rambam, Rashi Bābā Batrā 22a, *Ḥiddûšê HāRîṭbā, Bêt Habĕḥîrâ, Talmîd Hārašba*, second position found in *Nimmûqê Yôsēp*, Rab Yĕš'ayâ 'Aḥarôn); barber/bloodletter (Rabbênû Ḥanan'el [Arabic term *ḥajam*]).

24. For a full treatment of the transmission history of this list, see Wimpfheimer, "Legal Narratives," 412–24.

25. See Rabbênû Ḥanan'el, *Nimmûqê Yôsēp*, Rabbênû Bārûk in Moshe Yehuda Blau, *Šiṭat Ha-Qadmônîm 'al Šalôš Babôt* (New York: n.p., 1982), 239. *Ḥiddûšê Hāran* nuances the notion of public service by claiming that these individuals are public because the public pays them.

26. In this interpretation of Rābā's ruling, I am consciously assuming a double innovation—an extension of the exception and a limitation on the same. Others have chosen to credit Rābā with only one of these or with different innovations entirely.

27. This notion has been the subject of medieval debate. Rashi and Rambam take this to mean the specific performance of duty on behalf of the borrower. This view is adopted by R. Yiṣḥāq ben Šēšet (Rîbāš), Rab Yĕš'ayâ 'Aḥarôn and *Ḥiddûšê HāRîṭbā*. Ra'bad focuses on the "time of work" and limits liability to working hours as opposed to meals

or sleeping hours. This view is found already in Rabbênû Ḥanan'el, but is promulgated in Ra'bad's name by *Ḥiddûšê Hāran*, Rabbênû Měšûlām, Roš, *Nimmûqê Yôsēp*, and *Bêt Habĕḥîrâ*. *Bêt Habĕḥîrâ* mysteriously connects Rashi's position with Ra'bad's position, though this is nowhere evident.

28. Vatican 117 and Cremona T. IV 10 change the figure of this subsequent discussion to Rab 'Ašî. *Běhag Berlin* reads "Rab." See note 15 above for an explanation of the orthographic shift.

29. The English term "service" does not capture the double entendre of the Aramaic term *šě'îl* with its inherent linguistic replication of asking—as they are doing—and borrowing—which they are claiming.

30. For scholars as students in this context, see Friedman, *Talmûd 'ārûk*, Perush, 273, no. 39; Goodblatt, *Rabbinic Instruction in Sasanian Babylonia*, 286–88.

31. MS Florence II I 8 reads *'ikpar* (it is forgiven); this is probably an orthographic shift.

32. For a fuller treatment of Torah as capital, see Chapter 5.

33. Though Rābā seems here to change the currency from money to Torah, Rabbênû Bārûk continues within the monetary currency in order to argue that since Rābā is unpaid, he is not in the students' service. Rabbênû Měšûlām reaches for the well-known Ta'anît 7a homily of teachers learning *more* from their students. Rashi ad loc. suggests that the definition of service is determined by the intent of the endeavor. If the teacher controls the topic and picks subject matter for the purpose of furthering his own education, the students are in the teacher's service in the sense that the primary goal of the enterprise is the teacher's needs. Rîbāš rejects the idea that the service direction is unidirectional when he says in responsum no. 436: "just as the students need the teacher, the teacher needs the students."

34. Whether or not these are formal Mishnaic tractates or simply subjects.

35. Michel Foucault, *Power/Knowledge: Selected Interviews and Other Writings, 1972–1977*, ed. Colin Gordon (New York: Pantheon Books, 1980).

36. The variant reading "Rabbi 'Aqîbā" exists in Oxford Add. Fol. 23 (366), while the Pesaro and subsequent printed editions read "Rabbi Ḥanînā."

37. This word is missing in the print editions and is probably an explanatory addition.

38. This text is used by Ra'bad (cited in the commentary attributed to *Ḥiddûšê HāRiṭbā* ad loc.) to explain how the students can possibly be in Rābā's service. In other words, the students function as teachers, and Rābā is complimenting the students on their teacherliness.

39. This is more fully established below in Chapter 5.

40. See Gafni's *Yahadût Babel Û-Môsdôtehā Bi-Těqûpat Ha-Talmûd*; "Yěšîbâ Û-Měṭîbtā"; "Concerning D. Goodblatt's Article," *Zion* 46 (1981); and *Yěhûdê Babel Bi-Těqûpat Ha-Talmûd*; and Goodblatt's *Rabbinic Instruction in Sasanian Babylonia*.

41. Goodblatt, *Rabbinic Instruction in Sasanian Babylonia*, 155–65.

42. Brody, *Geonim of Babylonia*, 43–50. See also Goodblatt, *Rabbinic Instruction in*

Sasanian Babylonia, 161: "The picture which emerges from Amoraic sources is generally compatible with the description, in Geonic sources, of the *kallah* of Islamic times."

43. Brody, *Geonim of Babylonia*, 43.

44. Tosefta Mĕgîllâ 3:2.

45. Rubenstein, "Rise of the Babylonian Rabbinic Academy"; Rubenstein, *Culture of the Babylonian Talmud*. For Gafni's concession, see Gafni, "Political, Social and Economic History."

46. Daniel Boyarin, *Border Lines: The Partition of Judaeo-Christianity*, Divinations (Philadelphia: University of Pennsylvania Press, 2004), 152: "Institution (Yeshiva), founding and instituting text (Talmud), theological innovation (indeterminacy of meaning and halakhic argument), and practice (endless study as worship in and of itself) all come together at this time to produce the rabbinic Judaism familiar to us until this day."

47. For more on Torah capital, see Chapter 5.

48. The classic studies are Werner Wilhelm Jaeger, *Paideia: The Ideals of Greek Culture*, 2nd ed., 3 vols. (New York and Oxford: Oxford University Press, 1986); and Henri Irénée Marrou, *A History of Education in Antiquity*, trans. George Lamb (New York: Sheed and Ward, 1956).

49. Jaeger, *Paideia*; Marrou, *History of Education in Antiquity*, 196.

50. This is similar to those who have equated Torah with philosophy. See literature cited in Boyarin, *Socrates and the Fat Rabbis*, 243–44. The comparison is implicit in E. J. Bickerman, *The Jews in the Greek Age* (Cambridge, Mass.: Harvard University Press, 1988), 171.

51. William Boyd, *The History of Western Education* (London: A. & C. Black, 1921) 61: "There is a curious irony in the fact that the Jews, in seeking to save themselves from being overborne by the Greek culture, should have adopted the Hellenic institution of the school for their children and the Hellenic practice of disputation for their young men. It is a striking testimony to the tremendous power of that culture that the one Oriental people who succeeded in freeing themselves from its influence did so by making use of its educational methods." See also Eliezer Ebner, *Elementary Education in Ancient Israel During the Tannaitic Period (10–220 C.E.)* (New York: Bloch, 1956).

52. This argument is made extensively in Nathan Morris, *The Jewish School: An Introduction to the History of Jewish Education* (London: Eyre and Spottiswoode, 1937), and Fischel, "Story and History."

53. Morris (*The Jewish School*, 20–21) writes:

> That large numbers of children, both in Palestine and Babylonia, did not attend schools in the period under discussion is abundantly clear from the picture presented to us in talmudic literature. The existence of the uneducated, or illiterate class—the "am-haarez"—and the social and religious abyss between them and the adherents of the Pharisees, is in itself sufficient to destroy any idea of "compulsory" and "universal" education among Jews of those times. The contempt, even the hate, which is so often apparent in the

relations of the educated to the "am-haarez" reminds one strongly of the arrogant attitude of the Hellene towards the Barbarian, or even to the Helot. According to a famous rabbi of the second century C.E., "One is obliged to say three blessings every day: 'Who has not made me a heathen; who has not made me a woman; who has not made me an "am-haarez."'" I. H. Weiss hears in that an echo of the practice of Socrates to thank God every day for his having been born a human being and not an animal, a man and not a woman, a Greek and not a Barbarian. And the "am-haarez," we are told on good authority, did not give his children an education: There was nobody to compel him to do it.

54. Marc Hirshman (*Stabilization of Rabbinic Culture*) dates the stress on elementary education to Rābā on the basis of the material at Bābā Batrā 20a–22b which is treated in Chapter 5.

55. Moses Aberbach, *Ha-Ḥinûk Ha-Yĕhûdî Bi-Tĕqûpat Ha-Mišnâ Wĕha-Talmûd: Meḥqārîm Wĕ-'Iyûnîm* (Jerusalem: R. Mas; Baltimore: Baltimore Hebrew College, 1982).

56. Marrou, *History of Education in Antiquity*, 160. See interestingly Adam H. Becker, *Fear of God and the Beginning of Wisdom: The School of Nisibis and Christian Scholastic Culture in Late Antique Mesopotamia*, Divinations (Philadelphia: University of Pennsylvania Press, 2006), 2–3.

57. Bickerman, *Jews in the Greek Age*, 171, notes "that the Greek idea and ideal of *paideia*, of the notion that education forms a man, had already entered Jerusalem by the end of the third century B.C.E."

58. Fischel, "Story and History."

59. Marrou, *History of Education in Antiquity*, 172.

60. Fischel, "Story and History."

61. Morris, *The Jewish School*, 74, says:

It may be noted here that the method of the Jewish high school, the talmudic method of disputation, also dates from that early period and owes a great deal to Hellenistic influence. Thus we read, for example, of a famous scholar of the second century C.E., who could effectively argue on both sides of a case, proving the unclean (ritually) to be clean and vice versa. But this was the method of the Hellenistic rhetorical school, where the students were trained to speak for and against a given proposition. Some of these propositions, suitably translated into Hebrew or Aramaic, would easily pass as of talmudic origin. It is difficult to avoid the view that this method of study, which degenerated in later generations into a mere hair-splitting casuistry, was greatly stimulated by the example of the Hellenistic school—even if it was not entirely borrowed from there.

62. Peter Robert Lamont Brown, *Augustine of Hippo: A Biography* (London: Faber, 1967).

63. See also Boyarin, "Hellenism in Jewish Babylonia"; Boyarin, *Socrates and the Fat Rabbis*; Kalmin, *Jewish Babylonia*; and Becker, *Fear of God*. Becker's work is particularly apt since it situates a Christian academy operating within *paideia* modes of education adjacent to the Babylonian locales of amoraic disciple circles and stammaitic yeshivas.

64. It is important, of course, to remember that the structures of *paideia* were also fluid with emotionally charged boundaries. Marrou (*History of Education in Antiquity*, 160) writes: "The theoretical distinction between them did not always work out in practice, however; in the 'colonial' countries the educational system may not have been fully developed, but even elsewhere the same teacher might have two sets of pupils—this apparently was the normal situation in Rhodes, the great university city in the first century B.C.E., where Aristodemus of Nysa, for example, taught rhetoric in the morning and grammar in the afternoon. . . . the grammarians ended up by annexing part of the rhetors' field, whilst the grammatists may possibly have encroached on the grammarians."

65. David Stern ("The Alphabet of Ben Sira and the Early History of Parody in Rabbinic Literature," in *The Idea of Biblical Interpretation*, ed. Hindy Najman and Judith H. Newman [Leiden: Brill, 2004]) finds other evidence of this phenomenon in the alphabet of Ben Sira.

66. Morris, *The Jewish School*, 66, notes the specifically poor treatment of teachers in *paideia* while claiming a possible difference for the Jewish context:

> In Greece the teacher's calling was not such as to give him either dignity or self-respect. To call a man a teacher was almost an insult, and even his own pupils treated him with contempt. In Rome the position was even worse. The teachers of elementary schools were socially despised. Indeed, so many slaves and freed men were employed as teachers that this could not have been otherwise. Now, there was a fundamental difference between he Hellenistic and the Jewish schools. The former was a civil institution in which religion played relatively a minor part. The latter, especially in the later period when it was usually housed in the Synagogue, was essentially a religious institution, the instruction of children being regarded as the most sacred of all commandments. It was a duty which rested primarily on the father, who, in his turn, relegated it to the teacher. In the circumstances, it may be assumed that the Jewish teacher enjoyed a higher social status than his colleagues in Greece or Rome. We shall certainly never find him spoken of in such terms as "abominable schoolmaster," "object abhorred alike by boys and girls."

Just a page later, Morris writes: "And yet it would be a mistake to jump to the conclusion that his social position was in any way enviable. Talmudic literature abounds in expressions of the deepest respect and veneration for the teacher. But quite apart from the question how much these reflect real conditions, it must always be remembered that there was a sharp distinction between the sage, the recognised teacher of the 'Oral Law,' who occupied the highest rungs of the ladder, and his humble colleague at the bottom—the elementary teacher. This distinction existed all over the world from the days of ancient Greece down to modern times. *There is no doubt at all that it was very marked also among Jews in talmudic times*" (emphasis mine).

67. On the specific opprobrium for the 'am haarez in this passage in Bavli BT Pĕsāḥîm, see Rubenstein, *Culture of the Babylonian Talmud*; and Wald, *Pereq 'ēlû 'ôbrîn*.

68. Shaye J. D. Cohen, "The Rabbi in Second Century Jewish Society," in *The Cambridge History of Judaism*, vol. 3, *The Early Roman Period*, ed. William Horbury, W. D. Davies, and John Sturdy (Cambridge: Cambridge University Press, 1999).

69. PT Yĕbāmôt 12:7 (13a); and Genesis Rabbâ 81:2. These three identities are common to both texts. The Palestinian Talmud adds the duties of a sermonizer and a cantor to the list, an addition that was, presumably, not part of the original list.

70. Marrou, *History of Education in Antiquity*, 160.

71. Schwartz, *Imperialism and Jewish Society*, 121–24.

72. Marrou, *History of Education in Antiquity*, 308–9.

73. Paralleled at Ecclesiastes Rabbâ 7:28.

74. Though the verse contributes to the exaggerated numbers involved, there is little reason to assume that the scenario it describes is false.

75. PT Bĕrākôt 4:1 (7c); Taʿanît 4:1 (67c); and Mĕgîllâ 3:6 (74b).

76. BT Bĕrākôt 30b; Yĕbāmôt 40a; and Kĕtûbôt 56a.

77. Aberbach, *Ha-Ḥinûk Ha-Yĕhûdî*, 73, claims that such derogatory treatment of the schoolteacher is uniquely Palestinian since the two sources refer to Palestinian rabbis.

78. The term "great man" is unusual and the rhetoric reflects the point of the contrast.

79. Marrou, *A History of Education in Antiquity*, 196.

80. Ibid.

81. Peter Brown, "The Saint as Exemplar in Late Antiquity," in *Saints and Virtues*, ed. John Stratton Hawley (Berkeley and Los Angeles: University of California Press, 1987), 4, writes:

> We find ourselves in a world whose central elites were held together by what Henri-Irenée Marrou has brilliantly characterized as "The Civilization of the *Paideia*." The Greco-Roman world, in which the saints later appeared, was a civilization of *paideia* in the same way as our own is a civilization of advanced technology. It invariably tended to opt for the necessary self-delusion that all its major problems could be both articulated and resolved in terms of its one major resource—in this case, by the paradigmatic behavior of elites groomed by a *paideia* in which the role of ancient exemplars was overwhelming. The tendency to see exemplary *persons* as classics was reinforced by the intensely personal manner in which the culture of *paideia* was passed on from generation to generation. Intensive male bonding between the generations lay at the heart of the "Civilization of *Paideia*." No student ever went, as we do,

to a university conceived of as an impersonal institution of learning—to Cal, MIT, or "State" (how much these abbreviations speak of our desire to take the impersonality of learning absolutely for granted!). He would always have gone to a person—to Libanius, to Origen, to Proclus. The most poignantly expressed relation in the ancient and medieval worlds was that between teacher and pupil.

82. See also the semantic range of *ḥākām* at BT ʿErûbîn 36b.

83. From our own socioeconomic perspective, it is somewhat odd that the issue of a teacher's compensation is not raised in our passage. According to the one acontextual discussion of compensation for teaching Torah that is paralleled in both Bavli and Yerushalmi, it is clear that schoolteachers who taught reading and Bible were routinely paid, and that the second-level Mishnah teachers were paid. As for the highest level, the question of amora compensation is related to the question of bureaucratization. In Palestine, where the rabbinate may have been a bourgeois profession (see note 68 above), the amora could have been paid for rabbinical duties. In Babylonia, however, there is no evidence for lecturer compensation. As we will see in the next chapter more explicitly, Rābā is consistent in his assertion, against prior legal precedent, that rabbis are allowed and even encouraged to profit from their Torah knowledge and the stature accorded them as rabbis. Such a position works particularly well with the idea that the Babylonian amoraim were not formally remunerated by their communities for being rabbis. Rather, they were paid piecework for their adjudication, and their positions as judges enabled them to find other opportunities for profit.

84. Two versions of this name circulated among the original textual witnesses—"Mar" and "Mari"—though the latter had spellings with and without an aleph. The names eventually appeared in the early printed editions as consecutive words until *Ḥokmat Šĕlômô* 3:872 merged the two into one name, as it appears in the Vilna edition: Mĕrêmar.

85. Some witnesses have "Ḥananîyâ." Rabbinovicz, *Seper Diqdûqê Sôprîm*, 5: Rosh Hashanah, p. 24, cites several examples of variation between "Ḥanînā" and "Ḥananîyâ."

86. Though the Soncino printed edition supported by Florence II-I-8 has a plural form, the singular verb form inclines us toward the singular possessive noun found in other textual witnesses.

87. The translation treats *Bê Ḥôzāʾî* as the name of a collective of individuals, though the term literally means "the house of Ḥôzāʾî." Though it is possible that the text can mean, as *Pêrûšê Yônātān Milûnîl,* Bābā Mĕṣîʿā, 38, translates, "hired his mule to take them to Bêt Ḥôzāʾî," it is possible for it to mean the people of Ḥôzāʾî, as it does in Šabbāt 51b. The explicit rendering of this meaning in Florence II-I-8 as *libnê Ḥôzāʾî* is most likely the work of a reader who understood a gap between the phrase's meaning as a location and its use as a personal noun in the passage.

88. "With them" is missing in Hamburg 165.

89. Cremona T. IV 10 and Munich 95 have a third-person singular referring either to the case or to a single litigant.

90. The implicit bracketed phrase is explicated in Hamburg 165 and Cremona. T. IV 10.

91. The introduction "Is this the law?" found in Escorial G-I-3, Vatican 115, and Florence II-I-8 is borrowed from the preceding passage at Bābā Měṣiʿā 97a.

92. The verb lĕmêsar is from the Aramaic sûr, meaning "to supervise, or examine," rather than the Hebrew sûr, meaning "to remove."

93. Goodblatt, *Rabbinic Instruction in Sasanian Babylonia*, 272, claims that students acted as apprentice lawyers in the courts of their masters. Gafni, *Yĕhûdê Babel Bi-Tĕqûpat Ha-Talmûd*, concurs. According to this view, the only breach of etiquette is in the sharpness of the comment in this case.

94. Most of the commentators whose primary interest is the elucidation of the text have ignored this passage. Their silence may be the result of the clarity of earlier commentaries such as Rabênû Ḥananʾel who paraphrases the meaning as (Blau,1966, 330): "in other words, he erred in this judgment and his students bested him." Among those commentators interested primarily in determining Jewish law, there is unanimity that the students' opinion is correct. See *Bêt Habĕḥîrâ* 354, Rambam *Šĕêylâ ûpîqqādôn* 2:2, and *Talmîd Hārašba* 252.

95. It would seem that the only standard under which this might be considered owner presence is a noncontractual formal notion of presence. Even if one would point to the case of the wily lender who opened our passage as a model for this one, in that case the lender is explicitly asked by the borrower to pour prior to the ensuing actions. *Bêt Habĕḥîrâ* infers from this story that even de facto hiring is sufficient; this is an example of allowing the story to expand precedent as a statute as in the case of the Palestinian Talmud in Chapter 2. *Yônātān Milûnîl* creatively claims that the ambiguity of no contract is the basis for the story's eventual reinterpretation within the passage. Since there was no contract, it was never owner presence. Unfortunately, this interpretation is not supported by the text.

96. This is inferred from the oath that one who watches without compensation is forced to utter: "I have not been negligent in my watching."

97. Though the biblical exemption of owner presence is raised explicitly only in the context of the borrower, the Talmud extends it through an a fortiori argument to all cases of bailee liability.

98. In the *stam*'s treatment of the debate on BT Bābā Měṣiʿā 95a, both views begin with the assumption that on balance the owner presence exemption should win as an explicit biblical verse. But the view that insists on liability even in the face of owner presence presumes that the biblical inference does not extend to either the unpaid watch-person verse or anything derived logically on the basis of that verse. The presumption of the *stam* offers a possible explanation to the composition of a story that presumes the predominance of owner presence.

99. The debate also exists in PT Šĕbûʿôt 8:1;38c. See Friedman, *Talmûd ʿārûk*, II: 274.

100. PT Šĕbûʿôt 8:1 (38c). The Palestinian Talmud frames the question around the requirement of an oath in scenarios of exoneration owing to owner presence. By

inference, the requirement of an oath guaranteeing the absence of negligence only makes sense if negligence trumps owner presence. While this inference is a necessary ramification of the Palestinian Talmud's debate, the question is perhaps concerned with a more fundamental issue pertaining to the exception of owner presence. To wit, does the exoneration of owner presence become incorporated into the liability matrix, and is it treated like the exonerations for theft and force majeure?

101. The implicit bracketed statement is found in Cremona T. IV 10, Escorial G-I-3, Vatican 117, Munich 95, and printed editions.

102. The implicit bracketed statement is found in Cremona T. IV 10 and Munich 95.

103. See n. 87.

104. Bābā Měṣîʿā 96b. Joseph Zevi Hirsch Duenner, *Ḥiddushei haRitsad* (Jerusalem: Mosad Harav Kook, 1981), 218; Zvi Karl, *Dinei ʾArba>at Ha-Šomrim Bě-Mišpaṭ Ha-ʿIbrî*, Tarbiz 7, (1935): 276; and Henshke, *Mišnâ Rišônâ*, 249, all note that this was the status quo prior to Rābāʾs innovation.

105. Bābā Měṣîʿā 93a. This case is a classic example for the Rabbâ/Rābā confusion problem; see Chapter 1, note 82. Though the predominance of textual witnesses point to Rābā, Rabbinovicz, *Seper Diqdûqê Sôprîm*, 8: Bābā Měṣîʿā, 139 no. 00, suggests based on the comments of Rab Ḥîsdā and Rabbâ bar Rab Hûnā that this must be Rabbâ. The separation between these scholars' comment and Rabbâ/Rābāʾs makes it difficult to determine source-critically whether their statement—which places a claim in the mouth of the watchman—must be understood as commenting directly on the Rabbâ/Rābā statement. Eliezer Segal, *Case Citation*, 81, argues for Rābā by claiming that the figures Rabbinovicz uses to evidence Rabbâ may have uttered comments in a different context that were subsequently directed to Rābāʾs statement. In positing that this text is Rābā, I follow Segal, with the awareness that a final determination is probably impossible.

106. Bābā Měṣîʿā 36b. Rashi makes this intertext explicit in our passage within his comments on the *stam*'s rewritten story.

107. Though arguments of empathy are difficult to make within civil cases in light of the fact that one side's loss is another's gain, the context of bailees (at least in the Talmud) is generally one of economic imbalance. Siding with the bailee is tantamount, then, to siding with the poor. Though equity might demand that the poor receive no greater stake, this sort of leaning is often a necessary corrective to the real-world realities of judicial imbalance in the opposite direction. Within American law, this is often illustrated within the notion of unconscionability and *Williams v. Walker-Thomas*. A similar notion can be found in Isaiah 11:4, which associates true justice with a correction for the poor. Some might question such a reading of Rābā as inconsistent with the biblical law that mandates that neither the rich nor the poor receive unequal treatment in light of their differing monetary situations. Yet it is undeniably the case that when Rābā rules to accept the claim, "What should he have done?" he is doing precisely that, since the legal protections offered to the wealthy bailee are breached when the wealthy litigant is made to suffer a loss while seemingly under liability protection.

108. For a consideration of the relationship between storytellers and the *stam* see Chapter 6 below.

109. BT Gîṭṭîn 29b and 77b; Bābā Měṣî'ā 81a, 81b, and 97a; and 'Abôdâ Zārâ 22a.

110. Leib Moscovitz, "The Holy One Blessed Be He . . . Does Not Permit the Righteous to Stumble," in *Creation and Composition*, ed. Jeffrey L. Rubenstein (Leiden: Brill, 2005).

111. Friedman, *Talmûd 'Ārûk*, notes that the formula is almost unique to Rābā, with two exceptional cases with Rab Pāpā.

Chapter 5

1. Pierre Bourdieu, *The Rules of Art: Genesis and Structure of the Literary Field*, trans. Susan Emanuel (Cambridge: Polity Press, 1996).

2. Ibid., 3.

3. Ibid., 32.

4. The assumption of the randomness of talmudic composition and the discovery of deep structure animates Jacobs, *Structure and Form in the Babylonian Talmud*, and Jacobs, *Rabbinic Thought in the Talmud*.

5. Shamma Friedman, "Mibneh Siprûtî Šel Sûgîyôt Habablî," *Proceedings of the World Congress of Jewish Studies* 6, no. 3 (1977).

6. See Cohen, *Rereading Talmud*; Kraemer, *Mind of the Talmud*; and Kraemer, *Reading the Rabbis*.

7. Shamma Friedman, "Lĕ-'Aggādâ Ha-Hîsṭôrît Bĕ-Talmûd Ha-Bablî," in *Seper Ha-Zikārôn Lĕ-Rabbî Shaul Lieberman*, ed. Shamma Friedman (Jerusalem: Jewish Theological Seminary of America, 1993); Shamma Friedman, "The Further Adventures of Rav Kahana," in *The Talmud Yerushalmi and Graeco-Roman Culture*, ed. Peter Schafer (Tübingen: Mohr Siebeck, 2002); Shamma Friedman, "A Good Story Deserves Retelling: The Unfolding of the Akiva Legend," in *Creation and Composition*, ed. Jeffrey L. Rubenstein (Tübingen: Mohr Siebeck, 2005); and Rubenstein, *Talmudic Stories*.

8. Boyarin, *Carnal Israel*, 10–16; Rubenstein, *Talmudic Stories*, 3–15.

9. Hirshman, *Stabilization of Rabbinic Culture*.

10. Rab Dîmmî punctuates his point with a midrashic story that claims one of David's military mistakes was performed on the basis of a mispronunciation of the biblical text.

11. This passage contains several difficulties for translation. Rābā says that we do not fire the first teacher "lest he come to be slack." It's clear that the teacher who is being fired is the first, i.e., the less learned one. But the antecedent of "he" in Rābā's explanatory clause, "lest he become slack," is unclear. The ambiguity of the third person singular leaves open the possibility that we are talking about either of the two teachers. Also, only the print editions contain an intransitive verb form ("to become slack"); the other variants have a transitive verb form ("to slacken someone/something"). Within Rab Dîmmî's statement the problem of the ambiguous third singular is compounded by the fact that the first syllable *dĕ* of his term *dĕgārîs* can be taken either as a marker of indirect statement ("all the more so [it is the case that] he would learn") or as a relative pronoun

("all the more so [the one] who is [more] learned"). Moreover, some manuscripts read Rābā's explanatory clause in the plural: "lest they become/make slack."

Another problematic aspect of this debate is Rab Dîmmî's use of the "all the more so." This statement implies that his reasoning and Rābā's share a conceptual basis. These and other factors animate the commentarial debates of medieval interpreters. Rî Mîgāš assumes that the entire argument centers on the first teacher. To wit, Rābā is worried that the first teacher will become personally disappointed. Such disappointment will cause this teacher to stop learning and take a step backward because the teacher will forget what was already known. In order to make this argument, Rî Mîgāš understands Rab Dîmmî's statement as referring to the first teacher who, upon being fired, will be motivated to improve upon the second teacher. Rashi assumes the entire argument centers around the second teacher. The slackening is not in learning, but in teaching the students since this teacher, emboldened by competitive victory, does not fear being dismissed. Rab Dîmmî's response is that this is not true. Rather, the second teacher will be a better teacher because the original teacher might return out of jealous revenge and publicly embarrass the replacement. The difficulty with Rashi's interpretation is that it turns Rābā's position into a somewhat nonsensical straw position (this becomes even more apparent in the versions of Rashi's position found in *Pisqê Hārîd* and *Rabbênû Yônâ*). A teacher who was just hired in a competition would be aware of that competition and afraid for possible replacements.

Šiṭâ Lô Nôděʿa Lěmî, cited by *Šiṭâ Měqûbeṣet*, offers a less technically precise but more conceptually appealing version of the statement. In this account, the ambiguous pronouns refer to each and every possible teacher. As such, Rābā claims that every teacher will be dejected based upon the fear that the arrival of a more competent colleague will lead to unemployment. Rab Dîmmî responds (taking Rab Dîmmî's comment as a verb) that each teacher will study harder in order to be assured of job security. Ultimately, the aphorism solidifies this notion by claiming that every scholar will benefit from ensuring that another is not more qualified. Though this explanation has some difficulty with the singular language of Rab Dîmmî's initial statement, this difficulty can be justified since singular language is sometimes used when referring to the paradigmatic member of a collective group.

12. See note above regarding the alternative translation of this verb as an adjective.

13. M. H. Segal, *Sēper Ben Sîrā Ha-Šālem* (Jerusalem: Môsad Bialik 1958), 255.

14. The liturgy traditionally recited by Jews in celebration of the completion of a book, based on BT Běrākôt 28b, creates a negative comparison between Torah learners and market workers (Yehuda Septimus has alerted me to the uniquely Babylonian nature of this comparison since the Palestinian parallel compares Torah learners with public entertainers). Tosefta Bābā Měṣîʿā 2:30 = Hôrāyôt 2:5 says: "And which is his 'rab'? The 'rab' who taught him Torah, and not the 'rab' that taught him a profession." At Mishnah Qiddûšin 4:14, R. Něhôraʾî says, "I set aside all of the professions in the world and only teach my son Torah for one eats of its reward in this world and the principal lives on for the world to come."

15. A similar collapsing takes place with the contrasts of Mishnah Qîddûšîn 4:14 and BT Běrākôt 28b.

16. Pierre Bourdieu, *Outline of a Theory of Practice*, trans. Richard Nice (Cambridge and New York: Cambridge University Press, 1977), 183; Bourdieu, *Rules of Art*.

17. Aaron Levine, *Free Enterprise and Jewish Law: Aspects of Jewish Business Ethics* (New York: Ktav and Yeshiva University Press, 1980), and Dennis Carlton and Avi Weiss, "The Economics of Religion: Jewish Survival and Jewish Attitudes Toward Competition in Torah Education," *Journal of Legal Studies* 30, no. 1 (2001), use the problematic essentialized fact that "Jewish law" does not restrict competition within the knowledge economy to argue that such focus on education is the basis for Jewish survival in the diaspora.

18. Actually the text allows for two exceptions.

19. See text below at n. 64.

20. This dovetails with Rābāʾs claim at Šabbāt 119a referenced above in Chapter 3.

21. Gafni (*Yahadût Babel Ū-Môsdôtehā Bi-Těqûpat Ha-Talmûd*, 71 n. 41, and *Yěhûdê Babel Bi-Těqûpat Ha-Talmûd*, 102) connects rabbinic control over the market to the Greek concept of ἀγορανόμος (*agoranomos*).

22. ʾAvîʾāsāp, cited in *Mordecai* 518, says that the city can be forced to allow rabbinic visitors to establish a market, but Mordecai disagrees since Rābāʾs statement is explicitly not in accordance with Halakhah.

23. *Bêt Yôsēp* answers this question of unfairness by saying that any transfer of goods would violate only rabbinic and not biblical ordinances. Ḥatam Sôpēr, Ḥôšen Mišpāṭ, no. 79, is more in keeping with Rābāʾs approach when it says that the notion of grabbing the market illustrates that rabbis are empowered even over biblical monetary rules. Gafni, *Yěhûdê Babel Bi-Těqûpat Ha-Talmûd*, 103, posits that the relationship between the leadership (exilarch and amora) and the hoi polloi was no doubt strained by the creation of such economic exceptions.

24. Hamburg 165, Munich 95, Florence II-I-9, Paris 1337, Escorial G-I-3, and the Pesaro printed edition say "so they should not be bothered from their studies."

25. Moshe Beer, *ʾAmôraʾê Bābel* (Ramat Gan: Bar Ilan University, 1982), 220 n. 24, connects this argument to another statement of Rābāʾs that contributes to our general picture of Rābāʾs interest in the rabbinic hierarchy and rabbinic privilege. Bābā Batrā 144a narrates a story in which Rav Saprā invested his father's bequest and his siblings want to share the profits. When the case appears before Rābā, Rābā declares, "Rab Saprā is a great man; he would not abandon his study to labor on behalf of others."

26. Avinoam Cohen, *Rabînâ Wĕ-Ḥakmê Dôrô* (Ramat Gan: Bar Ilan University, 2001), 78 n. 65, references another instance at ʿErûbîn 65a in which Rabînā adjudicates in Bābel. Jacob Obermeyer, *Die Landschaft Babylonien im Zeitalter des Talmuds und des Gaonats: Geographie und Geschichte nach talmudischen, arabischen und andern Quellen* (Frankfurt am Main: I. Kauffmann, 1929), 304 n.14, infers from the story that Bābel was a large marketplace and that Jews had standing within it.

27. Cohen, *Rabînâ Wĕ-Ḥakmê Dôrô*, 68 n. 24, suggests from the order of names that this is the fifth-generation Ravina and not the sixth-generation colleague of R. ʾAšî.

28. This implicit explanation is made explicit in Oxford Opp. 249 (369), Vatican 115, Munich 95, Florence II-I-9, Paris 1337, and Escorial G-I-3.

29. Ayali, *'Ôṣar Kînûy 'ôbdîm*, 51, suggests that this term refers to both wool manufacturers and retailers.

30. Beer, *'Amôra'ê Bābel*, 168 n. 37, suggests that this is Rab Kahanā the teacher of R. 'Ašî, but discusses the problem of identifying the specific Rab Kahanā of whom this story is told. Oxford Opp. 249 (369) reads "Rābā."

31. Kalmin, *Sages, Stories, Authors, and Editors*, 223 n. 1.

32. The eight different variants produced here by the textual witnesses testify to the rarity of the original term. Sokoloff, *Dictionary of Jewish Babylonian Aramaic*, 299, prefers the version of *Midraš Hagādôl* "instead of gnawing" as translated here.

33. Goodblatt, *Rabbinic Instruction in Sasanian Babylonia*, 108ff.

34. Oxford Opp. 249 (369), Vatican 115, Munich 95, *'Aggādōt Hatalmûd*, and *'Êyn Ya'aqōb* add a line that sets the scene by saying "when he used to go to butcher to buy meat."

35. The implicit clause is explicated in Oxford Opp. 249 (369), Vatican 115, Florence II-I-9, Pesaro, *Midraš Hagādôl*, *'Aggādōt Hatalmûd*, *'Êyn Ya'aqōb*, *Sēper Hama'asîyôt* and the margin of Escorial G-I-3.

36. Like the schoolteacher, the butcher has an established communal bureaucratic position.

37. Rubenstein, "Rise of the Babylonian Rabbinic Academy."

38. For a brief review of other sources that determine that this is a row of the regular program of the study hall and not the *kallâ*, see Gafni, *Yĕhûdê Babel Bi-Tĕqûpat Ha-Talmûd*, 199 n. 94.

39. The stratified seating is a motif that appears in other late-redacted Bavli narratives. The story of Rab Kahanā at Bābā Qammā 117a–b. On this story, see Friedman, "Further Adventures of Rav Kahana"; and Daniel Sperber, "On the Unfortunate Adventures of Rav Kahana: A Passage of Saboraic Polemic from Sassanian Persia," *Irano-Judaica* (1982).

40. Compare BT Hôrāyôt 13b for a story in which rabbis plot to embarrass a teacher and another student secretly passes the necessary information along.

41. Friedman, "Lĕ-'aggādâ Ha-Hîstôrît Bĕ-Talmûd Ha-Bablî."

42. To be sure, I am not certain that this story was written after the Rab Naḥmān bar Isaac stories, which reflect a stammaitic institutional backdrop.

43. Cohen, *Rabînâ Wĕ-Ḥakmê Dôrô*, 72 n. 36, uses this story to argue that amoraim are given the honorific of "rabbi" anachronistically within stories.

44. This explanatory term appears in Florence II-I-9, in the Yemenite tradents' *Midraš Haggādôl* and *Sēper Hama'asîyôt*, and in the margins of Escorial G-I-3.

45. Beer (*'Amôra'ê Bābel*, 222 nn. 1, 2) suggests that the word can have the meaning of "taking" or of "delaying." Either would mean a monopoly on the market.

46. The variants disagree over the name of Rab 'Addā's father. Several (Oxford Opp. 249 (369), Vatican 115, Florence II-I-9, Paris 1337, *Midraš Haggādôl*, *Sēper Hama'asîyôt*,

Escorial G-I-3, *'Aggādōt Hatalmûd*, and *'Êyn Ya'aqōb*) have "''Ahabâ,'" while others (Hamburg 165, Munich 95, and Pesaro) have "''Abbā.'" Tosafot ad loc. cites Rabênû Ḥanan'el's "''Abā'" as preferable because there is another Rab 'Addā bar 'Ahabâ who lived earlier. The existence of two individuals of the same name is not uncommon in rabbinic literature, and I assume the name 'Ahabâ on the basis of *lectio difficilior* in light of the tosafist argument. Beer, *'Amôra'ê Bābel*, 250 n. 93, cites Heyman who has three entries under Rab 'Addā bar 'Ahabâ while Hanokh Albeck has only two individuals with this name.

47. The textual variants within the verb are helpful in constructing a stemmatic diagram. Oxford Opp. 249 (369), Vatican 115, Paris 1337, Escorial G-I-3, *'Aggādōt Hatalmûd*, and *'Êyn Ya'aqōb* use the verb root *'zl*. Hamburg, Munich, Florence, the Pesaro printed edition, and the Yemenite *Midraš Haggādōl* and *Sēper Hama'asîyôt* use the verb *npq*. Vilna follows Pesaro with *npq*, but adds *'zl* in brackets.

48. *Sēper Hama'asîyôt* and *Midraš Haggādōl* add an explicit statement that clarifies the tension between the vessel's status as a wooden vessel and its status as fecal matter.

49. Paris reverses the clauses, placing the striking with the sandal before Rab Dîmmî's assumption that Rab 'Addā bar 'Ahabâ is Rābā.

50. Kalmin (*Sages, Stories, Authors, and Editors*, 6 and n. 15) offers this meaning as well as the alternative meaning of striking on the sandal.

51. *Sēper Hama'asîyôt* and *Midraš Hagādōl* say that there "are many levels."

52. Three different versions of this clause emerge from the textual variants: "I am your master, the master of your master" (Oxford Opp. 249 (369), Munich 95, Paris 1337); "I am your master, and Rābā is your master's master" (Hamburg 165, Vatican 115, Paris 1337after change, Pesaro, *'Aggādōt Hatalmûd*, *'Êyn Ya'aqōb*); and "I am your master and Rābā and Rabbâ are the masters of your master" (Escorial G-I-3 with marginal note). The first version has four words and simply posits that Rab 'Addā is two steps removed from Rab Dîmmî. Any pun on Rābā's name is only implicit. Either to explicate the pun, or to lessen the extremity of Rab 'Addā's claim, the second version adds the term *wĕ-Rābā* within the first version's text. The third version, which appears only in the edited text of Escorial G-I-3 is most likely the result of an accidental *waw* placed before Rabbâ.

53. The implicit bracketed words are explicated in Munich 95, Florence II-I-9, Pesaro, *Midraš Haggādôl*, *Sēper Hama'asîyôt*, and Escorial G-I-3. Cohen, *Rabînâ Wĕ-Ḥ akmê Dôrô*, 254, cites this as a paradigm of the pattern in which full amoraic names are not explicitly mentioned the second time around. Halivni, *Mĕqôrôt Û-Mĕsôrôt: Nāšîm*, 560 n. 16, cites an extensive literature regarding the elimination of the father's name when a character is mentioned a second time.

54. That this line is additional can be determined from its absence from Munich and from the alternative: "for I am the story's protagonist" found in the Yemenite tradents. Though Sokoloff, *Dictionary of Jewish Babylonian Aramaic*, 709, translates this phrase generally as "one who knows the legal practice," here it must mean "the story's protagonist."

55. Aharon Oppenheimer, *Babylonia Judaica in the Talmudic Period*, in collaboration with Benjamin H. Isaac and Michael Lecker, Beihefte zum Tübinger Atlas des

Vorderen Orients, Reihe B, Geisteswissenschaften, no. 47 (Wiesbaden: L. Reichert, 1983), 188, follows Obermeyer, *Landschaft Babylonien*, 246, 57, in inferring from Rab Dîmmî's name that he travels from Něhardĕ'ā to Měḥôzā. I prefer to consider the name an honorific.

56. See note 21 above (Gafni links rabbinic control over the market to the Greek concept of *agoranomos*). Rî Mîgāš limits the monopoly to a situation in which the buyers are either non-Jewish consumers or Jews who retail to non-Jewish consumers. If the higher costs generated by the monopoly are paid by Jewish consumers, such a practice is inappropriate. By contrast, *Yad Ramâ* says that such practices cannot affect prices—the prices must remain the same or the monopoly is broken—and can only be applied in entirely Jewish markets. Otherwise, there is no advantage for the first seller.

57. See the versions of *Midraš Haggādôl* and *Sēper Hama'asîyôt* (Gaster, *Exempla of the Rabbis*, 147).

58. Kalmin, *Sages, Stories, Authors, and Editors*, 6, "Nevertheless, the question is very likely inappropriate as the initial greeting given to a visitor newly arrived in an unfamiliar locality. To use an imperfect modern analogy, discussion of the excretory functions of elephants might be perfectly appropriate in the context of a classroom or a professional conference. As the first words exchanged by two strangers, however, one of whom is a visitor from out of town, it is totally inappropriate."

59. The *stam* at Měnāḥôt 69a implies that the scenario raised by the question is one in which the elephant swallows reeds and they are transformed automatically in the digestive process into a basket. This scenario is chosen because the basket becomes capable of absorbing impurity as a reed basket (completion) simultaneous to its constitution as fecal matter. It is likely, though, that the intent of the original source concerned an elephant that swallowed a fully formed reed basket. In that scenario, the question could be twofold: first, does the digestive process reconstitute the basket as fecal matter, and second, even if it continues to be a reed basket, is digestion enough of a physical change to purify a basket that was not only capable of absorbing impurity but had actually become impure? Jeffrey Rubenstein, "The Thematization of Dialectics in Bavli Aggada," *Journal of Jewish Studies* 54, no. 1 (2003): 73 n. 11, contrasts this test to tests of dialectics. Whether this is a question of dialectics or not is a matter of interpretation. The question is the type of riddle that a dialectician might enjoy.

60. Reuben Margaliot, *Niṣôṣê 'ôr: He'ārôt Bě-Talmûd Bablî* (Jerusalem: Môsad ha-Rab Kook, 1965), 160; Obermeyer, *Landschaft Babylonien*, 258. Tosafot ad loc. and at Měnāḥôt 69a accepts the Talmud's assumption that the question of the basket itself is obvious from the tannaitic source and therefore assumes that Rab 'Addā's question is also about reeds that constitute themselves into a basket within the elephant's digestive tract. Nevertheless, Tosafot ask, why should Rab Dîmmî fail if the Talmud itself leaves the question unanswered in Měnāḥôt. They answer that the problem with Rab Dîmmî is his failure to attempt to answer the question through inferences and implications as the Talmud attempts in Měnāḥôt.

61. This is a cultural indicator of a teacher-student hierarchy. See Mô'ēd Qāṭān 25a

where the teacher is also the student's father and Bābā Qammā 32b. In both of those contexts, the slap is a punishment for answering a question with an apparently ludicrous suggestion. In our case, the ludicrous suggestion is that Rab 'Addā is Rābā.

62. Almut Hintze, "Treasure in Heaven: A Theme in Comparative Religion," *Irano-Judaica* 6 (2008).

63. It has also been noted in Hirshman, *Stabilization of Rabbinic Culture*, 113.

64. See text above at n. 19.

65. Aaron Hyman, *Seper Tôlĕdôt Tanā'îm Wĕ-'Amôrāîm* (London, 1910; repr., Jerusalem: Mākôn "Pĕrî ha-'Areṣ," 1986), 1:333. Hanokh Albeck, *Mābô La-Talmûdîm* (Tel Aviv: Devir, 1969), 361, turns Rab Dîmmî into a fourth-generation amora on account of this passage. Cohen, *Rabînâ Wĕ-Ḥakmê Dôrô*, 231 n. 73, assumes that this is because of the story. It is possible Albeck was motivated by the same problem the story was bothered by—the flat-footed legal debate between Rābā and Rab Dîmmî.

66. Marrou, *History of Education in Antiquity*, 172.

67. See Chapter 4 at n. 66.

68. Though the story of Rab Naḥmān bar Isaac might be later.

69. In light of the awareness of the bridge narrative as the final piece in the passage's composition, use of this story's explicit information for historiographical purposes must be reevaluated. The bridge narrative has been used by historians to argue that Rābā had political power as the exilarch's appointed *agoranomos*, that Rābā's study hall was around during Rab Joseph's period of activity, and that Rab Dîmmî lived a long life. These three points must be called into question by the story's provenance and the literary reasons for the story's features that have generated such historiographic claims.

70. The formulaic introductions to these stories provide the missing normative judgment. But I mentioned above that the judgment fits poorly, making this phenomenon a variation on the challenges of judging narrative that this book has been considering.

71. Ben-Menahem, *Judicial Deviation in Talmudic Law*.

Chapter 6

1. Some of the case stories treated in earlier chapters possess a clear layer of stammaitic interpretation; even so, one can often confidently retrieve an original source case story by separating out that addition or interpretation.

2. The Bridge Narrative of Chapter 5 is in this category.

3. Friedman, "Mābô Klalî 'al Derek Ḥeqer Ha-Sûgyā."

4. Friedman, "Lĕ-'aggādâ Ha-Hîsṭôrît Bĕ-Talmûd Ha-Bablî," "Further Adventures of Rav Kahana," and "A Good Story Deserves Retelling."

5. Friedman, " Lĕ-'aggādâ Ha-Hîsṭôrît Bĕ-Talmûd Ha-Bablî," "Further Adventures of Rav Kahana," and "A Good Story Deserves Retelling"; and Rubenstein, *Talmudic Stories* and *Culture of the Babylonian Talmud*.

6. I deliberately do not distinguish here among the source stories between legal and nonlegal narratives. The legal stories only present more explicit difficulty for subsequent readers because of their deliberate subversion of legal norms.

7. This includes story cycles of amoraic stories as well as liminal cases in which the level of stammaitic interpretation has not been completely smoothed out.

8. Much of what I say here is related to the recent call by scholars to clarify the specific literary process intended by scholarly analysis of "the *stam.*" See Boyarin, *Socrates and the Fat Rabbis*, 202–3; and Friedman, "A Good Story Deserves Retelling," n. 14.

9. Rubenstein, *Talmudic Stories*; Rubenstein, *Culture of the Babylonian Talmud*.

10. Kalmin, "Formation and Character of the Babylonian Talmud," 845–47; Kalmin, *Jewish Babylonia*, 10–11. Shamma Friedman ("A Good Story Deserves Retelling," 72) echoes some of this criticism when he writes: "These anonymous authors may have lent their hands to other types of literary creativity as well, such as composition and arrangement. On the other hand dialectic commentary was their forte, and they may well have left the other functions to specialists in those fields."

11. Kalmin, "Formation and Character of the Babylonian Talmud," 846.

12. Boyarin, *Socrates and the Fat Rabbis*, 193–242, draws attention to the same controversy and explains the genres much as they are articulated here. *Bārûk Šekiwantî*.

13. Zvi Septimus, "Trigger Words and Simultexts: The Experience of Reading the Bavli," in *Wisdom of Bat Sheva: The Dr. Beth Samuels Memorial Volume*, ed. Barry S. Wimpfheimer (Jersey City, N.J.: Ktav, 2009), collects all of the material borrowed from other places even while arguing against this kind of work.

14. At the end of his insightful analysis of this passage, Moulie Vidas ("The Bavli's Discussion of Genealogy in *Qiddushin* IV," in *Antiquity in Antiquity: Jewish and Christian Pasts in the Greco-Roman World*, ed. Gregg Gardner and Kevin L. Osterloh [Tübingen: Mohr Siebeck, 2008]) characterizes the narrative as simultaneously critical and conservative. This description captures my notion that the narrator is processing the rabbinic cultural world.

15. Yonah Fraenkel, "Šĕ'elôt Hermenûtîyôt Bĕ-Ḥeqer Sippûr Ha-'Aggādâ," *Tarbiz* 47 (1978); Rubenstein, *Talmudic Stories*, 8–10.

16. It is long established (Tal Ilan, *Mine and Yours Are Hers: Retrieving Women's History from Rabbinic Literature* [Leiden and New York: Brill, 1997]) that in earlier Bavli texts, Yaltā is an independent operator and is represented as Rab Naḥmān's wife only in later materials. This is a late story, and they appear to be married even though the text never explicitly communicates this.

17. The word *pôsēl* is literally translated as "disqualify." Vidas ("Bavli's Discussion of Genealogy") makes use of the ambiguity of how one disqualifies (physically or legally) in his reading.

18. Adiel Schremer, *Zākār U-Nĕqêbah Bĕrā'am: Ha-Nîśu'îm Bĕ-Šilhê Yĕmê Ha-Bayit Ha-Šēnî Ubi-Tĕqûpat Ha-Mišnâ Wĕha-Talmûd* (Jerusalem: Merkaz Zalman Shazar, 2003), 150, asserts that the immediate preceding text is a Babylonian *baraita* but does not comment explicitly on these lines. It seems to me that these two lines are independent of the preceding.

19. Vidas, "Bavli's Discussion of Genealogy," 307. Vidas's reading very insightfully notes the larger passage's transition from physical defilement to slander and uses this

transition as a central pivot for an observation regarding the passage in toto: namely, that the Bavli uniquely embraces the constructed (rather than natural) nature of genealogy.

20. For a collection of similar rabbinic psychological statements about genealogy, see ibid., 308 n. 41.

21. Vidas writes: "From the beginning, however, the story invites us to think about Rav Yehuda's motives . . . Rav Yehuda's original decision, then, is reduced to simple revenge" (ibid., 312).

22. For plot energy, see Brooks, *Reading for the Plot*.

23. That rabbinic law develops from the moral to the legal is treated in Jeremy Cohen, *Be Fertile and Increase, Fill the Earth and Master It: The Ancient and Medieval Career of a Biblical Text* (Ithaca, N.Y.: Cornell University Press, 1989); David Daube, *The Duty of Procreation* (Edinburgh: Edinburgh University Press, 1977); and Barry S. Wimpfheimer, "Interrupting Birth Control: Re-Reading a Famous Beraita," in *Wisdom of Bat Sheva: The Dr. Beth Samuels Memorial Volume*, ed. Barry S. Wimpfheimer (Jersey City, N.J.: Ktav, 2009).

24. Septimus, "Trigger Words and Simultexts."

25. The basic hypothesis of borrowing from Bābā Batrā is possible even if much of the parallel borrowed material found in text witnesses of Qiddûšîn is the product of scribal addition.

26. Martha Himmelfarb, *A Kingdom of Priests: Ancestry and Merit in Ancient Judaism*, Jewish Culture and Contexts (Philadelphia: University of Pennsylvania Press, 2006).

27. Geoffrey Herman, "Ha-Kōhanîm Bĕ-Babel Bi-Tĕqûpat Ha-Talmûd" (master's thesis, Hebrew University, 1998), 80–100; Rubenstein, *Culture of the Babylonian Talmud*.

28. Vidas ("Bavli's Discussion of Genealogy," 314) writes: "the punning used in Rav Yehuda's penultimate declaration . . . seems in this context to be a parody of the arbitrariness of the production of genealogical stratification." It is easy to conclude that this narrative is absurd; harder yet is determining whether the absurdity is self-conscious, self-aware, criticized, or simply reported. As a legal narrative, this story makes a claim to reality that is not undermined by redactorial framing. I would argue that it preserves cultural thickness, which is brought more blatantly to light in the late lengthy narrative.

29. Walter Benjamin, *Reflections: Essays, Aphorisms, Autobiographical Writing*, trans. Peter Demetz (New York: Schocken Books, 1986), 281, says: "one might consider the surprising possibility that the law's interest in a monopoly of violence vis-à-vis individuals is not explained by the intention of preserving legal ends, but, rather, by that of preserving the law itself; that violence, when not in the hands of the law, threatens it not by the ends that it may pursue but by its mere existence outside the law."

30. Vidas ("Bavli's Discussion of Genealogy," 312) comments: "I would like to suggest that both of the traditions Rav Yehuda uses, along with a third one, constitute an effort by Shmuel [Samuel] to remove genealogical stratification from daily interaction." Schremer, *Zākār U-Nĕqêbah Bĕrā'am*, 155, calls this "a space free of genealogical suspicion." Both characterizations fail to recognize the inherent problematic of the rabbinic monopolization over the power of slander.

31. Neusner, *History of the Jews in Babylonia*, 2:240–43.

32. Vidas ("Bavli's Discussion of Genealogy," 313) writes: "If these two traditions seek to preempt the abuse of genealogical language for the personal advantage of the speaker and to prevent further social stratification, Rav Yehuda uses them for precisely the opposite purpose."

33. Vidas (ibid., 316) says: "The Talmud's moves here are, as in other cases, at once 'conservative' and 'critical' in our terms. On the one hand, it avoids explicit criticism of the manipulation and use of genealogical information as vehicles of personal gain. It preserves and justifies the corrupted order of things. On the other hand, it acknowledges the contingency of this genealogical information and draws our attention to the conditions under which it is produced."

34. Herman, "Ha-Kōhanîm Bĕ-Babel Bi-Tĕqûpat Ha-Talmûd"; Richard Kalmin, "Genealogy and Polemics in Literature of Late Antiquity," *Hebrew Union College Annual* 67 (1996); Richard Kalmin, *The Sage in Jewish Society of Late Antiquity* (New York: Routledge, 1999), 51–60; Rubenstein, *Talmudic Stories*, 197–211; Rubenstein, *Culture of the Babylonian Talmud*, 80–101; Michael L. Satlow, *Jewish Marriage in Antiquity* (Princeton, N.J.: Princeton University Press, 2001), 133–61; and Schremer, *Zākār U-Nĕqêbah Bĕrā'am*, 147–58.

35. Vidas, "Bavli's Discussion of Genealogy," 310, insightfully observes that: "Throughout the story, legal and genealogical knowledge is represented as context-dependent in various ways." In footnote 45 Vidas highlights the significance of politics in the story's plot.

36. Ibid., 285. Describing the larger context, Vidas writes, "the Bavli presents a special interest in the social processes which lead to the production or manipulation of genealogical identities. It links this production with personal interest and political power."

37. Ibid., 310–11. Vidas notes the way the story attends not only to the contingent nature of genealogy, but to the political and local contexts for the production of such.

38. Ibid., 311.

39. Fraenkel, *Sippûr Ha-'Aggādâ*, 23, writes: "The talmudic story—without recourse to the question of its literary type—has a didactic purpose. It enters the world and is told in order to educate the listeners."

40. Bruner, "Narrative Construction of Reality."

41. One can use the same approach with the bridge narrative in the preceding chapter.

42. Boyarin, *Socrates and the Fat Rabbis*. Most of the examples used to support the notion of the talmudic grotesque are from lengthy narrative.

43. Vatican 111 adds that he originated in Nĕhardĕ'ā.

44. Ox. Opp. 248 (367) and Vatican 111 have a different verb meaning "wait."

45. Ox. Opp. 248 (367) has the verb *wĕnîtan*, but this is likely a *lectio difficilior*.

46. The bracketed phrase is absent from Venice and is not necessarily implicit; the man could have meant to utter this to himself.

47. Munich 95, Vatican 111, and the Spanish print edition add that R. Judah brought

out trumpets to announce the excommunication, a trope that appears frequently regarding excommunication in the Bavli and is likely a later addition to the original text.

48. Venice adds "because you are a great man," which is probably implied.

49. Both Ox. Opp. 248 (367) and Venice add this imperative, but in different places in the text.

50. It is interesting that the exilarchate is here referred to as the Nāsî.

51. The implicit bracketed phrase is explicated in Munich 95 and Vatican 111.

52. Vatican 111 adds that it was for his roof, no doubt drawing on the text of the biblical imperative.

53. Venice has "R. Hûnā bar 'Îddî" and Munich 95, Vatican 111, and the Spanish print edition have "R. Něhîla'î bar 'Îddî."

54. Munich, Vatican and Venice have "Samuel."

55. The Spanish print edition has the term for teaching.

56. This term is based on the Greek *krabatos*.

57. An etymologically Chaldean term.

58. Munich, Vatican 111, and the Spanish print edition have different versions here.

59. Ox. Opp. 248 (367) has a homeoteleuton here until the next Samuel.

60. Ox. Opp. 248 (367), Munich 95, and Vatican 111 turn the pronoun into the noun "Yaltā" on the basis of other sources that indicate that Yaltā was R. Naḥmān's wife. This is likely a later shift.

61. Venice has "like the other am haarez."

62. Ox. Opp. 248 (367), Vatican 111, and the Spanish print edition simplify the text here, but the instability of their text indicates that this is a later change. Ox. Opp. 248 (367) has another homeoteleuton here.

63. Or "linguistic ability."

64. The complete divergence of the witnesses marks this spot as difficult in some way. I have preferred in the translation to represent the Venice version.

65. Venice and the margins of Vatican 111 specify where he took it from.

66. Venice adds that R. Judah said, "this is the man and this is his summons."

67. Munich 95 adds that he deserved lashing, and the Spanish print edition has: "let the master lash him, because Rab would lash one who would pain the rabbinic emissary." Both witnesses have R. Judah responding that what he did was preferable to lashing.

68. Ox. Opp. 248 (367) and the marginal correction of Vatican 111 have "and does not speak of the praise of the world." One could translate the other witnesses to mean that the person who disqualifies never speaks praise (of others).

69. This line is missing in Ox. Opp. 248 (367) but this could be another homeoteleuton since the text as it stands does not flow. Similarly, the absence in the Spanish print edition juxtaposes two terms that make little sense.

70. Munich 95 has another name; Vatican 111 has the statement in the name of Rab Hûnā. Both the Spanish print edition and Venice *editio princeps* combine the two versions and add Rab Hûnā as an intermediate source.

71. Possibly, "they broadcast about him that he was a servant."

72. Ox. Opp. 248 (367) and Venice add a narrative support to Samuel's statement: "because there only remained from it one who went to the roof, raised her voice and said, 'whoever says I am descended from the house of the Hasmonean dynasty is a servant.' She fell from the roof and died." This text is borrowed from BT Bābā Batrā 3b.

73. The implicit bracketed phrase is explicated in Munich 95, Vatican 111, and Venice.

74. Munich 95 has "R. Naḥmān" in "Šeknĕṣîb." Vatican 111 and the Spanish print edition add this version after the one in the body. Ox. Opp 248 (367) places it after the Bar Batu declaration. Munich 95 puts the Rab Judah declaration in Něhardĕʿā.

75. On the appearance of Něhardĕʿā in some variants, see Schremer, *Zākār U-Něqêbah Běrāʾam*, 154 n. 120.

76. Schremer (ibid., n. 121) cites a responsum variant that conflates the two statements of this clause into a single statement: "'Adā and Yônātān, servants of Yiṣḥāq bar Pāppā are bastards."

77. Jeremiah 20:1 and Ezra 2:38.

78. Ox. Opp. 248 (367), Spanish print, and Venice add, "ʾAbayê says, "And they all sit in the market of Něhardĕʿā."

Bibliography

Aberbach, Moses. *Ha-Ḥinûk Ha-Yĕhûdî Bi-Tĕqûpat Ha-Mišnâ Wĕha-Talmûd: Meḥqārîm Wĕ-ʿIyûnîm*. Jerusalem: R. Mas; and Baltimore: Baltimore Hebrew College, 1982.

Adler, Rachel. *Engendering Judaism: An Inclusive Theology and Ethics*. Philadelphia: Jewish Publication Society, 1998.

Albeck, Hanokh. *Mābô La-Mišnâ*. Jerusalem: Môsad Bialik, 1966.

———. *Mābô La-Talmûdîm*. Tel Aviv: Devir, 1969.

Albeck, Shalom. *Batê Ha-Dîn Bî-Yĕmê Ha-Talmûd*. Ramat Gan: Bar Ilan University, 1980.

———. *Mābo La-Mišpaṭ Hā-ʿIbri Bi-Yĕmê Ha-Talmûd*. Ramat Gan: Bar Ilan University, 1999.

Alon, Gedalia. *The Jews in Their Land in the Talmudic Age, 70–640 C.E.* Jerusalem: Magnes Press, Hebrew University, 1980.

———. *Jews, Judaism, and the Classical World: Studies in Jewish History in the Times of the Second Temple and Talmud*. Jerusalem: Magnes Press, 1977.

Assaf, Simha. *Tĕšûbôt Ha-Gĕʾônîm*. Jerusalem:Darom, 1928.

Ayali, Meir. *ʾÔṣar Kînûy ʿÔbdîm Bĕ-Siprût Ha-Talmûd Wĕha-Midrāš*. Tel Aviv: Ha-Qibûṣ Ha-Mĕʾuḥād, 1984.

Bakhtin, M. M. *The Dialogic Imagination: Four Essays*. Edited by Michael Holquist. Translated by Caryl Emerson and Michael Holquist. University of Texas Press Slavic Series, no. 1. Austin: University of Texas Press, 1981.

———. *Rabelais and His World*. 1st Midland book ed. Bloomington: Indiana University Press, 1984.

Baron, Jane. "Law, Literature and the Problems of Interdisciplinarity." *Yale Law Journal* 108 (1999): 1059–85.

Baumgarten, Jean, and Jerold C. Frakes. *Introduction to Old Yiddish Literature*. Oxford and New York: Oxford University Press, 2005.

Becker, Adam H. *Fear of God and the Beginning of Wisdom: The School of Nisibis and Christian Scholastic Culture in Late Antique Mesopotamia*. Divinations. Philadelphia: University of Pennsylvania Press, 2006.

Beer, Moshe. *ʾAmôraʾê Bābel*. Ramat Gan: Bar Ilan University, 1982.

Benjamin, Walter. *Reflections: Essays, Aphorisms, Autobiographical Writing*. Translated by Peter Demetz. New York: Schocken Books, 1986.

Ben-Menahem, Hanina. *Judicial Deviation in Talmudic Law: Governed by Men, Not by Rules*. Jewish Law in Context, vol. 1. Chur, Switzerland, and New York: Harwood Academic Publishers, 1991.

Berlin, Adele. *Esther: The Traditional Hebrew Text with the New JPS Translation*. JPS Bible Commentary. Philadephia: Jewish Publication Society, 2001.

Bialik, H. N. *Kol Kitbê H. N. Bialik*. Tel Aviv: Dvir, 1947.

Bickerman, E. J. *The Jews in the Greek Age*. Cambridge, Mass.: Harvard University Press, 1988.

Blau, Moshe. *Šiṭat Ha-Qadmônîm ʿAl Šalôš Babôt*. Brooklyn, New York: n.p., 1982.

Blau, Moshe. *Šiṭat Ha-Qadmônîm: ʿAl Maseket Baba Mĕṣîʿâ*. Brooklyn, N.Y.: n.p., 1966.

Bourdieu, Pierre. *Outline of a Theory of Practice*. Translated by Richard Nice. Cambridge and New York: Cambridge University Press, 1977.

———. *The Rules of Art: Genesis and Structure of the Literary Field*. Translated by Susan Emanuel. Cambridge: Polity Press, 1996.

Boyarin, Daniel. *Border Lines: The Partition of Judaeo-Christianity*. Divinations. Philadelphia: University of Pennsylvania Press, 2004.

———. *Carnal Israel: Reading Sex in Talmudic Culture*. Berkeley: University of California Press, 1993.

———. *Dying for God: Martyrdom and the Making of Christianity and Judaism*. Stanford, Calif.: Stanford University Press, 1999.

———. "Hellenism in Jewish Babylonia." In *The Cambridge Companion to the Talmud and Rabbinic Literature*, edited by Charlotte Elisheva Fonrobert and Martin S. Jaffee, 336–63. Cambridge: Cambridge University Press, 2007.

———. "Lĕ-Leqsîqôn Ha-Talmûdî." *Tarbiz* 50 (1981): 164–91.

———. *Socrates and the Fat Rabbis*. Chicago and London: University of Chicago Press, 2009.

———. *Unheroic Conduct: The Rise of Heterosexuality and the Invention of the Jewish Man*. Contraversions: Critical Studies in Jewish Literature, Culture, and Society, 8. Berkeley: University of California Press, 1997.

Boyd, William. *The History of Western Education*. London: A. & C. Black, 1921.

Brandes, Yehudah. *ʾAggadâ Lĕ-Maʿaśeh: ʿIyûnîm Bĕ-Sugyôt Mišpāḥâ, Ḥebrâ, Wĕ-ʿabôdat Ha-Šēm*. Jerusalem: Eliner Library, Jewish Agency for Israel, Beit Morasha of Jerusalem, 2005.

Brody, Robert. *The Geonim of Babylonia and the Shaping of Medieval Jewish Culture*. New Haven, Conn.: Yale University Press, 1998.

Brooks, Peter. "The Law as Narrative and Rhetoric." In *Law's Stories: Narrative and Rhetoric in the Law*, edited by Peter Brooks and Paul D. Gewirtz, 14–23. New Haven, Conn.: Yale University Press, 1996.

———. "Narrativity of the Law." *Law and Literature* 14, no. 1 (2002): 1–9.

———. *Reading for the Plot: Design and Intention in Narrative*. New York: A. A. Knopf, 1984.

Brown, Peter Robert Lamont. *Augustine of Hippo: A Biography*. London: Faber, 1967.

———. "The Saint as Exemplar in Late Antiquity." In *Saints and Virtues*, edited by John Stratton Hawley, 3–14. Berkeley and Los Angeles: University of California Press, 1987.

Bruner, Jerome. "The Narrative Construction of Reality." *Critical Inquiry* 18, no. 1 (1991): 1–21.

Bruns, Gerald L. *Hermeneutics, Ancient and Modern*. New Haven, Conn.: Yale University Press, 1992.

Carlton, Dennis, and Avi Weiss. "The Economics of Religion: Jewish Survival and Jewish Attitudes Toward Competition in Torah Education." *Journal of Legal Studies* 30, no. 1 (2001): 253–75.

Cohen, Aryeh. *Rereading Talmud: Gender, Law, and the Poetics of Sugyot*. Brown Judaic Studies. Atlanta, Ga.: Scholars Press, 1998.

Cohen, Avinoam. *Rabînâ Wĕ-Ḥakmê Dôrô*. Ramat Gan: Bar Ilan University, 2001.

Cohen, Jeremy. *Be Fertile and Increase, Fill the Earth and Master It: The Ancient and Medieval Career of a Biblical Text*. Ithaca, N.Y.: Cornell University Press, 1989.

Cohen, Shaye J. D. "The Rabbi in Second-Century Jewish Society." In *The Cambridge History of Judaism*, vol. 3, *The Early Roman Period*, edited by William Horbury, W. D. Davies, and John Sturdy, 922–90. Cambridge: Cambridge University Press, 1999.

Cover, Robert M. *Narrative, Violence, and the Law: The Essays of Robert Cover*. Edited by Martha Minow, Michael Ryan, and Austin Sarat. Law, Meaning, and Violence. Ann Arbor: University of Michigan Press, 1992.

———. "The Supreme Court, 1982 Term—Foreword: *Nomos* and Narrative." *Harvard Law Review* 97, no. 4 (1983): 4–68.

Damrosch, David. *The Narrative Covenant: Transformations of Genre in the Growth of Biblical Literature*. San Francisco: Harper & Row, 1987.

Daube, David. *The Duty of Procreation*. Edinburgh: Edinburgh University Press, 1977.

Davies, Eryl W. "The Inheritance of the First-Born in Israel and the Ancient Near East." *Journal of Semitic Studies* 38, no. 2 (1993): 175–91.

Delgado, Richard. "Storytelling for Oppositionists and Others." *Michigan Law Review* 87 (1989): 2411–41.

Dimock, Wai-chee. "Deploying Law and Legal Ideas in Culture and Society: Rules of Law, Laws of Science." *Yale Journal of Law and the Humanities* 13 (2001): 203–25.

Dorff, Elliot N., Arthur I. Rosett, and Jewish Theological Seminary of America. *A Living Tree: The Roots and Growth of Jewish Law*. Albany, N.Y.: State University of New York Press, 1988.

Ebner, Eliezer. *Elementary Education in Ancient Israel During the Tannaitic Period (10–220 C.E.)*. New York: Bloch, 1956.

Elon, Menachem. *Jewish Law: History, Sources, Principles*. Translated by Bernard Auerbach and Melvin Sykes. 4 vols. Philadelphia: Jewish Publication Society, 1994.

Epstein, J. N., and E. Z. Melamed, eds. *Mĕkîltā Dĕ-Rabbî Šimʿôn Ben Yôḥaʾy*. Jerusalem: Mĕqîṣê Nirdāmîm, 1955.

Felman, Shoshana. *Jacques Lacan and the Adventure of Insight: Psychoanalysis in Contemporary Culture*. Cambridge, Mass.: Harvard University Press, 1987.

———. *The Juridical Unconscious: Trials and Traumas in the Twentieth Century*. Cambridge, Mass.: Harvard University Press, 2002.

Ferguson, Robert A. "Untold Stories in the Law." In *Law's Stories: Narrative and Rhetoric in the Law*, edited by Peter Brooks and Paul D. Gewirtz, 84–98. New Haven, Conn.: Yale University Press, 1996.

Finkelstein, Louis. *Akiba: Scholar, Saint and Martyr*. New York: Covici, 1936.

Finkelstein, Louis, and H. S. Horovitz, eds. *Sifre Deuteronomy*. Berlin: Ha-Aggûdâ ha-Tarbûtît ha-Yĕhûdîm bĕ-Germāniyâ, 1940.

Fischel, Henry A. "Story and History: Observations on Greco-Roman Rhetoric and Pharisaism." In *Essays in Greco-Roman and Related Talmudic Literature*, edited by Henry A. Fischel, 443–72. New York: Ktav, 1977.

Foucault, Michel. *Power/Knowledge: Selected Interviews and Other Writings, 1972–1977*. Edited by Colin Gordon. New York: Pantheon Books, 1980.

Fraade, Steven D. "Nomos and Narrative Before *Nomos and Narrative*." *Yale Journal of Law and the Humanities* 17, no. 1 (2005): 81–96.

Fraenkel, Yonah. *Darkê Ha-ʾAggādâ Wĕha-Midraš*. Masada, Israel: Yad la-Talmûd, 1991.

———. *ʿIyûnîm Bĕ-ʿOlāmô Ha-Rûhanî Šel Sippûr Ha-ʾAggādâ*. Tel Aviv: Ha-Kîbûṣ ha-mĕʾûḥād, 1981.

———. *Midraš Wĕ-ʾAggadah*. Tel Aviv: Open University, 1996.

———. "Šĕʾelôt Hermenûtîyôt Bĕ-Ḥeqer Sippûr Ha-ʾaggādâ." *Tarbiz* 47 (1978): 139–72.

———. *Sippûr Ha-ʾAggādâ: ʾAḥdût Šel Tōken Wĕ-Ṣûrâ*. Tel Aviv: Ben Ḥayîm, 2001.

Friedman, Shamma. "The Further Adventures of Rav Kahana." In *The Talmud Yerushalmi and Graeco-Roman Culture*, edited by Peter Schafer, 247–71. Tübingen: Mohr Siebeck, 2002.

———. "A Good Story Deserves Retelling: The Unfolding of the Akiva Legend." In *Creation and Composition: The Contribution of the Bavli Redactors (Stammaim) to the Aggada*, edited by Jeffrey L. Rubenstein, 71–100. Tübingen: Mohr Siebeck, 2005.

———. "Kĕtîb Ha-Šēmôt 'Rabbâ' Wĕ-'Rābā' Bĕ-Talmûd Ha-Bablî." *Sinai* 110 (1992): 140–64.

———. "Lĕ-ʾAggādâ Ha-Hîsṭôrît Bĕ-Talmûd Ha-Bablî." In *Seper Ha-Zikārôn Lĕ-Rabî Shaul Lieberman*, edited by Shamma Friedman. Jerusalem: Jewish Theological Seminary of America, 1993.

———. "Mābô Klalî ʿal Derek Ḥeqer Ha-Sûgyâ." In *Meḥqarîm Û-Mĕqorôt*, edited by H. Z. Dmitrovsky, 283–321. New York: Jewish Theological Seminary of America, 1978.

———. "Mibneh Siprûtî Šel Sûgîyôt Habablî." *Proceedings of the World Congress of Jewish Studies* 6, no. 3 (1977): 389–402.

———. "*Nomen est Omen*—Dicta of the Talmudic Sages Which Echo the Author's Name" (in Hebrew). In *These Are the Names: Studies in Jewish Onomastics*, vol. 2, edited by Aaron Demsky, 51–77.

———. *Talmûd ʿārûk: Pereq Ha-Ṣôḥēr Et Ha-'Ûmanîn*. 2 vols. Jerusalem: Jewish Theological Seminary of America, 1990.

Gafni, Isaiah. "Concerning D. Goodblatt's Article." *Zion* 46 (1981): 52–56.

———. "Maʿăśēh Bêt Dîn Bĕ-Talmûd Ha-Bablî." *Proceedings of the American Academy of Jewish Research* 49 (1982): 23–40.

———. "The Political, Social, and Economic History of Babylonian Jewry, 224–638 CE." In *The Cambridge History of Judaism*, vol. 4, *The Late Roman-Rabbinic Period*, edited by Steven T. Katz, 792–820. Cambridge: Cambridge University Press, 2006.

———. *Yahadût Babel Û-Môsdôtehā Bi-Tĕqûpat Ha-Talmûd*. Jerusalem: Zalman Shazar Center, 1975.

———. *Yĕhûdê Babel Bi-Tĕqûpat Ha-Talmûd*. Jerusalem: Zalman Shazar Center, 1990.

———. "Yĕšîbâ Û-Mĕtîbtā." *Zion* 43 (1978): 12–37.

Gaster, Moses. *The Exempla of the Rabbis*. New York: Ktav, 1968.

Geertz, Clifford. *The Interpretation of Cultures: Selected Essays*. New York: Basic Books, 1973.

Geiger, Abraham. *Ha-Miqrā Wĕ-Targûmāyw*. Translated by Y. L. Barukh. Jerusalem: Môsad Bialik 1949.

Gerber, Jane S. "My Heart Is in the East." In *The Illustrated History of the Jewish People*, edited by Nicholas De Lange, 140–97. New York: Harcourt Brace, 1997.

Goodblatt, David. "The History of the Babylonian Academies." In *The Cambridge History of Judaism*, vol. 4, *The Late Roman-Rabbinic Period*, edited by Steven T. Katz, 821–39. Cambridge: Cambridge University Press, 2006.

———. *Rabbinic Instruction in Sasanian Babylonia*. Studies in Judaism in Late Antiquity, vol. 9. Leiden: Brill, 1975.

Graetz, Heinrich. *History of the Jews*. 6 vols. Edited by Bella Löwy. Philadelphia: Jewish Publication Society of America, 1891–98.

Gray, Alyssa M. *A Talmud in Exile: The Influence of Yerushalmi Avodah Zarah on the Formation of Bavli Avodah Zarah*. Providence, R.I.: Brown Judaic Studies, 2005.

Greenblatt, Stephen. "The Touch of the Real." *Representations* 59 (Summer 1997): 14–29.

Grossman, Avraham. "The Sources of Kiddush Hashem in Early Ashkenaz." In *Sanctity of Life and Martyrdom: Studies in Memory of Amir Yekutiel*, edited by Isaiah Gafni and Aviezer Ravitzky, 99–131. Jerusalem: Hebrew University, 1991.

Halbertal, Moshe. *People of the Book: Canon, Meaning, and Authority*. Cambridge, Mass.: Harvard University Press, 1997.

Halevy, Isaak. *Dôrôt Ha-Rišônîm*. Frankfurt am Main: Slobotzky, 1901.

Halivni, David Weiss. *Mĕqôrôt Û-Mĕsôrôt: Bābā Mĕṣîʿā*. Jerusalem: Magnes, 2003.

———. *Mĕqôrôt Û-Mĕsôrôt: Bābā Qammā*. Jerusalem: Magnes, 1993.

———. *Mĕqôrôt Û-Mĕsôrôt: ʿĒrûbîn Û-Pĕsaḥîm*. Jerusalem: Jewish Theological Seminary of America, 1982.

———. *Mĕqôrôt Û-Mĕsôrôt: Mĕ-Yômā ʿad Ḥăgîgâ*. Jerusalem: Jewish Theological Seminary of America, 1975.

———. *Mĕqôrôt Û-Mĕsôrôt: Nāšîm*. Tel Aviv: Dvir, 1968.

———. *Měqôrôt Û-Měsôrôt: Šabbāt.* Jerusalem: Jewish Theological Seminary of America, 1975.
———. *Midrash, Mishnah, and Gemara: The Jewish Predilection for Justified Law.* Cambridge, Mass.: Harvard University Press, 1986.
Harris, Jay Michael. *Nachman Krochmal: Guiding the Perplexed of the Modern Age.* Modern Jewish Masters Series. New York: New York University Press, 1991.
Hasan-Rokem, Galit. *Riqmat Ḥayyîm.* Tel Aviv: ʿAm ʿÔbēd 1996.
Henshke, David. *Mišnâ Rišônâ Bě-Talmûdam Šel Tanā'îm 'Aḥărônîm: Sugyôt Bě-Dînê Šômrîm.* Ramat Gan: Bar Ilan University, 1997.
Herman, David. *Story Logic: Problems and Possibilities of Narrative.* Frontiers of Narrative. Lincoln: University of Nebraska Press, 2002.
Herman, Geoffrey. "Ha-Kōhanîm Bě-Babel Bi-Těqûpat Ha-Talmûd." Master's thesis, Hebrew University, 1998.
———. "Rāšût Ha-Gôlâ Bě-Babel Bi-Těqûpat Ha-Talmûd." Ph.D. dissertation, Hebrew University, 2005.
Himmelfarb, Martha. *A Kingdom of Priests: Ancestry and Merit in Ancient Judaism.* Jewish Culture and Contexts. Philadelphia: University of Pennsylvania Press, 2006.
Hintze, Almut. "Treasure in Heaven: A Theme in Comparative Religion." *Irano-Judaica* 6 (2008): 9–36.
Hirshman, Marc G. *The Stabilization of Rabbinic Culture, 100 C.E.–350 C.E.: Texts on Education and Their Late Antique Context.* New York: Oxford University Press, 2009.
Hyman, Aaron. *Seper Tôlědôt Tanā'îm Wě-'āmôrā'îm.* 3 vols. London, 1910. Reprint, Jerusalem: Mākôn "Pěrî ha-'Areṣ," 1986.
Ilan, Tal. *Mine and Yours Are Hers: Retrieving Women's History from Rabbinic Literature.* Leiden and New York: Brill, 1997.
Isaiah ben Mali. *Pisqê Ha-Rîd.* Jerusalem: Mākôn ha-Talmûd ha-Yiśra'elî ha-Šalem, 1964.
Jacobs, Louis. *Rabbinic Thought in the Talmud.* Edgware, Middlesex, and Portland, Ore.: Vallentine Mitchell, 2005.
———. *Structure and Form in the Babylonian Talmud.* Cambridge and New York: Cambridge University Press, 1991.
———. *Studies in Talmudic Logic and Methodology.* London: Vallentine, 1961.
Jaeger, Werner Wilhelm. *Paideia: The Ideals of Greek Culture.* 2nd ed. 3 vols. New York and Oxford: Oxford University Press, 1986.
Jastrow, Marcus. *A Dictionary of the Targumim, the Talmud Babli and Yerushalmi, and the Midrashic Literature.* Brooklyn: Traditional Press, 1975.
Jewish Publication Society (JPS). *Tanakh: A New Translation of the Holy Scriptures According to the Traditional Hebrew Text.* Philadelphia: Jewish Publication Society, 1985.
Jost, I. M. *Allgemeine Geschichte des israelitischen Volkes, sowohl seines zweimaligen Staatslebens als auch der zerstreuten Gemeinden und Sekten bis in die neueste Zeit . . . aus den Quellen.* Berlin: C. F. Amelang, 1832.

Kahana, Menahem, ed. *Siprê Zûṭā on Deuteronomy: Citations from a New Tannaitic Midrash* (in Hebrew). With text of Jeshua ben Judah's commentary on Deuteronomy. Jerusalem: Magnes, 2002.

Kahn, Paul W. *The Cultural Study of Law: Reconstructing Legal Scholarship*. Chicago: University of Chicago Press, 1999.

Kalmin, Richard. "The Formation and Character of the Babylonian Talmud." In *Cambridge History of Judaism*, vol. 4, *The Late Roman-Rabbinic Period*, edited by Steven T. Katz, 840–76. Cambridge: Cambridge University Press, 2006.

———. "Genealogy and Polemics in Literature of Late Antiquity." *Hebrew Union College Annual* 67 (1996): 77–94.

———. *Jewish Babylonia Between Persia and Roman Palestine*. New York: Oxford University Press, 2006.

———. *The Sage in Jewish Society of Late Antiquity*. New York: Routledge, 1999.

———. *Sages, Stories, Authors, and Editors in Rabbinic Babylonia*. Brown Judaic Studies, no. 300. Atlanta, Ga.: Scholars Press, 1994.

Kanarfogel, Ephraim. "Realia (Metsiut) and Halakhah in Ashkenaz: Surveying the Parameters and Defining the Limits." *Jewish Law Annual* 14 (2002): 201–16.

Kertzer, David I. *Ritual, Politics, and Power*. New Haven, Conn.: Yale University Press, 1988.

Kraemer, David Charles. *The Mind of the Talmud: An Intellectual History of the Bavli*. New York: Oxford University Press, 1990.

———. *Reading the Rabbis: The Talmud as Literature*. New York: Oxford University Press, 1996.

Kugel, James. "Two Introductions to Midrash." *Prooftexts* 3, no. 2 (1983): 131–55.

Labov, William, and Joshua Waletzky. "Narrative Analysis: Oral Versions of Personal Experience." In *Essays on the Verbal and Visual Arts*, edited by June Helm, 12–44. Seattle: University of Washington Press, 1967.

Lehto, Adam. "Divine Law, Asceticism and Gender in Aphrahat's *Demonstrations*, with a Complete Annotated Translation of the Text and Comprehensive Syriac Glossary." Ph.D. dissertation, University of Toronto, 2003.

Levine, Aaron. *Free Enterprise and Jewish Law: Aspects of Jewish Business Ethics*. New York: Ktav and Yeshiva University Press, 1980.

Levine, Lee I. *The Rabbinic Class of Roman Palestine in Late Antiquity*. Jerusalem: Yad Izhak Ben-Zvi; New York: Jewish Theological Seminary of America, 1989.

Levinson, Joshua. "An-Other Woman: Joseph and Potiphar's Wife—Staging the Body Politic." *Jewish Quarterly Review* 87, nos. 3–4 (1997): 269–301.

Lewin, Benjamin Manasseh, ed. and pub. *'Ôṣar Ha-Gĕ'ônim*.[12 vols.] Haifa, 1928–42.

Libson, Gideon. "Halakhah and Law in the Period of the Geonim." In *An Introduction to the History and Sources of Jewish Law*, edited by Neil S. Hecht, B. S. Jackson, S. M. Passamaneck, D. Piattelli, and A. M. Rabello, 197–242. Oxford: Oxford University Press, 1996.

———. *Jewish and Islamic Law: A Comparative Study of Custom During the Geonic*

Period. Harvard Series in Islamic Law 1. Cambridge, Mass.: Islamic Legal Studies Program, Harvard Law School, 2003.

Lieberman, Saul. *Šĕqî'în*. Jerusalem: Wahrmann, 1970.

Lifshitz, Berachyahu. "'Aggādâ Bĕ-Tôlĕdôt Tôrâ Šebĕ-'al Peh." *Shenaton Hamishpat Haivri* 22 (2004): 233–328.

———. "Minhāg Mĕbaṭēl Halākâ." *Sinai* 86, nos. 1–2 (1980): 8–13.

Lorberbaum, Yair. "Reflections on the Halakhic Status of Aggadah." *Dînê Yiśra'el* 24 (2007): 29–64.

———. *Ṣelem 'Elôhîm: Halākâ Wĕ-'aggādâ*. Jerusalem: Schocken Press, 2004.

Lukinsky, Joseph. "Law in Education: A Reminiscence with Some Footnotes to Robert Cover's *Nomos and Narrative*." *Yale Law Journal* 96, no. 8 (1987): 1836–59.

Margaliot, Reuben. *Niṣôṣê 'ôr: He'ārôt Bĕ-Talmûd Bablî*. Jerusalem: Môsad ha-Rab Kook, 1965.

Marrou, Henri Irénée. *A History of Education in Antiquity*. Translated by George Lamb. New York: Sheed and Ward, 1956.

Mermelstein, Benjamin. "Ṣûrbā Mērabbānān " In *Abhandlungen zur Erinnerung an Hirsch Perez Chajes*, edited by V. Aptowitzer and A. Z. Schwartz, 223–30. Vienna: Alexander Kohut Memorial Foundation, 1933.

Minow, Martha. "Stories in Law." In *Law's Stories: Narrative and Rhetoric in the Law*, edited by Peter Brooks and Paul D. Gewirtz, 24–36. New Haven, Conn.: Yale University Press, 1996.

Moore, Carey A. *Esther: Introduction, Translation and Notes by Carey A. Moore*. Anchor Bible, vol. 7B. Garden City, N.Y.: Doubleday, 1971.

Morris, Nathan. *The Jewish School: An Introduction to the History of Jewish Education*. London: Eyre and Spottiswoode, 1937.

Morson, Gary Saul, and Caryl Emerson. *Mikhail Bakhtin: Creation of a Prosaics*. Stanford, Calif.: Stanford University Press, 1990.

Moscovitz, Leib. "The Holy One Blessed Be He . . . Does Not Permit the Righteous to Stumble." In *Creation and Composition: The Contribution of the Bavli Redactors (Stammaim) to the Aggada*, edited by Jeffrey L. Rubenstein, 125–79. Leiden: Brill, 2005.

Neusner, Jacob. *A History of the Jews in Babylonia*. 5 vols. Studia Post-Biblica. Leiden: E. J. Brill, 1965.

———. *A Life of Yohanan ben Zakkai, ca. 1–80 C.E.* 2nd ed. Studia Post-Biblica, vol. 6. Leiden: Brill, 1970.

Obermeyer, Jacob. *Die Landschaft Babylonien im Zeitalter des Talmuds und des Gaonats: Geographie und Geschichte nach talmudischen, arabischen und andern Quellen*. Frankfurt am Main: I. Kauffmann, 1929.

Ochs, Vanessa L. *Words on Fire: One Woman's Journey into the Sacred*. San Diego: Harcourt Brace Jovanovich, 1990.

Oppenheimer, Aharon. *The Am Ha-Aretz: A Study in the Social History of the Jewish People in the Hellenistic-Roman Period*. Translated from the Hebrew by I. H. Levine.

Arbeiten zur Literatur und Geschichte des hellenistischen Judentums 8. Leiden: E. J. Brill, 1977.

———. *Babylonia Judaica in the Talmudic Period*. In collaboration with Benjamin H. Isaac and Michael Lecker. Beihefte zum Tübinger Atlas des Vorderen Orients, Reihe B, Geisteswissenschaften, no. 47. Wiesbaden: L. Reichert, 1983.

Paul, Shalom M. *Studies in the Book of the Covenant in the Light of Cuneiform and Biblical Law*. Supplements to Vetus Testamentum. Leiden: E. J. Brill, 1970.

Pigeaud, Jackie. *La maladie de l'âme: Étude sur la relation de l'âme et du corps dans la tradition médico-philosophique antique*. Collection d'études anciennes. Paris: Société d'édition "Les Belles lettres," 1981.

Rabbinovicz, Raphael Nathan Nata. *Seper Diqdûqê Sôprim*. 12 vols. Jerusalem: 'Ôr ha-Ḥokmâ, 2002.

Rajak, Tessa. "Dying for the Law: The Martyr's Portrait in Jewish-Greek Literature." In *The Jewish Dialogue with Greece and Rome*, edited by Tessa Rajak, 99–133. Leiden: Brill, 2001.

Riessman, Catherine Kohler. *Narrative Analysis*. Qualitative Research Methods. Newbury Park, Calif.: Sage Publications, 1993.

Ross, Tamar. *Expanding the Palace of Torah: Orthodoxy and Feminism*. Brandeis Series on Jewish Women. Hanover: Brandeis University Press, published by University Press of New England, 2004.

Roth, Joel. *The Halakhic Process: A Systemic Analysis*. Moreshet Series. New York: Jewish Theological Seminary of America, 1986.

Rubenstein, Jeffrey L. *The Culture of the Babylonian Talmud*. Baltimore: Johns Hopkins University Press, 2003.

———. "The Rise of the Babylonian Rabbinic Academy: A Reexamination of the Talmudic Evidence." *Jewish Studies, an Internet Journal* 1 (2002): 55–68.

———. *Talmudic Stories: Narrative Art, Composition, and Culture*. Baltimore: Johns Hopkins University Press, 1999.

———. "The Thematization of Dialectics in Bavli Aggada." *Journal of Jewish Studies* 54, no. 1 (2003): 71–84.

Ryle, Gilbert. *Collected Papers*. 2 vols. London: Hutchinson, 1971.

Sarat, Austin, and Thomas Kearns. "Making Peace with Violence: Robert Cover on Law and Legal Theory." In *Law's Violence*, edited by Austin Sarat and Thomas Kearns, 211–50. Ann Arbor: University of Michigan Press, 1995.

Sarna, Nahum M. *Understanding Genesis*. Heritage of Biblical Israel. New York: Jewish Theological Seminary of America, 1966.

Satlow, Michael L. *Creating Judaism: History, Tradition, Practice*. New York: Columbia University Press, 2006.

———. *Jewish Marriage in Antiquity*. Princeton, N.J.: Princeton University Press, 2001.

Schechter, S., Louis Ginzberg, and Israel Davidson. *Ginzê Shekhter*. 3 vols. Texts and Studies of the Jewish Theological Seminary of America. Jerusalem: Hôṣa'at Maqôr, 1969.

Schiffman, Lawrence H. *From Text to Tradition: A History of Second Temple and Rabbinic Judaism.* Hoboken, N.J.: Ktav, 1991.

Schlag, Pierre. *The Enchantment of Reason.* Durham, N.C.: Duke University Press, 1998.

Schremer, Adiel. "Stammaitic Historiography." In *Creation and Composition: The Contribution of the Bavli Redactors (Stammaim) to the Aggada,* edited by Jeffrey L. Rubenstein, 219–35. Tübingen: Mohr Siebeck, 2005.

———. *Zākār U-Něqêbah Běrā'am: Ha-Nîśu'îm Bě-Šilhê Yěmê Ha-Bayit Ha-Šēnî Ubi-Těqûpat Ha-Mišnâ Wěha-Talmûd.* Jerusalem: Merkaz Zalman Shazar, 2003.

Schwartz, Seth. "Historiography on the Jews in the Talmudic Period." In *The Oxford Handbook of Jewish Studies,* edited by Martin Goodman, Jeremy Cohen, and David Sorkin, 79–114. Oxford: Oxford University Press, 2002.

———. *Imperialism and Jewish Society, 200 B.C.E. to 640 C.E.* Jews, Christians, and Muslims from the Ancient to the Modern World. Princeton, N.J.: Princeton University Press, 2001.

———. "The Political Geography of Rabbinic Texts." In *The Cambridge Companion to the Talmud and Rabbinic Literature,* edited by Charlotte Elisheva Fonrobert and Martin S. Jaffee, 75–96. Cambridge: Cambridge University Press, 2007.

Segal, Eliezer. *Case Citation in the Babylonian Talmud: The Evidence of Tractate Neziqin.* Brown Judaic Studies, no. 210. Atlanta, Ga.: Scholars Press, 1990.

Segal, M. H., ed. *Sēper Ben Sîrā Ha-Šālem.* Jerusalem: Môsad Bialik 1958.

Septimus, Zvi. "Trigger Words and Simultexts: The Experience of Reading the Bavli." In *Wisdom of Bat Sheva: The Dr. Beth Samuels Memorial Volume,* edited by Barry S. Wimpfheimer, 163–85. Jersey City, N.J.: Ktav, 2009.

Simon-Shoshan, Moshe. "Halachah Lemaʿaseh: Narrative and Legal Discourse in the Mishnah." Ph.D. dissertation, University of Pennsylvania, 2005.

Sokoloff, Michael. *A Dictionary of Jewish Babylonian Aramaic of the Talmudic and Geonic Periods.* Ramat Gan, Israel: Bar Ilan University Press; and Baltimore: Johns Hopkins University Press, 2002.

———. *A Dictionary of Jewish Palestinian Aramaic of the Byzantine Period.* 2nd ed. Ramat Gan, Israel: Bar Ilan University Press; and Baltimore: Johns Hopkins University Press, 2002.

Soloveitchik, Haym. "Halakhah, Hermeneutics, and Martyrdom in Medieval Ashkenaz (Part I of II)." *Jewish Quarterly Review* 94, no. 1 (2004): 77–108.

Soloveitchik, Joseph Dov. *Halakhic Man.* Philadelphia: Jewish Publication Society of America, 1983.

Sperber, Daniel. "On the Unfortunate Adventures of Rav Kahana: A Passage of Saboraic Polemic from Sassanian Persia." *Irano-Judaica* (1982): 83–100.

Stern, David. "The Alphabet of Ben Sira and the Early History of Parody in Rabbinic Literature." In *The Idea of Biblical Interpretation,* edited by Hindy Najman and Judith H. Newman, 423–48. Leiden: Brill, 2004.

———. "The Captive Woman: Hellenization, Greco-Roman Erotic Narrative, and Rabbinic Literature." *Poetics Today* 19, no. 1 (1998): 91–127.

Stone, Suzanne Last. "In Pursuit of the Countertext: The Turn to the Jewish Legal Model in Contemporary American Legal Theory." *Harvard Law Review* 106, no. 4 (1993): 813–94.

Ta-Shma, Israel M. *Minhag 'Aškĕnaz Ha-Qadmôn: Ḥēqer Wĕ-'îyûn*. Jerusalem: Magnes, Hebrew University, 1992.

———. "Suicide and Murder for the Sake of Kiddush Hashem." In *Facing the Cross: The Persecutions of 1096 in History and Historiography*, edited by Y. T. Assis et al., 150–56. In Hebrew. Jerusalem: Hebrew University, 2000.

Tchernowitz, Chaim. *Tolĕdôt Ha-Pôsqîm*. New York: n.p., 1946.

Toohey, Peter. "Love, Lovesickness and Melancholy." *Illinois Classical Studies* 17 (1992): 265–86.

Tur-Sinai, Naphtali Herz. *Pĕšûṭô Šel Miqrā*. Jerusalem: Qiryat Sēper, 1962.

Vidas, Moulie. "The Bavli's Discussion of Genealogy in *Qiddushin* IV." In *Antiquity in Antiquity: Jewish and Christian Pasts in the Greco-Roman World*, edited by Gregg Gardner and Kevin L. Osterloh, 285–326. Tübingen: Mohr Siebeck, 2008.

Wack, Mary Frances. *Lovesickness in the Middle Ages: The Viaticum and Its Commentaries*. Middle Ages Series. Philadelphia: University of Pennsylvania Press, 1990.

Wald, Stephen G. "Am Haarez." In *Encyclopaedia Judaica*, edited by Fred Skolnick and Michael Berenbaum, 66–70. Detroit: Macmillan Reference, 2007.

———. *Pereq 'ēlû 'ôbrîn: Bablî Pĕsāḥîm, Pereq Šĕlîšî*. New York: Jewish Theological Seminary of America, 2000.

Weiss, Abraham. *'Al Ha-Yĕṣîrâ Ha-Siprûtît Šel Ha-'Amôra'îm*. New York: Horeb Yeshiva University, 1961.

———. *Lĕ-Ḥēqer Ha-Talmûd*. New York: Feldheim, 1954.

Weiss, Isaac Hirsch. *Dôr Dôr Wĕ-Dôrshāyw*. 5 vols. Vilna: Romm, 1904..

Weiszburg, Y. "'Ôdôt Batê Ha-Dîn Bi-Zĕman Ha-Talmûd." In *Seper Ha-Yôbel Lĕ-Kabod Moshe Aryeh Bloch*. Budapest: Singer és Wolfner, 1905.

West, Cornel. *Keeping Faith: Philosophy and Race in America*. New York: Routledge, 1993.

White, Hayden V. *Tropics of Discourse: Essays in Cultural Criticism*. Baltimore: Johns Hopkins University Press, 1978.

———. "The Value of Narrativity in the Representation of Reality." *Critical Inquiry* 7, no. 1 (1980): 5–27.

Williams, Patricia J. *The Alchemy of Race and Rights*. Cambridge, Mass.: Harvard University Press, 1991.

Wimpfheimer, Barry S. "Interrupting Birth Control: Re-Reading a Famous Beraita." In *Wisdom of Bat Sheva: The Dr. Beth Samuels Memorial Volume*, edited by Barry S. Wimpfheimer, 247–74. Jersey City, N.J.: Ktav, 2009.

———. "Legal Narratives in the Babylonian Talmud." Ph.D. dissertation, Columbia University, 2005.

Yassif, Eli. *The Hebrew Folktale: History, Genre, Meaning*. Translated by Jacqueline S. Teitelbaum. Folklore Studies in Translation. Bloomington: Indiana University Press, 1999.

Yerushalmi, Yosef Hayim. *Zakhor, Jewish History and Jewish Memory*. Samuel and Althea Stroum Lectures in Jewish Studies. Seattle: University of Washington Press, 1982.

Zeitlin, Solomon. "The Am Haarez: A Study in the Social and Economic Life of the Jews Before and After the Destruction of the Second Temple." *Jewish Quarterly Review* 23, no. 1 (1932): 45–61.

Zunz, Leopold. *Die gottesdienstlichen Vorträge der Juden, historisch entwickelt: Ein Beitrag zur Alterthumskunde und biblischen Kritik, zur Literatur-und Religionsgeschichte*. Berlin: A. Asher, 1832.

Zussman, Yaakov. "Wĕ-Šûb Lĕ-Yĕrûšalmî Nĕzîqîn." In *Mehqārê Talmûd* 1, edited by Yaakov Zussman and David Rosenthal, 55–133. Jerusalem: Magnes, 1990.

Subject Index

'Abayê, 117, 135-37, 141-42
'Addā bar 'Ahabâ, Rab, 135-43, 145, 153
aggadah and halakhah: in modern scholarship, 35-40, 147, 159-60, 166; as literary genres, 2, 7-8, 31-37, 44-45, 57-62, 130, 147, 159-60, 166-67; as reading practices, 5, 7-8, 31-32, 44-45, 57-62, 147, 159-60, 166-67; in traditional post-rabbinic commentary, 32-37, 147, 166
'Aggadōt Hatalmûd, 34, 36-38
'Aḥā, Rab,115-16
'Aḥā, Rab, son of Rab 'Îqqā, 46-48, 51, 57
Alfasi, Rav Yiṣḥaq (Hilkōt Rabbātî), 25, 34, 36, 38
'Amêmar, 86-87
am haarez, 79-83, 88-90, 107-10, 155. See also rabbis, and non-rabbis
Aphrahat, 72, 74
Aristotle, 19

Bakhtin, Mikhail, 13-15, 20-22, 27-28, 45, 56, 159
ben Běṣalēl, Rabbi Ḥayyîm, 11-12, 14
Benjamin, Walter, 157
Ben Sira, 105, 128
Bialik, Haim Nahman, 2, 35
Bible: critical study of, 9, 23; as a law code, 9, 23; and legal narrative, 9, 15-18, 23
Bourdieu, Pierre, 122-23, 128, 130, 132, 145-46
Boyarin, Daniel, 6, 21 n.66, 27 n.91, 35, 43 n.49
Brandes, Yehudah, 35-36
Bruner, Jerome, 19

calumny, 151-52, 156-58
capital, 122-25, 128-33, 135-38, 140-46, 153-54, 157-58

carnival, 27-29
caste, 149, 154, 156-59. See also priesthood; status, legal
codification: critique of, 11-14; impulse toward, 9-11, 14, 34
Cohen, Shaye, 109
comedy, 27-29, 90-92, 100-102
commerce. See capital; competition
competition, 122-25, 127-38, 140-45, 153-54, 158
Cover, Robert, 13-20, 23, 53, 165
curriculum. See rabbis, pedagogy of
curses, 24, 29, 138-40, 142

dialogical relationships: and cultural discourses, 21-24, 56-57, 159-60; between individuals, 21; and legal discourses, 22, 45; and legal narrative, 22-24, 44-46, 56-58, 61, 159-60, 164-67
Dîmmî, Rab, of Něhardě'ā', 126-30, 139-44

education. See rabbis, pedagogy of
'El'āzār, R., 41, 45-47, 75 n.36, 141
'El'āzār ben Dama, R., 55-56
'Elî'ezer, R., 73-75, 107
'Eprayim, Rabbênû, of Qal'at Ḥamad, 25
equity, judicial, 68-70, 76-90, 92-93, 95, 131-35, 154-55, 159
ethics, rule-based, 14
excommunication, 150-52, 158
exilarch, 82, 97, 131, 139-40, 142, 150, 158
'Êyn Ya'aqōb, 34, 36-38

Flaubert, Gustave, 122, 124-25
Foucault, Michel, 102
Fraenkel, Yonah, 37-40, 44, 57-58, 158-60
Friedman, Shamma, 6, 50, 99 n.17

Subject Index

Gafni, Isaiah, 65, 103–4
Gamĕlîēl, R., 73–75
Geertz, Clifford, 16, 20, 22, 85–86, 89, 92
geonim: as composers of legal codes, 11, 34; and the creation of rabbinic academies, 32–34, 37, 81, 97, 103–4, 111; and Jewish legal authority, 32–34, 93–94
Goodblatt, David, 65, 81, 97, 103–4, 136
Greenblatt, Stephen, 85–86

ḥābēr, 80, 89–90. *See also* purities
halakhah. *See* aggadah and halakhah
Halakōt Gĕdōlōt, 34, 36
Halakōt Pĕsûqōt, 34
Halēvî, Rab Zĕraḥyâ, 25
Halivni, David Weiss, 6, 50
Hasmonean dynasty, 151–53, 156
Herman, Geoffrey, 154
hierarchy: as a central concern for Babylonian rabbis, 72–75, 79–92, 95, 101–12, 118–21, 123, 128, 135–44; and courtroom posture, 68–76, 80–84, 86–95, 154–55
Ḥisdā, Rab, 110–12
Hûnā, Rab, 70–71, 75, 89–92, 129, 150
Hûnā, Rab, son of Rab Joshua, 74–75, 129, 137–38

Isaac, R., 52, 57–61
Isaac, R., son of R. Judah, 74–75
Isaac bar Naḥmān, Rab, 44
Ishmael, R., 55–56
Isserles, Rabbi Moshe, 11–12

Jacob bar 'Îddî, Rab, 44
Jeroboam, 71–72
Joseph, Rab, 76–79, 88, 93, 129–30, 139–40, 142–44, 155–56
Joshua, R., 58, 73–74
Josiah, Rab, 131–32, 136
Judah, R., 69–71, 75–76, 79–80, 87–89, 91–92, 94–95
Judah, Rab (son of Ezekiel), 36, 150–56, 158
Judah the Patriarch, Rabbi (Rabbî), 102, 109

Kahanā, Rab, 134, 141
kallâ (public lectures in Babylonian academies), 103–5, 111, 120
Kalmin, Richard, 135, 137–38, 141, 148–49
Karo, Rabbi Joseph (*Shulḥan Arukh*), 3, 9, 11
kings, Davidic, 71–72

law: commercial, 126–34; in contemporary Judaism, 3–4, 12, 164; and courtroom procedure, 68–71, 75–84, 86–95, 112–14, 120; as cultural discourse, 3–7, 12–24, 48, 52, 56–61, 141, 145, 164–67; and custom, 94; formalistic interpretation of, 23–27, 44–48, 68–70, 83, 89–93, 99–100, 118–20; and narrative (*see* Talmud, Babylonian, and legal narrative); normative function of, 9, 11, 15–18, 22, 28–30, 44–46, 48–50, 60–61; and positivism, 70; practice of, 4, 15–20, 68–71, 75–95, 112; as statute, 3–4, 9–19, 21–30, 39–40, 44, 48–50, 53, 60–61, 65, 69, 78, 89, 113–14, 117, 141, 147, 164–67; as a system, 12–21, 48, 53; "law and literature," 5, 15, 35
Levi ben Sisi, 109
liability, bailee, 97–101, 112–20
Libson, Gideon, 94
Lorberbaum, Yair, 36
lovesickness, 36, 38, 40–57, 60–61, 117

Maimonides (*Mishneh Torah*), 2–3, 9 n.2, 93–95
Mar bar Ḥanînā, 112–21
Mar bar Rab 'Ašî, 77, 79
Margōlîyōt, Rab 'Eprayim Zalmān, of Brody, 25–26
market, market protection. *See* competition
marriage, in Jewish law, 149–51, 157–58, 166
martyrdom, 55–56
Mar Zûtrā, 86
Matneh, Rab, 151–53
Mĕḥôzā, 131, 136, 139–40, 156
Mĕnā, Rab, 110
Merî, Rab, 74–75
midrash, 10, 32, 37, 76
Minow, Martha, 20, 22
Mishnah: as a law code, 9–11, 32; and midrash, 10, 32, 39; redaction of, 10
monological relationships, and legal discourse, 21–22, 29, 45–46, 48, 56–58, 149, 153, 155, 159–60, 164–67

Naḥmān, Rab, 71–72, 78, 89–92, 150–52, 154–56, 158
Naḥmān bar Isaac, Rab, 137–39, 142
narrative, theory of, 6–7, 19–22, 26–28, 35, 38, 53, 85–86, 113, 122–25, 128, 158–60, 164–67

Subject Index

Nātān Ṣûṣîtâ, 43, 55
Neusner, Jacob, 64–66
New Criticism, 6, 35, 38–39, 124
nomos. See law, as cultural discourse
novel, 13–14, 21, 27, 65–66, 122–25, 159

Obadiah, Rab, 131–32, 136

paideia, 105–7, 109–11, 125, 130, 144–45
Pāppā, Rab, 46–48, 51, 57, 74–75, 88–89, 99 n.17, 137–38
patriarchy, 97, 109
Pigeaud, Jackie, 56
Pinḥās, Rab, son of Rab Ḥîsdā, 74–75
poetics, 13–14, 20–21, 52, 57, 60
priesthood, 131, 154, 156–57. *See also* caste; status, legal
Pûmbĕdîtâ, 136, 140, 150, 156, 158
purities, 90. See also *ḥaber*

Rab, 36, 140
Rab bar Šĕbā, 88
Rābā, 74–75, 77, 79, 99–105, 107, 109, 111–21, 126–33, 135–44, 153, 156
Rabbâ, 24–30
Rabbâ bar Rab Hûnā, 79–81, 83–89, 93, 155
rabbis: anxiety of, 7, 59–61, 66, 80, 107–8, 112, 154–55; authority of, 4, 7, 23, 53–61, 66, 81–83, 88–93, 95, 97, 101–5, 109–12, 120, 123, 131–37, 140–42, 156–60, 166; and the disciple circle, 101–7, 110, 112, 117–21, 135–36; and Greco-Roman culture, 54–56, 60–61, 105–7, 109–11, 144; hagiographic attitude toward, 119–20; and hierarchy (*see* hierarchy, as central concern for Babylonian rabbis); history of, in Babylonia, 6–8, 63–68, 72, 81–83, 96–97, 103–12, 123–45, 154–58, 166; history of, in Palestine, 64–66, 68, 71–72, 97, 105–10, 154; and non-rabbis, 68–69, 76–83, 88–93, 95, 104–5, 107–12, 123, 131–36, 141–42, 150, 153–58, 166; pedagogy of, 5, 32–34, 37, 67–68, 96–97, 100–112, 117–21, 125–30, 135–45; and scholarly envy, 110, 126–129, 135–45; and secular authorities, 67, 97; social dynamics of, 7–8, 66, 68–93, 96–97, 100–121, 123, 125–45, 153–58, 166; spouses of, 77, 89–92, 150, 154; status within Jewish society, 64, 66–67, 81–90, 95, 104–5, 107–12, 120, 131–36, 141–42, 153–58

Rabînā, 115–16, 133–34, 141
Rashi, 23 n.78, 43, 79 n.51, 101 n.33, 126 n.11, 131
Rehoboam, 71–72
responsa, 32–33, 93. *See also* geonim
Rubenstein, Jeffrey, 80–81, 104, 141 n.59, 148–49
Ryle, Gilbert, 85–86

Ṣādôq, R., 73–75
Samuel, 140, 151–53, 156–58
Samuel bar Naḥmēnî, Rab, 44
sanhedrin, 33, 81
scandal. *See* calumny
Sĕʿadîyâ Gāōn, 32, 36, 38
Segal, Eliezer, 9–10
sex, illicit, 42–44, 46–47, 49, 52
shame, 46–48, 57, 112–21
Simeon ben Gamĕlîēl, R., 58
Simeon ben Šeṭaḥ, 87
Simeon ben Yĕhôṣādāq, Rab, 42
sin, cardinal, 42–44, 47, 49, 53, 55
Šîšā bar Rab ʾÎddî, Rab, 84
sociology, 122–25, 12
stam: and the Babylonian yeshiva, 103–5, 120, 137–38, 145; lateness of, 5, 50–51, 57, 67; and the redaction of the Babylonian Talmud, 5, 46, 50–52; and reinterpretation of amoraic material, 41, 46, 50–52, 54, 57, 60–61, 67, 77–79, 81, 84, 86–89, 91–93, 103–5, 116–17, 119–21, 126–27, 131–35, 147–49, 153–55, 159–60, 164–67. *See also* Talmud, Babylonian, redaction of; yeshiva (Babylonian)
status, legal, 149–54, 156–59. *See also* caste; marriage, in Jewish law; priesthood
sugyot (Talmudic textual units), 41–42, 67, 123–25, 130–31, 139, 147, 164–66. *See also* Talmud, Babylonian, genre of
ṣûrbā mērabbānān, 77, 79–83, 89 n.93, 155

Talmud, Babylonian: anonymous voice of (see *stam*); Aramaic in, 33, 148, 153; critical scholarship of, 5–6, 24, 35–40, 50–51, 63–67, 79–82, 123–27, 147–49, 154, 158–60, 164–67; genre of, 1–3, 7–11, 31–42, 67–68, 79, 82–83, 100, 123–24, 147–48, 164–67; as a historiographic source, 7–8, 63–68, 81–83, 96–97, 103–12, 117, 123–30, 143, 154–58, 166–67; impulse to resolve contradictions, 3, 11, 23–27, 41–50, 52–53, 57, 60–61, 117, 164, 167; as a law code, 3, 9–11, 33–34; and legal narrative, 2–12, 14, 18–32, 36–46, 48–49, 52–53, 56–58, 60–61, 65–66, 68, 76, 78, 82–83, 86–93, 100, 112–13, 117–21, 124–25, 130–35, 143–45, 147–49, 158–60, 164–67; and the lengthy narrative, 147–60, 167; and Mishnaic code, 9–11; and nonnormative (nonlegal) narrative, 124–25, 130–31, 135–39, 142–45, 158–60; and post-talmudic scholarship, 9–12, 25–26, 32–38, 44, 93–95, 100–101, 113, 131, 140; redaction of, 46, 51–52, 120, 123–24, 135–38, 141, 147–48, 153, 164; status of, in Jewish culture, 1–3, 5, 27–29, 33–34

Talmud, Palestinian: anonymous voice of, 41, 46–50; genre of, 41–42; impulse to resolve contradictions, 41–42, 44–46, 48–50, 61; and legal narrative, 40–46, 48–50, 61; redaction of, 41, 46, 48–50

Temple, destruction of, 52, 58–60, 107, 154

ʿÛllā, 70–71, 75, 78, 87, 154

violence, 88, 157

Wack, Mary, 56
Wald, Stephen, 79–80
White, Hayden, 65–66
wisdom, 128–29
Wissenschaft des Judentums, 6, 37

Yalta, 150, 154
Yann'ay (Alexander Jannaeus), 87
Yann'ay, Rab, 110
Yêmar, Rab, 86–87
yeshiva (Babylonian), 5, 32–34, 37, 81, 97, 103–6, 111, 135–39. *See also* geonim, and the creation of rabbinic academies
Yôḥānān, Rab, 42
Yôḥānān ben Zakka'y, Rabban, 64
Yôsî, R., 58

Zêrā, Rab, 24–29
Zussman, Yaakov, 51

Source Index

Hebrew Bible

Exodus
  18:8, 73
  18:13, 70–71
  22:6–14, 97–99
Leviticus
  19:15, 76
Numbers
  35:33, 78 n.46
Deuteronomy
  19:16 (Sĕpôrnô ad loc.), 17 n.50
  19:17, 69–71
  21:15–17, 15–19
1 Kings
  12:27, 71–72
  12:28, 72
Isaiah
  11:4, 118 n.107
Amos
  2:1, 139
Zechariah
  10:5 (Targûm ad loc.), 54
Psalms
  137:5–6, 58 n.81
Proverbs
  9:17, 52, 58; 9:18, 58 n.79
Ecclesiastes
  8:13, 75 n.36; 10:8, 55

Apocrypha and Pseudepigrapha

Ben Sira
  38:24, 128

Midrashic literature

Mĕkîltā Dĕ-Rabbî Šim'ôn bar Yôḥa'y (ed. Epstein and Melamed)
  131–32, 74
  206–7, 98 n.8
Siprā Qĕdôšîm
  2:4, 69 n.20
Genesis Rabbâ
  81:2, 109
Leviticus Rabbâ
  2:1, 110
Ecclesiastes Rabbâ
  7:28, 110 n.73
'Ābôt Dĕrabbî Nātān
  A 10, 69 n.20
Yalqûṭ Šim'ôn
  Yitrô 270, 70 n.24
Midraš Hagādôl
  Deuteronomy 19:17, 70 n.24

Mishnah

'Erûbîn
  1:4, 58 n.83
Sôṭâ
  9:12, 58–59
  9:15, 107–9
Qîddûšîn
  4:14, 128 nn.14–15
Bābā Mĕṣî'ā
  7:9, 114–15
  8:1, 98–99
Šĕbû'ôt
  8:1, 114–15

Tosefta

Měgîllâ
  3:2, 104 n.44
Sôṭà
  15:10-15, 58 n.81
Bābā Měṣîʿā
  2:30, 128 n.14
  8:20-21, 98-99
Sanhedrîn
  6:2, 69 n.20
Hôrāyôt
  2:5, 128 n.14

Palestinian Talmud

Běrākôt
  4:1 (7c), 110 n.75
Šabbāt
  14:4 (14d), 40-51, 53, 55 n.75, 61
Pěsāḥîm
  5:10 (34d), 72 n.29
Yômā
  5:7 (43b), 69 n.20
Taʿanît
  4:1 (67c), 110 n.75
Měgîllâ
  3:6 (74b), 110 n.75
Yěbāmôt
  12:7 (13a), 109
Sôṭâ
  7:7 (21a), 72 n.29
Bābā Měṣîʿā
  8:1, 98 n.8
  11:3-4, 98 n.8
Sanhedrîn
  3:8 (21c), 69 n.20
Šěbûʿôt
  4:7 (35b), 69 n.20
  8:1 (38c), 115-16
ʿAbôdâ Zārâ
  2:2 (40d), 40-51, 53, 55 n.75, 61

Babylonian Talmud

Běrākôt
  8a, 59 n.83
  28b, 128 nn.14-15
  30b, 110 n.76
Šabbāt
  23b, 79 n.57
  30b, 100
  51b, 112 n.87
  67a, 54 n.65
  108a, 140-41
  119a, 77, 79
ʿErûbîn
  36b, 112 n.82
  46b, 11 n.11
  65a, 133 n.26
Pěsāḥîm
  49a, 107-9
Yômā
  25a, 72 n.29
  69b, 72 n.29
Taʿanît
  7a, 101 n.33, 102
Měgîllâ
  2a, 28 n.94
  7b, 24-30
Môʿēd Qāṭān
  25a, 142 n.61
Yěbāmôt
  31b, 110
  40a, 110 n.76
Kětûbôt
  56a, 110 n.76
  105b, 78 nn. 43, 45, 87 n.85
Nědārîm
  62a-b, 131, 136
Gîṭṭîn
  29b, 119 n.109
  57b, 44
  58a, 55
  77b, 119 n.109
Qîddûšîn
  32b-33b, 73-75
  70a-b, 149-63
Bābā Qamā
  32b, 142 n.61
  60b, 32 n.6
  117a-b, 138n39
Bābā Měṣîʿā
  33a (Rashi ad loc.), 23 n.78
  36b, 117 n.106
  59a, 76-77

81a–b, 99 n.17, 119 n.109
86a, 11 n.13
93a, 117 n.105
95a, 98n8, 115–16
96b, 117 n.104
97a, 97, 99–105, 107–9, 111–21
Bābā Batrā
   3b, 153
   20a–22b, 100 n.22, 105 n.54, 123, 125–46, 153–54
   81b, 141
   144a, 132 n.25
Sanhedrîn
   19a, 87
   31b (Rashi ad loc.), 43 n.49
   75a, 36, 38, 40–61
   101b, 71–72

Šĕbûʿôt
   30a–b, 68–71, 75–81, 83–95, 154–55
   41a, 89 n.93
ʿAbôdâ Zārâ
   22a, 119 n.109
   39a, 90
Hôrāyôt
   13b, 138n40
Zĕbāḥîm
   16a, 86 n.83
Mĕnāḥôt
   69b, 141
Bĕkôrôt
   35b, 77 n.42

Acknowledgments

This book would not have appeared without the feedback, encouragement, and support of so many people, and the funding and research assistance offered by various institutions.

I have had the good fortune of being mentored extensively by the two leading scholars of the Babylonian Talmud, David Weiss Halivni and Shamma Friedman. It was their respective work on the layered composition of the Talmud and the import of its anonymous redactors that first lured me from traditional Talmud study, and their impact on me has only increased with time. Professor Halivni has always made himself available to me to discuss any and every aspect of a talmudic text. His legendary recall is more than matched by his personal warmth.

Through my ḥabrûtâ with Shamma Friedman in Jerusalem, I had the weekly opportunity to observe a prolific scholar in action. Had I not witnessed it, I would not have imagined the creative energy that could flow from a devotion to explaining every last feature of a talmudic text. I am grateful to have had this opportunity and for Professor Friedman's continued correspondence and friendship.

Various academic contexts allowed me to present and critique some of what appears in this book. An early version of "The Lovesick Man" was critiqued by Robert Post and Nan Goodman at the Law and Humanities Junior Scholar Workshop. Another version of this work was published as "Talmudic Legal Narrative: Broadening the Discourse of Jewish Law" in a special issue of *Dine Yisrael* (2007), and I am grateful to Suzanne Last Stone for her editorial comments and suggestions. Early drafts of Chapter 4 were written in dialogue with David Damrosch and Pericles Lewis. A version of those drafts appeared as "'But It Is Not So': Toward a Poetics of Legal Narrative in the Talmud" in *Prooftexts* (Winter 2004) thanks to the enthusiasm and constructive editing of David Stern.

I have had a number of institutional homes while writing this book. Penn

State was my first scholarly home, and I am particularly grateful for the collegial friendships of Brian Hesse, Lila Corwin Berman, Daniel Berman, Aaron Rubin, and Markus Asper. I am also grateful to the Center for Jewish Studies at Harvard for providing the opportunity, as a Harry Starr Fellow, to engage with Michela Andreatta, Marc Caplan, Haim Gertner, Geoffrey Herman, Rabbi Joseph Levi, Shulamith Furstenburg-Levi, Marcus Pyka, and David Wacks.

My current residence is Northwestern University's Department of Religious Studies (née Religion) and Law School. My colleagues at Northwestern have provided the kind of intellectual camaraderie every academic craves.

Michael Stanislawski, director of Columbia's Institute for Israel and Jewish Studies, provided constructive feedback on much of this volume. Elizabeth Castelli has taught me so much, both formally and by example. I am grateful to Alan Segal and Jeffrey Rubenstein for their comments and critiques on earlier research that is the basis for this book.

Several scholars have mentored me or provided me with helpful feedback. I would like to thank Elizabeth Shanks Alexander, Moshe Benovitz, Beth Berkowitz, Jeremy Dauber, Charlotte Fonrobert, Moshe Halbertal, Christine Hayes, Menachem Kahana, Joshua Levinson, Shlomo Naeh, Jonathan Schofer, and Holger Zellentin for their feedback. I am grateful that Idana Goldberg, Ricky Hidary, Meir Katz, Jon Levisohn, Tova Mirvis, Asha Moorthy, Tzvi Novick, Shai Secunda, and Zvi Septimus responded to cries for help. Special thanks go to Alyssa Henning for her research assistance.

Since the initial submission of this monograph to the University of Pennsylvania Press, I have received extensive constructive feedback from editors of the Press's Divinations series, Virginia Burrus and, especially, Daniel Boyarin. I have been enamored of Boyarin's work for some time, and his development of some of my insights within his own recent book honors me greatly. Our work has been in dialogue for the past few years, and I am pleased that this volume will appear in Divinations. I am also grateful to Jerry Singerman, who has been the perfect editor for me. I am extremely indebted both to Jennifer Shenk for her meticulous copyediting and to Erica Ginsburg for masterfully shepherding the monograph through final production.

Particular friends need to be singled out for their assistance. For several years I saw more of Daniel Reifman than anyone else, including my wife. Though our formal ḥabrûtâ has been over for some time, Daniel has always encouraged this project and has lent an incredibly learned ear to both the ideas herein and the many rejected along the way. I must also acknowledge

Daniel for suggesting (at the head of a much appreciated committee of friends) the book's title.

Though we are no longer in the same city, Jonathan Milgram and I speak often, and I value those conversations. I first met Jonathan in rabbinical school, where we connected over our mutual interest in academic Talmud scholarship. Jonathan is a terrific Talmudist (and a great friend) and I appreciate the ways in which he keeps my work grounded in the finest tradition of Talmud textual scholarship.

Though I have never formally trained with Ravit Reichman, her influence on my work cannot be overstated. At Yale's Slifka Center we discovered a shared interest in the cultural side of law. Ravit has beautifully rewritten some of my prose, and I have learned much from her own scholarship.

Eliyahu Stern and I bonded at Yeshiva University over our mutual admiration for the world of ideas. During the years since, we have become each other's sounding boards, and I am forever grateful for his friendship, for his thoughts, and for responding helpfully and almost instantly to written drafts.

My son, Adin, was born shortly after I arrived in Chicago, and I have spent the last three years enjoying his company. Whenever I have told Adin that I am writing a book, he has responded by telling me about the book he is writing; I eagerly await Adin's publication.

This book is scheduled for print just after my fifteenth wedding anniversary. For the past fifteen years Shana has been my best friend, my life partner, my most ardent cheerleader, and my most constructive critic. I am regularly awed by her analytic mind, her clarity of thought, and her ability to quickly penetrate to core principles and emotions. I dedicate this book to her, with love, in gratitude for all she has done for it and me.

Breinigsville, PA USA
08 February 2011
255061BV00001B/1/P